Edinburgh University Library

Books may be recalled for return earlier than due date;
if so you will be contacted by e-mail or letter.

Due Date	Due Date	Due Date
– 3 MAY 2009		

CHAUCER STUDIES VIII

CHAUCER AND PAGAN ANTIQUITY

CHAUCER STUDIES

ISSN 0261-9822

I
MUSIC IN THE AGE OF CHAUCER
Nigel Wilkins

II
CHAUCER'S LANGUAGE AND THE PHILOSOPHERS' TRADITION
J. D. Burnley

III
ESSAYS ON TROILUS AND CRISEYDE
Edited by Mary Salu

IV
CHAUCER SONGS
Nigel Wilkins

V
CHAUCER'S BOCCACCIO
Sources of Troilus *and the* Knight's *and* Franklin's Tales
Edited and translated by N. R. Havely

VI
SYNTAX AND STYLE IN CHAUCER'S POETRY
G. H. Roscow

VII
CHAUCER'S DREAM POETRY
Sources and Analogues
B. A. Windeatt

CHAUCER AND
PAGAN ANTIQUITY

A. J. MINNIS

D. S. BREWER · ROWMAN & LITTLEFIELD

First published 1982 by D. S. Brewer
240 Hills Road, Cambridge
an imprint of Boydell & Brewer Ltd, PO Box 9,
Woodbridge, Suffolk IP12 3DF
and Rowman & Littlefield Inc, 81 Adams Drive,
Totowa, New Jersey N.J. 07512, USA

British Library Cataloguing in Publication Data

Minnis, A. J.
    Chaucer and pagan antiquity.—(Chaucer studies; 8)
    1. Chaucer, Geoffrey—Religion and ethics
    2. Paganism in literature
    I. Title   II. Series
    ISBN 0-85991-098-9

For Florence

Photoset in Great Britain by
Rowland Phototypesetting Ltd, Bury St Edmunds, Suffolk
and printed by St Edmundsbury Press
Bury St Edmunds, Suffolk

Preface

Felix qui potuit rerum cognoscere causas. The ultimate cause or origin of this book was a series of lectures by Éamonn Ó Carragáin on *Beowulf*, which I attended as an undergraduate at the Queen's University of Belfast. He invited his class to speculate on the implications of the fact that this Old English epic was a profoundly Christian poem which treated the pagan past with a surprising yet pleasing degree of objectivity and a modicum of explicit moralizing. By a happy coincidence, at that time I had just become fascinated by Chaucer's literary paganism, and so those seeds fell on good ground, if not in the place which the sower had intended.

A more immediate and general cause is the wish for some degree of certainty in literary interpretation, in a period in which new interpretations, approaches and critical theories seem to appear almost daily. I am writing with an undergraduate audience in mind, hoping to demonstrate that historical criticism can check the drift towards solipsism and channel imaginative energy into areas of possible interpretation which may be validated by reference to the ideas, thought-structures and literary traditions available to the author. Historical criticism based on 'primary literature' need not be dogmatic, though some of its advocates may have given that impression; it can open at least as many doors as it closes—and many of those doors richly deserve to be closed, since they lead to dim and distant lands far removed from the texts themselves. This book is a testimony of faith in a type of source-study which goes beyond the listing of verbal parallels (though I would wish to defend that time-honoured scholarly activity) yet stops far short of 'source determinism', i.e. the belief that what the author wrote was rigidly determined by what he read. None of the poems discussed below was determined by its sources, but comparative study of Chaucer's sources can throw much light on his interests and purposes in writing, thereby helping to establish firm standards of validity in interpretation. For example, it may be taken as axiomatic that, in a case in which all the changes Chaucer made to his sources tend in a certain direction, any interpretation which runs counter to that direction should be rejected.

I have chosen to concentrate on two major poems, *Troilus and Criseyde* and *The Knight's Tale*, because therein Chaucer's treatment of pagan antiquity is at its most complex and sophisticated. Other poems, of course, fall within the same basic terms of reference—notably *The Squire's Tale*, *The Franklin's Tale* and *The Legend of Good Women*—but they present special problems which I intend to treat separately in the future. Moreover, the two chosen poems form a distinctive pair in so far as they are 'creative translations' of works by Boccaccio. In each case Chaucer 'medievalizes' his Italian source, and I have attempted to quantify that process through examination of the attitudes to antiquity which he encountered in the writings of 'classicizing' clerics of the later Middle Ages. The title of this book is a deliberate echo of the title of Beryl Smalley's pioneering book, *English Friars and Antiquity in the Early Fourteenth Century*.

To Miss Smalley I am indebted for, among other things, many stimulating conversations about medieval theologians. When this book was a mere gleam in my eye Piero Boitani encouraged my research and allowed me to read his unpublished Cambridge doctoral thesis, comprising a complete translation of Boccaccio's *Il Teseida*. Meg Twycross gave me permission to consult her unpublished Oxford B. Litt. thesis on the representation of the pagan deities in Middle English Literature, a fine piece of careful scholarship and interesting criticism which, regrettably, has not seen the light in print. I am most grateful to two of my colleagues at the University of Bristol, Professor John Burrow and Miss Myra Stokes, for reading the penultimate draft of this book and making valuable comments and suggestions. John Burrow kindly allowed me to read his unpublished paper on 'Chaucer's *Knight's Tale* and the Ages of Man'. Dr Brian Scott, Reader in Latin at the Queen's University of Belfast, provided invaluable advice on several puzzling passages of Medieval Latin, and Mr Edward Bower, formerly Senior Lecturer in Latin at the same university, translated the extracts from Nicholas Trevet's commentary on Boethius which are printed in the Appendix.

I owe a special debt to the late Professor E. T. Silk, formerly of Yale University, for supplying me with a copy of his (unfinished) edition of that commentary by Trevet and generously allowing me to use it in whatever way I thought fit.

This book is dedicated to my wife Florence, to whom my debt is as incalculable as it is large.

Alastair Minnis
Bristol, 1982

Contents

INTRODUCTION

The Popular Pagans

'The pagans are wrong and the Christians are right!', exclaims the hero of the
late eleventh century *Chanson de Roland*.[1] By contrast, in the *Roman de la Rose*
(c.1277) Jean de Meun assures his audience that 'It is good to believe the
pagans, for we may gain great benefit from their sayings'.[2] By Jean's time the
pagans had attained a considerable degree of respect, even of popularity.
Sometimes they were wrong, sometimes they were right, and often they were
half-right, or right in a limited way.

Christians of the thirteenth and fourteenth centuries were fascinated by
classical or pagan lore of every kind. Pagan philosophers were recognized as
experts in such subject-areas as natural science, ethics and politics; pagan poets
were supposed to have written fables which, when interpreted allegorically,
were found to contain profound truths.[3] It was generally accepted that
contemporary Christians, the *moderni*, had much to learn from the sages of
antiquity, the *antiqui*.[4] After all, many of them had been monotheistic,
believing in an omnipotent god who could be identified with the one true God
of Christianity. Some of them, moreover, had been prophets or forerunners of
the faith to come. Virgil had foretold the coming of Christ in his fourth
eclogue;[5] the testimony of David had been supported by the Sibyl:

> Dies irae, dies illa,
> solvet saeclum in favilla,
> teste David cum Sibylla.[6]
>
> [The day of wrath, that awful day,
> will dissolve the world in ashes.
> David and the Sibyl bear witness to this.]

But the authority of pre-Christian writings was limited: the Christian estab-
lishment pronounced them to be in error on matters relating to the nature of
God and His characteristic operations, and any scholar who was enticed by
pagan notions about, for example, astral determinism or the eternity of the
world, ran the risk of being condemned by Holy Church. Once the pagans'
errors had been identified, however, one could carefully avoid them and freely
exploit the abundance of lore which was left—hence the need for a work like
Giles of Rome's *Errores Philosophorum* (written between 1270 and 1274), which
lists the mistakes made by Aristotle and his Arabian interpreters, and the great
Jewish scholar Maimonides.[7] Concomitant with the assimilation of heathen
knowledge to Christian doctrine was the investigation of the final end of those
ancients who had taught the moderns so much both by precept and by virtuous
example. Were Socrates, Aristotle, Cato, Seneca, Virgil, Trajan, Ripheus and

the rest in heaven or in hell? This interest in the pagan past was not confined to schoolmen and academic theologians. It was shared by vernacular writers like, in the case of England, William Langland, John Gower, the anonymous authors of *Patience* and *St Erkenwald*, the native tellers of tales of Alexander and redactors of the matter of Troy, Greece and Rome—and Geoffrey Chaucer, whose literary paganism is the subject of this book.[8]

Chaucer's three great pagan poems, *Troilus and Criseyde*, *The Knight's Tale* and *The Franklin's Tale*, belong, at bottom, to a particular species of the genus of romance, the *roman d'antiquité*. As such, they bear comparison with, for example, the *Roman de Thebes* (c.1150, based on Statius), the *Roman d'Eneas* (c.1160, based on Virgil's *Aeneid*), and Benoît de St Maure's *Roman de Troie* (c.1160, based on Dares and Dictys; a minor source for *Troilus and Criseyde*). These French works succeed in making the past come alive, and display some sense of historical perspective. Therein the noble pagans of ancient Troy, Greece and Rome are depicted 'in a natural environment, observing laws and customs that they felt were true, performing duties and obligations in which they believed, doing the best that they knew, and occasionally exceeding the virtue and moral excellence of Christians'.[9] Chaucer, therefore, was not unusual in presenting his pagan characters in this way; what was unusual was the subtlety and profundity with which he did so, notably the way in which Troilus, Theseus and other ancients are characterized in accordance with quite sophisticated contemporary notions about what pagan antiquity was like.

Although Chaucer's pagans are generally fatalistic, polytheistic and idolatrous, on occasion the best of them pushes his recognition that Jupiter is the supreme god to a monotheistic vision which anticipates Christian belief. Troilus at the end of book III of *Troilus and Criseyde* and Theseus at the end of *The Knight's Tale* sound rather like those 'friends of God' described in the Book of Wisdom 7.27, 'And being but one, she [i.e. Wisdom] can do all things: and remaining in herself the same, she reneweth all things, and through nations conveyeth herself into holy souls, she maketh the friends of God and prophets'. Expounding this text in his *Postilla Litteralis* (completed 1331), Nicholas of Lyre, 'the best-equipped Biblical scholar of the Middle Ages', states that, according to the Old Testament, there were many gentile prophets as well as hebrew ones, as is obvious from the case of St Job, who was a gentile.[10] The Erithrean Sibyl had the spirit of prophecy, as Augustine says. Similarly, Lyre continues, in the histories of the Romans we read that during the time of the Emperor Constantine and his mother Helen a certain sepulchre was found, in which lay a man with a golden blade on his breast, on which was written, 'Christ will be born of the Virgin, and I believe in Him. O Sun, in the time of Helen and Constantine you will see me again', i.e. you will cause me to be seen. Chaucer, of course, does not go so far as to suggest that his good pagans have received a special grace whereby advance information about Christ has been revealed to them: his interest is rather in the moral and martial achievements which they attained through wisdom, identified by Lyre as a gift of the holy Spirit. From the martial point of view, Duke Theseus resembles the patriarchal conquerors celebrated in the Old Testament; from the moral and intellectual point of view, he resembles those virtuous pre-Christian philosophers whose exemplary lives were recorded in the anonymous *Liber Philosophorum Moralium Antiquorum*, the sixth book of the *Speculum Historiale* of Vincent of Beauvais, the *Compendiloquium de Vitis Illustrium Philosophorum* of John of

Wales, and Walter Burley's *Liber de Vita et Moribus Philosophorum*.[11] The case of Chaucer's Troilus is a more complex one, as I hope to show in Chapter III below.

The timeliness of Chaucer's pagan poems deserves some comment at the outset, since it is difficult for us to grasp just how controversial the alleged achievements and limitations of the pagans could be in Chaucer's day, and to appreciate the wider implications of some of the philosophical ideas he was handling. In 1270 and 1277 Stephen Tempier, Bishop of Paris, 'condemned and excommunicated' a series of pagan errors 'together with all who should knowingly teach or affirm them'; Robert Kilwardby, Archbishop of Canterbury, followed suit at Oxford.[12] Among these errors were the propositions that man's will acts from necessity, and that all that happens in the sublunar world is subject to the necessity of heavenly bodies. Absolute necessity and astral determinism were thereby identified as distinctively pagan beliefs which no Christian could accept—a point which must be taken into account in any appreciation of Chaucer's fatalistic pagans. Certainly, it is impossible to accept the tentative suggestions of T. O. Wedel that our poet might have 'favoured a kind of determinism' and that 'his mature judgment decided in favour of a fatalistic philosophy'.[13] What Wedel's account of Chaucer's literary use of astrology fails to recognize is the fine sense of historical perspective that operates in *Troilus*, *The Knight's Tale*, and *The Franklin's Tale*: Chaucer's pagans act and think as pagans were supposed to. The narrator of *Troilus* briefly but firmly condemns the rascally gods and cursed old rites of the pagans; the Franklin laboriously criticizes

> swiche illusiouns and swiche meschaunces
> As hethen folk useden in thilke dayes.
>
> (V, 1292-3)

A consideration of the traditional aspects of these literary stances is included in Chapter III.

The nature of pagan achievement was as open to question as the nature of pagan limitation, a point which will be discussed in Chapter II. Precisely what was the basis of such knowledge as the heathen possessed, and what degree of perfection was possible to them? Nominalist theologians made much of the idea that the man who does his best naturally (*qui facit quod in se est ex puris naturalibus*) will receive divine aid in acquiring knowledge and effecting his salvation.[14] Robert Holcot (d.1349), whose popular commentary on the Book of Wisdom was known to Chaucer,[15] claimed that God would not refuse the grace necessary for salvation to people who 'did what was in them' and observed assiduously the best law they had, whether it was the natural law (available to pagans), the Mosaic Law (available to Old Testament figures) or the New Law (available since the passion of Christ). Such views were castigated as semi-pelagian by Thomas Bradwardine (d.1349), one of the foremost Augustinian theologians of the fourteenth century, by which he meant that the nominalists inclined to the belief that an individual could merit salvation through his own efforts. Holcot's position was far more complex than that, as shall be explained below. Suffice it to mention here one interesting attack on the *facere quod in se est* principle by a contemporary of Chaucer's, which (to the best of my knowledge) has not hitherto been recognized for what

3

it is. In the second book of *The Scale of Perfection*, the English mystic Walter Hilton (d. 1395) emphasizes that Jews and pagans do not receive the benefits of the passion since they do not believe in it.[16] From the beginning of the world until its end, no-one was ever saved, nor will be saved, except through belief in Jesus Christ and His coming. Therefore, Hilton continues, it seems to him a serious mistake for anyone to say that Jews and Saracens may be saved by keeping their own law, even though they do not believe in Jesus Christ in the manner of Holy Church, inasmuch as their own faith is supposed to be good and sufficient for their salvation, and in that faith they seem to perform many good deeds. It is sometimes assumed that they will be saved, and that if they knew that the Christian faith was better than their own, they would renounce their own faith and accept Christianity.

> Sen þis is soþ, þen þink me þat þese men gretly & greuously erre þat saien þat Iewes & Sareʒeins bi keping of þeir own law moun be mad saf þawʒ þei trowe not in Iesu Crist als Haly Kirke trowes; in als mikel as þei wene þat þeir owne trowþ is good & siker & suffisaunt to þair saluacioun, & in þat trouþ þei doo as it semes many gode dedes of riʒtwisnes, & perauenture if þei knewe þat Cristen feiþ ware better þen þaires is þei wold leue þeire own & take it, þat þei þerfore schuld be saf.[17]

All these ideas may be found in the writings of Nominalist theologians. Their point of view is untenable, Hilton argues, because Christ, God and man, is both the way and the end; He is the mediator between God and man, and without Him no soul can be reconciled to God or come to heavenly bliss. This major difference of opinion helps to explain Chaucer's reticence about making any definite statement concerning the ultimate destiny of his noble pagans, although it can be argued that he is implying more than he wished to make explicit.[18] He was prepared, however, to have his Squire praise the pagan 'Tartre Cambyuskan', king of Tzarev, for keeping his own law to such an extent that he possessed all the regal and chivalric virtues:

> Hym lakked noght that longeth to a kyng.
> As of the secte of which that he was born
> He kepte his lay, to which that he was sworn;
> And therto he was hardy, wys, and riche,
> And pitous and just, alwey yliche;
> Sooth of his word, benigne, and honurable;
> Of his corage as any centre stable;
> Yong, fressh, and strong, in armes desirous
> As any bacheler of al his hous.
>
> (V, 16–24)

One may compare the manner in which Chaucer's Knight, the Squire's father, depicts the 'pitous and just' Theseus, the heathen ruler of ancient Athens.

Chaucer's portrait of a Tartar king, and Hilton's reference to 'sareʒeins', will serve to remind us that plenty of pagans were living in Chaucer's day, whose presence was proof positive that there were viable value-systems other than Christianity. The term 'Saracen' was 'used by medieval writers of the Arabs generally and later applied to the infidel and Mohammedan nations against whom the crusaders fought'.[19] The crusades having failed, some Western Christians sought to conquer the Muslims by argument rather than by force.[20] To take but one notable example, Raymond Lull (d.1316), who dedicated his life to the conversion of infidels, seems to have been the prime mover behind the decision at the Council of Vienne in 1311 to institute language schools in Arabic, Hebrew and Syriac, at Paris, Oxford, Bologna, Avignon and Salamanca.[21] This, presumably, was designed to facilitate a dialogue between the religions with a view to conversion. As the frontiers of the known world were pushed back new candidates for conversion were revealed. Thomas Bradwardine read with horror Marco Polo's account of the Tartar deity Natigai, an earthly god who watches over children, beasts and crops.[22] Late-medieval debates on the salvation of the heathen may seem remote and re-cherché to us, but they were stimulated by current affairs of great importance.

For the most part, Chaucer did not respond directly to those current affairs—a point which may be made effectively by contrasting his literary paganism with that of a major poet who was fascinated by the interaction of Christian and pagan characters, Wolfram von Eschenbach. In Wolfram's *Willehalm* (c.1217) the hero's wife, a converted pagan, begs the assembled Christian leaders to spare the pagans, should they win the crucial battle.[23] The Saracens are the creation of God's own hand; whatever they may have done they should be forgiven, even as Christ forgave those who put him to death. After all, the first man God made was a heathen, as were Elias, Enoch, Noah, and Job—and all these men were just. When the battle has been fought and won, Wolfram speaks *in propria persona* to accuse the Christians of having sinned by killing many heathen, and has his hero command that the bodies of the fallen Saracens should be carried home to their own country in order to receive burial according to the rites of Islam. Wolfram's pagans are misguided and limited, but not wilful enemies of the one true God, who cares for all his creatures and offers salvation to all.[24] Moreover, in *Willehalm* religious values are complemented by chivalric ones, valid for all knights, so that in those terms a Saracen may be equal in worth to a Christian. We have come a long way from the *Chanson de Roland*, wherein the pagans, although not lacking in courage, are underhand, hot-tempered, stupidly idolatrous, and generally despicable; they all go to hell after death.

Chaucer's interests and emphases were very different from Wolfram's. *The Man of Law's Tale* is the only work of his in which pagans and Christians confront each other, and there the stress is on the divine providence which sees Constance safely through her intricate and marvellous adventures rather than on the nature of Islam or the relative merits of the different faiths. The wickedness of the Sultan's mother cannot be ascribed simply to her wish to defend 'the hooly lawes of our Alkaron' (II, 332): the point is rather that she, as a daughter of Eve, is the willing instrument of Satan's malice (see II, 358–71). Although Chaucer's Knight has seen honourable service both with and against present-day pagans (I, 60–66) he prefers to tell a pagan tale of long ago. It could be suggested that his experience of Saracen chivalry and honour has coloured the way in which he portrays the martial exploits of ancient Athenians and Thebans, but the pagan world of *The Knight's Tale* is essentially remote, 'closed', and self-contained—a description which applies equally well to the pagan world of *Troilus and Criseyde*. In those works, and to a lesser extent in *The Franklin's Tale*, Chaucer was concerned to present an image of antiquity, to write as an 'historial' poet about events which had long since passed and beliefs which had been rendered obsolete.[25]

What is meant by calling Chaucer an 'historial' poet will be made clear in our first chapter, through discussion of medieval attitudes to history and poetic fiction respectively. The differences between *historia* and *fabula* (or *fictio*) have for long fascinated literary critics and theorists. In his *Apology for Poetry* (1581–3), Sir Philip Sidney, adopting certain precepts of Italian literary theory for his own polemical purposes, had argued that poetical fiction is superior to historical fact because 'Poetry ever setteth virtue out in her best colours' whereas history is obliged to record every kind of event and deed, whether edifying or not: 'the historian, being captived to the truth of a foolish world, is many times a terror from well-doing, and an encouragement to unbridled wickedness'.[26] Chaucer and his circle would have found this argument difficult to accept (as, indeed, did many of Sidney's contemporaries) since for them 'the reading of history was an exercise second only to the study of Holy Writ in its power to induce good morality and shape the individual into a worthy member of society'.[27] The good pagans presented in Chaucer's poems about pagan antiquity attain heights of virtue and wisdom which should put many a so-called Christian to shame (to apply the late-medieval cliché). On the other hand, Chaucer was perfectly aware that the heathen had made numerous mistakes and were limited in many ways, partly through their own fault and partly through the historical accident of having been born at the wrong time, before the advent of Christ. Yet Chaucer did not write exemplary history in the strict late-medieval and Renaissance sense of the term. His concern was with truth-to-life, with verisimilitude, rather than with moral truth; instead of wishing to score moral points through and off his pagans he wanted to show how they thought and behaved in their historical time and place.

Viewed from the vantage point of our own age, Chaucer's pagan poems are intriguing hybrids: they are at once anachronistic and historically accurate. Their anachronism mainly consists in such things as the late-medieval manners, fashions, ideals of chivalry, and doctrines of *fin' amors* which Chaucer imposed on his pagan materials in an attempt (how conscious we will never know) to up-date the past slightly, to make it more meaningful in contemporary, 'modern' terms. But when we consider such matters as pagan philosophy and faith, *Troilus* and *The Knight's Tale* are as historically accurate as Chaucer, as an Englishman of his time, could have made them. In order to understand precisely what Chaucer did to the primary sources of his pagan poems, it is necessary to investigate those attitudes to pagan antiquity which were current in fourteenth-century England, a task which (it will be argued in Chapter I) involves the reading of such philosophical, theological, encyclopaedic, historical and 'fabulous' works as Chaucer and his contemporaries read. Here one may find the basis for an understanding of Chaucer's poetry which takes stock of both his celebration of the achievements of good pagans and his fundamental detachment from their limitations.

CHAPTER I

An Historical Approach
to Chaucerian Antiquity

When attempting to enter Chaucer's pagan world the modern critic is faced with a twofold problem. In the first place, he is approaching Chaucer's poems as fourteenth-century writings, which display late-medieval attitudes, preconceptions, prejudices and ideals. In the second place, he is approaching them as depictions of antiquity, with its pagan attitudes, preconceptions, prejudices and ideals. The critic is looking back into the medieval past at Chaucer's poems; Chaucer was looking back into the ancient past at pre-Christian societies.

The task of disentangling what was 'ancient' and what was 'modern' to Chaucer is a difficult one. It is all too easy for us to mistake what was, in Chaucer's opinion, an authentically pagan attitude for a fourteenth-century notion, as may be illustrated by reference to the most problematic of all the ancient themes treated by Chaucer, namely, pagan love. Emelye in *The Knight's Tale* has been regarded as the archetypal 'courtly lady' of the Middle Ages, the unmoved mover who stands aloof from the trials and tribulations which her suitors are suffering, content to accept the lover whom a spectacular trial of strength proves to be the better man. Similarly, Troilus in *Troilus and Criseyde* has been regarded as the ideal 'courtly lover' who, under the guidance of the trusted *ami* Pandarus, pursues his *fin'amors* according to the book, the book being the *Roman de la Rose* of Guillaume de Lorris and Jean de Meun. In fact, neither Emelye nor Troilus are typical of the courtly ladies and lovers of romance tradition. Emelye is simply too passive and acquiescent to keep company with the heroines of, for example, Chrétien de Troyes' *Eric et Enide*, *Cliges* and *Yvain*, or (to go somewhat down-market), the anonymous *Sir Degrevant*, *William of Palerne*, *Sir Isumbras* and *Floriant and Florete*. Troilus is so ideal a courtly lover that he renders himself ineffectual: the reader may be forgiven for suspecting that, had Pandarus not helped him into bed with Criseyde (which he does, literally, at one point), there would have been no love-affair and hence no poem.

When it is realised that they are pagans, however, the behaviour of Emelye and Troilus becomes more comprehensible. As I hope to show below, Emelye's acquiescence is an aspect of her fatalism, the world-view which, according to late-medieval clerics, had been held by the vast majority of ancient heathen. Troilus, too, is imbued with the fatalism endemic to pagan society: if he is slow to act, this is because he cannot believe in the efficacy of human action in any situation. Faced with the impending loss of his beloved Criseyde, Troilus exclaims that

> 'al that comth, comth by necessitee:
> Thus to ben lorn, it is my destinee'.
>
> (IV, 958–9)

In *The Knight's Tale* and *Troilus and Criseyde* Chaucer is demonstrating how certain virtuous heathen attempted, in the words of the supremely noble Duke Theseus, to 'maken vertue of necessitee', to ennoble what, in their opinion, must be by accepting it with courage and dignity.

Emelye and Troilus are 'ancients' rather than 'moderns', products of a culture different from Chaucer's own, and therefore 'modern' norms of behaviour and codes of conduct do not apply to them. Of course, his interest in the pagan past was not narrowly antiquarian: Chaucer endowed the old stories with new vigour, making them come alive for his modern reader. It is hardly surprising that human love, a topic of perennial fascination and a literary obsession of the fourteenth century, is the area of *Troilus and Criseyde* where, as it were, the pagan colouring has been applied most lightly. But to mistake the 'ancient' elements of Chaucer's works for the 'modern', and vice-versa, is to run the risk of misunderstanding the writer's purpose and achievement. The personality of Criseyde cannot be reduced to an amalgam of (supposedly) pagan hopes and fears. Yet she would not be what she is had late-medieval historians, mythographers and theologians conceived of the pre-Christian era in different terms.

The terms in which such people did conceive of pagan antiquity provide the substance of this book, which is offered as an essay in historical criticism. To some extent it supports and illustrates the opinion of E. D. Hirsch that authorial intention is 'the only practical norm for a cognitive discipline of interpretation. . . . The reader should try to reconstruct authorial meaning, and he can in principle succeed in his attempt'.[1] Comprehensive study of the sources which informed and influenced Chaucer's attitudes to pagan antiquity can, I suggest, be of the first importance in reconstructing authorial meaning in *Troilus and Criseyde* and *The Knight's Tale*. More generally, our historical approach to Chaucerian antiquity involves the reclamation of Chaucer's own sense of history; the extent to which, and the manner in which, he was aware of the 'pastness' and 'otherness'—what a contemporary critic might call the 'alterity'—of past experience.[2]

This chapter, therefore, offers a twofold response to the twofold problem presented at its beginning. First, an explanation is provided of the source-based historical criticism which is practised in the following pages. Secondly, an attempt is made to discover what Chaucer's sense of history was and how it determined the form of literary procedure in which he wrote about pagan antiquity. This course of action will, it is hoped, give both our historical awareness and Chaucer's historical awareness their due.

I   AN HISTORICAL APPROACH TO CHAUCER

My discourse on method must involve a certain amount of apologia and justification, in view of the current uncertainty—some would call it a failure of nerve—which in some quarters is afflicting medieval studies.[3] The type of literary study practised nowadays can be, like death, a great leveller. Not very long ago medieval texts were considered predominantly as philological documents and linguistic constructs, little attention being paid to considerations of literary merit and quality. The 'New Criticism' has been preoccupied with literary quality, but in a narrow sense—literary quality as dictated by what the words on the medieval page mean to a select group of modern readers. This approach has tended to place the cultured modern reader in the position of importance rightly occupied by the medieval author, and to deny determinate meaning to his text. Contemporary literary theory can be reductionist too, in so far as it can encourage a lumping-together of diverse medieval writings as (for example) semiotic records or reflections of social infrastructures, thereby precluding considerations like genre, style, and authorial intention. The present time of literary-critical ferment is ripe for the introduction of fresh approaches to literature and the reappraisal of established ones. My own method is a personal blend of old and new: a type of all-embracing source study which is broadly structuralist in principle in so far as it places a premium on the ideological structures which determine the semantic area and range within which a given Chaucer text operates, yet which takes full cognizance of Chaucer's personal exploitation of the medieval structures of ideas which he transmitted.

Study of an author's sources has, until very recently, been regarded as indispensable in literary scholarship, and I for one am convinced that it should maintain this position. Indeed, I would go further, by arguing that study of the materials which Chaucer employed in producing his works must be allowed its *full* value in our modern approach to Chaucer, since by this means we can avoid what Hirsch has happily called 'the fallacy of the homogenous past'.[4] In the case of Chaucer, this fallacy may be identified by citation of a few random examples: since certain attitudes were held by late-medieval rhetoricians, or writers on the art of memory, or 'doctors of signs', or commentators on Ovid, then Chaucer—being a man of his age—must also have held these attitudes. But in the late Middle Ages, ideas did not travel in the air, in the water supply, or in the wine, any more than they do now. In each and every case of ideological influence, there was a specific process of transmission, whether textual or oral, and the critic must make some attempt to explain that process. If one wishes to argue that Chaucer was influenced by a certain idea, the criterion of historical plausibility must be satisfied with reference to its two facets, namely, dissemination and provenance. The senses in which these two terms are used derive from the theory of editorial technique and textual criticism.

Concerning dissemination, we should inquire if the idea under investigation was present in a text which we know that Chaucer knew. If the answer is in the negative, a weaker case might still be made. Was the idea recherché or commonplace, was it restricted to works of a highly specialized nature or was it reiterated in many works which enjoyed a wide readership? In other words, is the extent and/or level of dissemination right? Did the idea exist in a text or texts of a type or genre which Chaucer read or could have read?

Concerning provenance, ideally we should be able to prove that the source containing the idea in question was in the right place at the right time for Chaucer to have read it. If the evidence for this is lacking, it might yet be possible to posit an 'ideological provenance': was the idea close to ideas which can be identified precisely in Chaucer's work, being part of a system or complex of ideas which was familiar to Chaucer? If this weaker claim cannot be

9

made either, the modern critic should recognize the danger of solipsism and bow out gracefully.

Moreover, it is not enough for the individual ideas offered by the interpreter of Chaucer to be authentically 'late-medieval': their structure and inter-relationship, as described by the critic, must also be authentically late-medieval. Otherwise we are being given fragments of fact yoked together with violence. The individual pieces may be old but, having been taken from their original contexts and brought together in a new collage, they have lost their historical identity. Study of Chaucer's sources in their entirety—not just the extracts which provide close literal parallels with Chaucer passages—is essential. The full context of the key passage in the source, what medieval commentators called 'the circumstances of the letter', must be investigated fully.[5] (It has been suggested that I call these two aspects of the source the 'microsource' and the 'macrosource' respectively, but I retain the view that jargon should not be multiplied beyond necessity.) From the 'circumstances of the letter' can be obtained information about the ideological structure within which the ideas in question functioned and took on their original meaning. Modern structuralism should alert us to the integrity of medieval structures of ideas.

Applying all this theory to Chaucer's literary practice, we come up with a richer range of sources for his depiction of antiquity than is usually brought to bear on the two major 'pagan' poems, *Troilus and Criseyde* and *The Knight's Tale*. As is well known, the main source of Troilus was Boccaccio's *Il Filostrato* (probably composed between 1335 and 1338); of *The Knight's Tale*, Boccaccio's *Il Teseida* (c. 1340–2).[6] With the knowledge of hindsight, we may detect a distinctive 'Renaissance' quality in the classicism of *Il Filostrato* and *Il Teseida*, and it is precisely this quality which Chaucer eliminated in *Troilus* and *The Knight's Tale* respectively. His 'medievalization' of Boccaccio resulted in splendid representations of pagan society which are consonant with the attitudes to antiquity expressed in other, more distinctively 'medieval', sources. These other sources will briefly be characterized in turn, since the pagan world they evoke has much more in common with Chaucerian antiquity than has the pagan world described by Boccaccio, and so they provide the basis for our attempted reconstruction of authorial meaning in *Troilus and Criseyde* and *The Knight's Tale*.

It is generally accepted that important details in *Troilus* derive from three major Troy-books, Benoît de Sainte-Maure's *Roman de Troie* (c. 1160), Joseph of Exeter's *De Bello Trojano* or *Iliad* (c. 1188), and Guido delle Colonne's *Historia Destructionis Troiae* (completed in 1287).[7] Guido's *Historia* is a translation, with additional material, of Benoît's Old French *roman d'antiquité*, and some of that additional material was supplied by Joseph of Exeter.[8] Somewhat surprisingly, no systematic attempt has yet been made to relate to *Troilus and Criseyde* the representations of pagan antiquity provided in these long-acknowledged sources.

Most of the philosophy in Chaucer's three major pagan poems is taken from the *De Consolatione Philosophiae* of Boethius, which Chaucer appears to have read with the aid of Nicholas Trevet's commentary (completed before 1307).[9] In order to understand the full 'circumstances of the letter' in the case of Chaucer's use of *De Consolatione Philosophiae*, the late-medieval significance of the fact that this was a consolation *of philosophy* must be grasped. In twelfth-century divisions of the sciences, the term *philosophia* could denote the whole spectrum of knowledge and inquiry, including theology, which was classed as theological or speculative science.[10] Such a division is outlined, for example, in William of Conches's commentary on *De Consolatione Philosophiae* I pr. 1, and throughout this commentary William does not hesitate to employ theological knowledge (including quotations from Scripture) in expounding his author.[11] Thirteenth-century schoolmen, however, drove a wedge between theology and philosophy, the latter being regarded as the inferior of the former.[12] Theology was supposed to rest on the authority of revelation, whereas in philosophy truth was reached by the use of reasoning: to either discipline was 'reserved its proper province and its own sphere of action and investigation'.[13] Hence, St Albert the Great (d. 1280) could state that, while in matters of faith and morals Augustine was to be preferred to the philosophers, in philosophy and in the natural sciences he rather believed 'Aristotle and those who are expert in these sciences'.[14] The same demarcation is evinced by John of Wales, who claimed (slightly misquoting Aristotle) that philosophy is not concerned with contemplation but with making us good.[15] This explains why Nicholas Trevet's commentary on Boethius is rigorously philosophical, with no use being made of theological knowledge as such. For Chaucer, then, the doctrine of *De Consolatione Philosophiae* pertained to philosophy in the strictest possible sense of the term, a specialist discipline which was grounded on natural reason and in which most of the experts were pagans. The material which he extracted from this source would, therefore, have seemed perfectly germane to his pagan characters.

Other key notions concerning the pagan past are found in the following books that we believe that Chaucer knew: the *Speculum Maius* of Vincent of Beauvais (written between 1247 and 1259, and consisting of three parts, the *Speculum Naturale, Speculum Doctrinale* and *Speculum Historiale*),[16] the *Communiloquium* of John of Wales (regent master at Oxford c. 1260),[17] Robert Holcot's highly popular commentary on the Book of Wisdom then attributed to King Solomon (1334–6),[18] and the *Ovidius Moralizatus* which comprises the fifteenth book of Pierre Bersuire's *Reductorium Morale*.[19] The second recension of Bersuire's 'Moralized Ovid' (made around 1350) was the version used by Chaucer: it has additional material from the Old French *Ovide Moralisé* (1316–28), which also was known to Chaucer, and from John Ridevall's *Fulgentius Metaforalis* (before 1333), a re-moralization of the fifth-century *Mythologiae* of Fulgentius. All of these works were produced by 'classicizing' scholars, i.e. clerics who sought to show how pagan science, history and mythology could serve and support Christian doctrine.[20] Here we have sources which illuminate Chaucer's own brand of classicism.

Chaucer seems to have known at least by reputation some of the work of another 'classicizing' scholar, Thomas Bradwardine, who was consecrated Archbishop of Canterbury in 1349. In *The Nun's Priest's Tale* mention is made of 'Bishop Bradwardyn', and his name is linked with that of St Augustine, the main precursor of the theology in Bradwardine's monumental *De Causa Dei contra Pelagium et de Virtute Causarum* (completed 1344). Several of the most important arguments used in this work are found also in a sermon which Bradwardine preached before Edward III and his lords on the occasion of the English victories at Crécy and Neville's Cross.[21] The triumphant army was assured that God alone, and not any secondary cause such as the stars, fate or fortune, was to be thanked for the victory: those superstitious soldiers who, on the eve of the battle of Crécy, tried to foretell its outcome would have been better employed in placing their trust in God. Since such plain speaking on an auspicious occasion is the stuff of which reputations are made, I have cited the *Sermo Epinicius* along with the *De Causa Dei*.

Other works quoted below satisfy the (less strict yet still demanding) criteria of 'right level of dissemination' and 'ideological provenance'. For example, astrological lore and classical mythology have been taken from the fifth book of Bersuire's *Reductorium Morale* as well as from the fifteenth book which Chaucer certainly knew. This is more of a procedural leap than might appear initially since, being a self-contained 'Moralized Ovid', the fifteenth book circulated independently of the rest of the *Reductorium*. However, we may be reassured by the fact that the ideas in the fifth book were commonplace and frequently reiterated. Indeed, most of them derive from the *De Proprietatibus Rerum* of Bartholomaeus Anglicus (begun between 1225 and 1231 at Oxford). The first fourteen books of Bersuire's work consist of a systematic revision of this earlier work with emphasis being placed on its moral sense and symbolism, hence the title *Reductorium Morale*—Bartholomaeus's science has been 're-duced' or traced back to its moral significance. Therefore, it seems reasonable to quote Bartholomaeus along with Bersuire. John Trevisa's translation of *De Proprietatibus Rerum* (1398) has been used because it may readily be compared with Chaucer's English.

Vincent's *Speculum Historiale* was a major source for Ralph Higden's *Polychronicon*, by far the most popular history book in fourteenth-century England, which has been quoted in the translations by Trevisa (1387) and an anonymous fifteenth-century writer. Another important compilation, the *Communiloquium* of John of Wales, seems to have been known to Chaucer, but since John's attitudes to pagan knowledge and virtue are sometimes expressed more succinctly in another of his works, the *Compendiloquium de Vitis Illustrium Philosophorum*, I have resorted to it as well.

In order to preserve the integrity of medieval structures of ideas, the works mentioned above, and others, have been quoted at some length. This has been done even when the writer in question is heavily dependent on some earlier writer, since our main interest is in that ideological structure which was closest in time and culture to Chaucer.[22] For example, many of the theories concerning fate and providence found in our Bradwardine extracts are amalgamations of ideas promulgated by St Augustine and Boethius, but in order to gain insight into how these ideas were understood and applied in the fourteenth century we must concentrate on Bradwardine.

From the writings of Vincent, John of Wales, Holcot and the rest we can obtain a rich harvest of ideas relating to the pagan past as seen from the medieval present. In subsequent chapters an attempt will be made to show how Chaucer adopted some of those ideas and rejected others, bringing his individual talent to bear on the traditions concerning antiquity. But in order to understand better the full 'circumstances of the letter' in respect of Chaucer's handling of such ideas, it is necessary to identify the relevant forms and modes of procedure which were available to him as a writer. Having described the basis of our historical approach to Chaucer, we may now proceed to discuss the basis of Chaucer's historical approach to antiquity.

As a Christian poet—by which I mean simply a poet whose mind and attitudes were shaped by Christian culture and learning—Chaucer could have deployed his 'matter of antiquity' in one of two fundamental ways. First, he could have composed moralized fables after the manner of the Old French *Ovide Moralisé* or Bersuire's *Ovidius Moralizatus*. Secondly, he could have placed pagan lore within a firm historical perspective that stressed both its antiquity and its limitations. Chaucer's reaction to these options will now be considered, beginning with his attitude to the moral sense of fiction, what Dante regarded as the 'allegory of the poets'.[23] Since some modern critics are inclined to regard medieval fable-interpretation as a simple extension of Scriptural exegesis, it will be necessary to include the 'allegory of the theologians' in our discussion.

According to a famous passage in Dante's *Il Convivio*, the first or 'literal' sense of a piece of writing is that sense which does not go beyond the strict sense of 'the letter', whereas the second or allegorical sense is 'disguised under the cloak' of the literal story and is 'a truth hidden under a beautiful fiction'.[24] By contrast, in accordance with the 'allegory of the theologians' sacred Scripture could be expounded in four senses, the literal and historical, the moral or tropological, the allegorical or typological, and the anagogical. Theologians often explained this exegetical method through the example of Jerusalem: literally, Jerusalem signifies a city, once the most important city in the kingdom of Judea; morally, it signifies a faithful soul; allegorically, it is the church militant; anagogically, it betokens the heavenly Jerusalem, the church reigning in bliss.[25] Here is the version of this explanation found at the beginning of Nicholas of Lyre's monumental *Postilla Litteralis* on the whole Bible, as englished by the Lollard translators of Scripture:

> The lettre techith what is doon; allegorie techith what thou owist for to bileeue; moral techith what thou owist for to do; anagogic techith whedir thou owist to go; and of these iiij. sensis, either vndirstondingis, may be set ensaumple in this word Jerusalem; for bi the literal vndirstonding Jerusalem singnefieth a cyte, that was sumtyme the cheef citee in the rewme of Jude, and Jerusalem was foundid first of Melchisedech, and aftirward it was alargid, and maad strong bi Salomon; bi moral sense it signefieth a feithful soule, bi which sense it is seid in iij.ᵗᵗ c. of Apoc., 'I siʒ the hooly citee newe Jerusalem comynge doun fro heuene, as a spouse ourned to hire housbonde;' bi sence anagogik it singnefieth the chirche rengninge in blisse, bi this sence it is seid in iiij.ᵗc. to Galat. 'thilke Jerusalem which is aboue, which is oure modir, is free . . .'[26]

The extent to which such theological allegory influenced the 'allegory of the poets' is a highly controversial issue in the criticism of medieval literature. Commentators on Dante's *Divine Comedy* were interested in the literal, moral, allegorical and anagogical senses of the poem, and, if the *Epistle to Can Grande della Scala* is authentic, Dante himself had suggested that it could be read in this way.[27] Boccaccio's *De Genealogia Gentilium Deorum* contains some four-fold interpretation, but this is the exception rather than the rule.[28] At any rate,

13

literary attitudes in Italy, when placed in the full context of late-medieval Europe, are seen to be unique and ahead of their time, and so it would altogether be improper to cite them in discussing the very different scene in other countries. The norm for fourteenth-century France and England is represented by the anonymous compiler of the *Ovide Moralisé*, John Ridevall, and Pierre Bersuire. Their method of interpretation, which is applied most elaborately in Bersuire's *Ovidius Moralizatus*, is not to be confused with the 'allegory of the theologians'.

Bersuire interprets the pagan gods and goddesses literally, historically, naturally and spiritually.[29]. The literal reading is an astrological one. Saturn, for example, is the planet with the longest orbit.[30] As he admits in the prologue of the *Ovidius Moralizatus*, Bersuire is not greatly concerned with this type of interpretation.[31] He had, after all, reiterated the planetary lore of Bartholomaeus Anglicus in the fifth book of the *Reductorium Morale*. Naturally, the deities can be understood in terms of natural elements and process, Saturn being all-devouring time.[32] The historical interpretation had its rationale in the euhemeristic theory of the origin of the gentile gods: historical personages like Saturn and Jupiter, with the passage of time, had come to be worshipped as gods, through either fear, misplaced reverence, or misunderstanding of their true nature.[33] Hence, Saturn was really a Cretan king who, having failed to escape the downfall which his brother had predicted, was exiled by his son Jupiter.[34] Exposition of the spiritual or allegorical sense meant moralization, and here Bersuire's imagination takes wing. Saturn is interpreted both *in malo* and *in bono*.[35] Viewed in the worst possible light, he represents the tyrant who subjugates his state by guile or force, or he personifies the sin of greed. Viewed in the best possible light, he represents the upright prelate who feeds the poor and 'devours' or corrects his spiritual children, or he personifies the virtue of prudence, as is stated 'in the treatise on the *Mythologiae* of Fulgentius' (i.e. in Ridevall's *Fulgentius Metaforalis*). The proliferation of alternative allegories is bewildering. Bersuire seems to be struggling to provide a moral for every occasion. His enthusiastic classicism is appealing, even if one wonders how many practising preachers found that it met their needs.

The kind of allegory found in the *Ovidius Moralizatus* is at once encyclopaedic and structured. All things and systems which are true in some sense— whether literally, naturally, historically or morally—are placed in parallel so that they become mutually illuminating.[36] The four senses of poetic fiction according to Bersuire are quite different from the four senses of Scripture according to the theologians. It is, however, interesting to note that the late-medieval growth of interest in the moral sense of fiction corresponded to a decline of interest in the spiritual sense of Scripture.[37] The great Dominican scholars Albert the Great (d. 1280) and Thomas Aquinas (d. 1274) had emphasized the primacy of the literal sense of Scripture, which they defined as the sense intended by the inspired human authors.[38] Aristotelian epistemology gave the human faculties a new dignity; the 'body' of Scripture, its literal sense, was afforded a corresponding dignity.[39] Moreover, a more rigorous logical method was applied in exegesis. Thomas Aquinas made much of Augustine's remark that an argument can be drawn only from the literal sense, and for Aquinas 'argument' meant strictly logical argument, proceeding by means of premiss and syllogism.[40] Allegorical senses, which involve significative *things*, are of no use to the logician, who is confined to the literal sense.[41] There are, however, various kinds of literal sense: sometimes an author may speak plainly; sometimes he may employ figurative expressions. For Aquinas all kinds of figurative language, including metaphors and parables, involve significative *words* and therefore are part of the literal sense. Nicholas of Lyre, who was greatly influenced by Aquinas, accused his predecessors of obscurantism.[42] Although the ancient exegetes said many good things, they spent little time on the literal and historical sense but multiplied the spiritual senses to such an extent that the literal sense was partly suffocated. Lyre therefore decided to concentrate on the literal sense of Scripture in his *Postilla Litteralis*, only occasionally inserting short spiritual expositions. He was admirably equipped for the task, with a knowledge of Hebrew and rabbinic exegesis, including that of Rashi. Aquinas's theory and Lyre's practice dealt a powerful blow to the status of allegory as a scholastic procedure.

I have stressed this waning of interest in the spiritual senses within scholastic Bible-study because of the surprising tenacity of the oft-refuted opinion that the 'allegory of the theologians' permeates Chaucer's works, in some way or other (opinion being varied concerning the exact manner). According to D. W. Robertson, the tropological, allegorical, and anagogical levels of meaning express the central cultural and intellectual ideals of the Middle Ages, namely, those relating to the furtherance of Christian charity, the love of God and one's neighbour, and the repudiation of cupidity, the love of one's self.[43] Chaucer, in his opinion, wrote with these ideals in mind, intending each and every passage to be read in terms of one or other of the three spiritual senses which had been identified most articulately by the theologians. *Troilus and Criseyde*, therefore, should be interpreted as a Christian tragedy in which the 'three stages of tragic development correspond to the three stages in the tropological fall of Adam: the temptation of the senses, the corruption of the lower reason in pleasurable thought, and the final corruption of the higher reason . . .'.[44] Similarly, in *The Knight's Tale* the love and death of Arcite should be interpreted as frustrated concupiscence leading 'to wrath which in time causes self-destruction'.[45] In my opinion, this (hypothetical) type of writing would simply not have been a valid literary option for Chaucer.[46] Quite apart from the fact that the 'allegory of the theologians' had, as Lyre's strictures on earlier exegesis illustrate, undergone drastic reappraisal during the late-medieval period, the scholastic literary theory of Chaucer's day had unequivocally identified the Bible as being unique within the world of books. It would have been a considerable breach of literary decorum, to put it mildly, for Chaucer to have written in studied imitation of the unique divine style.

Of course, on occasion in *The Canterbury Tales* Chaucer compared his literary procedure with those found in the Bible.[47] When, in the General Prologue, he justified his practice of speaking 'rudeliche and large' after the manner of the Canterbury pilgrims, Chaucer was able to cite the precedent of a *modus loquendi* found in the Gospels: 'Crist spak hymself ful brode in hooly writ, / And wel ye woot no vileynye is it' (I, 739–40). Defending his translation of *Melibee* on the grounds that it preserved the *sententia* of the original text, Chaucer could refer to the fact that, although the words of the Four Evangelists often differ, their profound meaning is single and uniform (VII, 943–52). But these statements can be understood only within the full context of the changing attitudes to literature which characterize the later Middle Ages. The crucial notion (which has already been mentioned, in Aquinas's formulation) is that figurative language of whatever kind is part of the literal sense of Scripture.

By the time of Chaucer, the stylistic gap between sacred poetry and profane poetry had narrowed considerably in the minds and treatises of many academics.[48] Peter Auriol believed that songs of joy, love and sorrow had been composed by both pagan and Scriptural poets.[49] Ulrich of Strassburg emphasized the importance of the *modus poeticus* or fabulous mode as a Biblical form of treatment, while Thomas of Ireland and Pierre Bersuire offered examples of Scriptural *fabulae*.[50] Scriptural authors were read literally, with close attention being paid to those poetic devices that were facets of the literal sense; pagan *poetae* were read allegorically or moralized—and thus the twain could meet. In such an intellectual climate a writer could justify his own literary procedure by appeal to a Scriptural model, without seeming arrogant or without implying that he was concerned with the spiritual sense. This accounts for Chaucer's references to Christ's 'brode' manner of speaking and to the common 'sentence' of Matthew, Mark, Luke and John. Thomas Usk (d.1388) invoked both Aristotle and David in describing his own literary activity.[51] The general prologue to John Gower's *Vox Clamantis* contains the suggestion that the mode of procedure of this poem is similar to that employed by St John in the Apocalypse.[52] The fact that these English writers could act in this way testifies not to the large-scale incursion of the 'allegory of the theologians' into secular literature but rather to the emergence of the literal-historical sense—with all the literary variety which it comprised—as the most important sense of Scripture.

What, then, was Chaucer's reaction to the 'allegory of the poets', this being a valid literary option for a writer of his time? Having established that fable moralization is not to be confused with, or seen as a mere appendage of, Scriptural exegesis, we are now in a position to consider whether or not Chaucer was influenced by the techniques of *moralizatio* found in, for example, the *Ovide Moralisé* and Bersuire's *Ovidius Moralizatus*, works which we know that he knew well. My impression is that his interest was (to apply Bersuire's categories) literal and historical but rarely, if ever, spiritual or moral. That is to say, he inclined towards the astrological interpretation of the pagan deities (whom he portrayed as planet-gods) and he had a euhemeristic habit of mind (tending to see classical gods and heroes in the most human of terms), but moral allegory held no attraction for him, save as an object of humour or irony.[53] These attitudes of Chaucer's may emerge very clearly if they are considered in relation to the similar views held by two writers who influenced him considerably, Jean de Meun and Nicholas Trevet.

Jean de Meun reacted against the common twelfth-century practice of moralizing tales in moral and/or cosmological terms.[54] His own attitude was unflinchingly literal,[55] and on occasion we may even detect him regarding the procedure of moralization with amusement. For example, in the *Roman de la Rose*, 21619–32 Jean's narrator compares the difficult sexual penetration of his virgin rose with the excessive toil of Hercules in breaking down the gate which protected Cacus the cattle-thief. In William of Conches's commentary on the *De Consolatione Philosophiae* of Boethius, which Jean used in writing several passages of the *Roman*, the entry of Hercules into the cave of Cacus formed part of an elaborate allegory about the moral progress of the wise man (the *sapiens* so beloved of medieval mythographers and commentators).[56] Like Chaucer after him, Jean eliminated the 'wonder-element' of the story of Hercules, ignored any possible allegory which could be derived from it, and related its incidents in an earthy way. In *The Monk's Tale* the story of Hercules and Dianira is rendered in a prosaic, even domestic, manner.

But the most spectacular manifestation of Jean's 'demythologizing' approach occurs during Reason's justification of his use of words like *coilles* ('testicles') which some people would regard as obscene. In *Le Roman de la Rose*, 5533–42 there is a jocular reference to the fable of the birth of Venus: Jupiter cut off Saturn's testicles 'as if they were sausages' and flung them into the sea, whence Venus, the goddess of love, was generated.[57] In a subsequent reference to this passage (7153–84) Reason remarks that ancient philosophers were wont to cover their useful truths with fictional garments (*integumenz*), and therefore these fables are expounded in the schools.[58] But she, for her part, has used certain words which should be understood literally, without a gloss:

> 'Mais puis t'ai teus deus moz renduz,
> E tu les as bien entenduz,
> Qui pris deivent estre a la letre
> Tout proprement, senz glose metre'.

> ['But afterwards I pronounced these two
> words—and you understood them well—
> which should be taken quite strictly
> according to the letter, without gloss'.]

The dubious words in question are not part of an integument to be explained away; they function within a perfectly literal account of Jean's theory of love.

William of Conches gives the impression of having been interested in pagan mythology in so far as he could moralize it. By contrast, Nicholas Trevet, whose commentary on Boethius is heavily dependent on William's, was more concerned with explanations which were literal and historical.[59] Trevet reduced considerably the amount of exposition *per integumentum* and increased the historical reference; when explaining those fables which have no historical sense his emphasis is on character and on sequence of events rather than on the profound truths figured thereby. Moralization has receded before narration.

Chaucer seems to have shared, on the one hand, Jean de Meun's mild amusement at the excesses of mythography, and, on the other, Trevet's interest in euhemerism. Considerable insight into his personal tastes can be gained by discovering precisely what he did to those sources which contained moralization. Materials from the *Ovide Moralisé* and Bersuire's *Ovidius Moralizatus* are consistently demythologized, as Chaucer fastens on the narrative element and either ignores, questions or literalizes the allegorical import.[60] Hence, in his tale of Seys and Alcyone the allegorical import is ignored, in *The Manciple's Tale* it is questioned, while in the Knight's account of the temple of Mars it is literalized. These examples will now be considered in turn, together with the Nun's Priest's predominantly jocular version of an Aesopian *fabula*.

In *The Book of the Duchess* the *fabula* of Seys and Alcyone, a pagan tale from long ago, is denuded of the *moralizatio* provided for it in one of the major sources of this Chaucer poem, the *Ovide Moralisé*.[61] In the Old French work, the ship in which Seys sails is the human body, the sea is mortal life, the wind that causes the storm is sin, and so on: the fable warns us against putting our trust in earthly things, for the pleasures of this life are fleeting, like birds. All this Chaucer ignored. Indeed, he also cut short the ending of the *narratio*, omitting all reference to the metamorphosis of the lovers into sea-birds. In Ovid's Latin text the gods had taken pity on Seys and Alcyone; in John Gower's version of the fable their transformation becomes a reward for the queen's 'trowthe of love' (*Confessio Amantis*, IV, 2927–3123).[62] But Chaucer could hardly have incorporated this happy ending: it was quite inappropriate to the circumstances in which he wrote the poem, as was the *moralizatio* warning against over-valuing earthly things. The bereaved John of Gaunt, one may imagine, would not have been impressed with either 'solution'. Instead, Chaucer had his narrator make 'game' of the ancient story: the reading of the fable is 'play', like playing at chess or tables; a mock-moralization is provided when the narrator derives from the tale a cure for his insomnia (221–69).

The passage in *The Book of the Duchess* in which Chaucer describes the book of 'fables' in which he found the story of Seys and Alcyone (44–61) seems to echo the very beginning of the *Ovide Moralisé*, in which the anonymous Franciscan justifies his translation of 'les fables de l'ancien temps' into French ('en romans').[63] From the origin of the world until the advent of Christ (i.e. the period in which pagans lived in accordance with natural law, what Chaucer calls 'the lawe of kinde'[64]), mention is made of fables which, although they all seem false, contain nothing but truth. If one gets to know the sense of such fables, the French poet continues, the truth contained in them is obvious. It is perfectly proper to enlist pagan material in the service of Christian doctrine since 'All that is written is written for our doctrine' (Romans 15.4):

> Se l'escripture ne me ment,
> Tout est pour nostre enseignement
> Quanqu'il a es livres escript,
> Soient bon ou mal escript.[65]

> [If the Scriptural passage does not lie to me,
> whatever is written in books is all for our doctrine,
> be the writings good or ill.]

These lines may have influenced the ending of the Nun's Priest's Aesopian fable, in which the audience is reminded that within the *integumentum* or 'chaf' is found the 'fruyt' of truth:

> But ye that holden this tale a folye,
> As of a fox, or of a cok and hen,
> Taketh the moralite, goode men.
> For seint Paul seith that al that writen is,
> To oure doctrine it is ywrite, ywis;
> Taketh the fruyt, and lat the chaf be stille.
> (VII, 3438–43)

Here 'Sir John' seems to be encouraging us to moralize *The Nun's Priest's Tale* in the way in which contemporary mythographers and preachers were used to moralize *fabulae*. Indeed, it is perfectly possible to find much 'moralite' in the tale, which warns against flattery, exemplifies the sin of pride, and reminds the reader that sexual 'solas' does not make one's problems disappear.[66] Yet one wonder if Chaucer's appeal to the genre of 'moral fable' is in some way ironic.[67] He may have wished to exploit the contrast between what the audience is led to expect (a fable with the moral heavily stressed) and what it actually gets (a 'myrie' tale with its own integrity). For example, the hearers would have anticipated a full *moralizatio* to follow the *narratio* (as in Henryson's *Morall Fabillis of Esope*), but all they are offered is a glib 'take note of the moral, for *all* that is written is written for our doctrine—St Paul says so!'. Chaucer could be implying that if one can moralize *The Nun's Priest's Tale* one can moralize anything. At the very least, he has succeeded in 'defamiliarizing' a typical moral fable by presenting it to us in a highly unusual way.

Whether all these suggestions be accepted or not, it is at least clear that in this poem, as in Chaucer's tale of Seys and Alcyone, *moralizatio* has receded before *narratio*. In *The Manciple's Tale*, which is based on the fable of Phoebus and Coronis as retold and interpreted in the *Ovide moralisé*, Chaucer seems to be calling in question the traditional relationship between literally-fictitious *narratio* and allegorically-true *moralizatio*.[68] The Manciple is an unsympathetic character, and his tale is a sordid one—Chaucer may have been influenced by an antifeminist passage in Guido's *Historia Destructionis Troiae* in which Clytemnestra is attacked for having defiled her marriage bed with a man who was far inferior to her husband Agamemnon.

Nam, eius pudore postposito, matrimonialem thorum cum quodam Egisto nomine uiolauit. In cuius amore Clitemestra in tantum exarserat quod ex eo quandam susceperat filiam, que Erigona uocabatur, cui dare promiserat pro certo regnum suum, licet Egistus regie non esset originis nec ducis aut comitis nobilitate decorus, sed hoc certum est inter femineas voluptates quod cum in sui corporis deliramenta labuntur, numquam appetunt cum aliquo commisceri qui marito suo sit melior nec equalis, semper enim ad uiliora declinant. Et cum ipse honoris earum prodige facite sint, in personis suis non horrent committere uilitates, sed non nisi cum uilibus eas committunt, quamuis eo cum melioribus uiris suis eciam et seipsis aut mundi maioribus committerent, scelus esse putarent.

[Having put aside her modesty, she had defiled her marriage bed with a man named Aegisthus. Clytemnestra had been enflamed by his love to such an extent that she bore him a daughter, who was called Erigona, to whom she had promised certainly to give the kingdom, although Aegisthus was not of royal birth nor honoured by the noble rank of duke or count. It is certain among lascivious women that when they fall into wantonness of their bodies, they never desire to join with anyone who would be better to or equal to their husbands, but they always descend to a lower person. Since they have become careless of their honour, they do not shrink from doing base deeds in their own right, but they only do these things with base fellows, since they would think it a crime if they did these things with men better than their husbands and themselves, or of higher rank in the world.][69]

19

Similarly, Coronis (not named by the Manciple) has a lustful encounter with 'a man of litel reputacioun' (IX, 199), as the Crow reports to its master with more relish than prudence:

> 'Phebus', quod he, 'for al thy worthynesse,
> For al thy beautee and thy gentilesse,
> For al thy song and al thy mynstralcye,
> For al thy waityng, blered is thyn ye
> With oon of litel reputacioun,
> Noght worth to thee, as in comparisoun,
> The montance of a gnat, so moote I thryve!
> For on thy bed thy wyf I saugh hym swyve'.
>
> (IX, 249–56)

Phebus kills his wife in a rage, then proceeds to blame the Crow for all his misfortune. The Manciple's *moralizatio* of this fable emphasizes the importance of keeping one's mouth shut and, by implication, never reporting vice—a conclusion which no *sapiens* could accept. Chaucer has highlighted the arbitrary nature of this moral, thereby showing (among other things) how the technique of *moralizatio* can be misused or abused by a moralizer of dubious moral standards.

An excellent example of the way in which Chaucer literalized fabulous material is provided by his adaptation of passages from Bersuire's *Reductorium Morale* in *The Knight's Tale*. In the *Ovidius Moralizatus* which constitutes book 15 of his *Reductorium*, Bersuire had described the pagan gods as they were 'painted' by the ancients. This notion of 'painting' goes back at least to the *Mythologiae* of Fulgentius; in his moralization of this work John Ridevall used it extensively.[70] Ridevall, and Bersuire after him, were thinking of literary images rather than visual art, whether paintings or statues: each and every 'picture' was the work of the poets (*pingitur a poetis*). They provided the framework for extensive moralization, as may be illustrated by Bersuire's 'picture' of Mars. The figure of Mars, Bersuire explains, takes the form of a fiery man sitting in a chariot, with a helmet on his head and a whip in his hand.[71] In front of him a wolf is painted, because this animal was specially dedicated to Mars by the ancient gentiles. The name 'Mars' comes from *Mavors*, i.e. *mares vorans*, 'devouring males'. First, a brief 'literal' interpretation is offered: the poets wished this figure to be understood in terms of the nature and complexion of the planet Mars, which is hot and dry, and therefore the man in the chariot is said to have a choleric complexion. Then Bersuire proceeds to moral allegories. Mars signifies earthly princes and tyrants, and especially bellicose men, who are said to be sitting in a chariot because of their lack of stability. I Kings 25.29 states that 'the impious will go round and round like a cart', and Ecclesiasticus 33.5 assures us that 'the feelings of the impious man are like the wheel of a cart'. The wolf in front of Mars designates rapacious and wolvish retainers, since worldly princes and tyrants are invariably accompanied by cruel officials. On the other hand, Bersuire continues, the chariot in which the impious sit may signify the din and tumult of vices, its four wheels being the four evil feelings or the four kinds of pride. Alternatively, Mars signifies the sin of discord which is seated in the chariot of the evil soul, drawn by four wheels which are the four spiritual vices, namely, avarice, pride, detraction, and injury.

Chaucer ignored all this moralizing and concentrated on the visual details provided by Bersuire. An extensive account of the 'portreiture' which is 'peynted' on the walls of the temple of 'myghty Mars the rede' has as its climax a description (unparalleled in Boccaccio) of the central icon in this temple, a statue of armed Mars in his chariot and accompanied by a male-devouring wolf:

> The statue of Mars upon a carte stood
> Armed, and looked grym as he were wood . . .
> This god of armes was arrayed thus.
> A wolf ther stood biforn hym at his feet
> With eyen rede, and of a man he eet;
> With soutil pencel depeynted was this storie
> In redoutynge of Mars and of his glorie.
>
> (I, 2041–50)

The temples of Venus and Diana are described in the same literal way (I, 1918–66; 2051–88). Chaucer is thinking of real paintings and statues, of actual physical objects which exist in the empirical world and are located in historical time and place. At the end of his 'picture' of Diana the Knight even comments on the lifelike quality of the artifact and the expense of the artist's materials:

> Wel koude he peynten lifly that it wroughte;
> With many a floryn he the hewes boghte.
>
> (I, 2087–8)

Read in the light of the Bersuire excursus paraphrased above, these lines seem utterly deflating, even bathetic. Their down-to-earth realism is far removed from the arcane extrapolation of the mythographers. In short, Chaucer has reduced the many layers of mythographic meaning to a single sense, namely, the literal-historical.

Our brief survey of Chaucer's reactions, in four different poems, to fabulous materials indicates that his genius did not lie in the direction of moral allegory.[72] This general conclusion emerges after every possible allowance has been made for the requirements of the individual literary situation. In order that falsity may serve truth, Bersuire proclaimed, a moral sense must be extracted from fables. Chaucer, it would seem, was not interested in extracting moral truth through allegorical exposition of classical gods, heroes and narratives. His concern was with literal truth, with the historical sense. This, I suggest, was related to a finely-developed sense of history.

Chaucer was acutely aware of the essential differences between the pagan past and the Christian present, and to some extent he tried to avoid imposing 'modern' criteria and classifications on 'ancient' experience, striving to present it with historical plausibility. In keeping with the standard contrast between the pagan world under natural law and the Christian world under grace, he writes with a large measure of consistency, and only a few exceptions, of the Trojans and Greeks in *Troilus and Criseyde* and the Athenians and Thebans in

The Knight's Tale as if they were reasonable and virtuous heathen believing in one supreme God and in the basic moral law.[73] In the personal comments of the narrator of *Troilus* and Chaucer's Knight we find, as is fitting, Christian allusions and phraseology. But the settings and the characters are as consciously pagan as he could make them. Chaucer created his historical settings and characterized his pagans with the latest information available to him in the most influential encyclopedias, history books, mythographies and theological treatises of the day. When no information was available, he improvised by converting Christian beliefs and 'modern' mores into their pagan equivalents. The result is poetry of impressive verisimilitude, judged by the standards of the late fourteenth century.

The manner in which Chaucer's understanding of his literary role as a purveyor of paganism was influenced by the typical justifications and disavowals of medieval historians and compilers will be considered in a later chapter, since it may be understood better after we have grasped the problematic nature (from the orthodox Christian point of view) of much of the material which they were handling. Suffice it to claim here that Chaucer approached antiquity as a sympathetic observer rather than as a dogmatic exegete, that he conceived of himself as a writer of *historia* rather than *fabula*.

Precisely what did *historia* mean in the age of Chaucer; what kind of 'sense of history' can we credit him with? A suitable point of departure is provided by one of the standard dictionaries of the day, the *Expositiones Vocabulorum Biblie* of William Brito, also known as the *Summa Britonis*. This work, compiled between 1250 and 1270, drew heavily on two earlier dictionaries, by Papias and Hugutio of Pisa, and 'soon competed with them on equal terms throughout western Europe'.[74] Brito's entry under *historia* directs us to his discussion of *allegoria*, where he explains each of the four methods of expounding Scripture (historically, allegorically, anagogically and tropologically) in that order. The definition of *historia*, taken from Isidore of Seville's *Etymologiae*, is as follows:

> Historia . . . est narratio rei geste per quam ea que in preterito facta sunt dignoscuntur. Dicitur autem historia ab historin grece quod est videre latine vel cognoscere. Apud veteres enim nemo conscribebat historiam nisi is qui interfuisset et ea que scribenda essent vidisset.[75]

> [History . . . is the narration of an action performed, by which the things done in the past are known. Now, it is called history from the Greek *historein* which in Latin is *videre* (to see) or *cognoscere* (to know). For among the ancients no-one wrote history except one who had been present and had seen the events which had to be written about.]

Others say, Brito adds, that *historia* derives from *historon* which means 'gesticulator', whence the historian is called a gesticulator in that he represents 'gests' or events. In sum, the historian is someone who narrates or reports events which actually occurred in the past, and originally history was written only by those who had witnessed the things about which they wrote. These qualities distinguish it from *fabula*, which Brito (again following Isidore) derives from *fando* ('by speaking') because fables are not factual things but spoken fictions, i.e. literary artifacts: *non sunt res facte sed loquendo ficte*.[76] A more elaborate form of this distinction between history and fable occurs in the two standard textbooks for the teaching of rhetoric in the Middle Ages, the *Rhetorica ad Herennium* and Cicero's *De Inventione*.[77] *Historia* is defined as an account of actual occurrences (*gesta res*) removed in time from the recollection (*memoria*) of our age, whereas *fabula* comprises events which are neither true nor probable.

The notion of history as eyewitness testimony lies behind the claims of Dares and Dictys (who provided the main sources of the medieval Troy-story) to have been present at the Trojan war, Dictys being on the Greek side and Dares on the Trojan.[78] To later historians, unable to adduce personal participation in the events they chronicled, Dares and Dictys were *auctores* ('authorities'), whose written records were to be accepted as authentic and trustworthy. History records events removed in time from the recollection of our age, as Cicero said, and because of the weakness of human powers of recollection—what Vincent of Beauvais described as the 'slippery' nature of memory—the written word preserved the past.[79] In the prologue to his *Polychronicon*, Ralph Higden claimed that the use of letters was a divine gift designed to remedy this imperfection of man, and that the recording of history results in the perpetual conservation of things which are mortal and transitory.[80] As Chaucer himself put it, old books are the key of remembrance.[81] Hence, Guido delle Colonne could praise the 'writings of the ancients, faithful preservers of tradition' which 'depict the past as if it were the present, and, by the attentive readings of books, endow valiant heroes with the courageous spirit they are imagined to have had, just as if they were alive—heroes whom the extensive age of the world long swallowed up by death'.[82] Therefore, he continues, it is fitting that the fall of Troy 'should not be blotted out by a long duration of time'. Attitudes such as these help us to understand why the forgeries of Dares and Dictys received such unwarranted respect for so long. Any 'modern' writer who wished to recount some incident from the story of Troy had to attest his reliance on the proper authorities, and on the face of it Dares and Dictys seemed to be the most 'ancient'. Benoît de Sainte-Maure stated that he was following Dares and Dictys, as did Guido delle Colonne—who, for the most part, was actually translating Benoît.[83] Joseph of Exeter proclaimed his debt to 'the Phrygian master, Dares', and he knew Dictys as well.[84]

The crucial distinction between history and fable is reflected by medieval contrasts of Dares as a reliable historian with Homer as a mischievous mythmaker who invented lies about the Trojan War. In the letter which prefaces his translation of the *De Excidio Troiae Historia* of Dares, the translator Cornelius Nepos denigrates Homer in favour of Dares, 'who lived and fought at the time the Greeks stormed Troy'.[85] 'When the Athenians judged the matter', he continues, 'they found Homer insane for describing gods battling with mortals'. Subsequent writers criticised Homer on these two counts. He wrote at a date later than the eyewitness Dares, and he mingled with historical truth poetical fictions concerning divine intervention in human affairs. Such objections are found in Joseph of Exeter's *De Bello Trojano* and Guido's *Historia Destructionis Troiae*. 'Should I admire Homer, that old man of Maeonia', Joseph asks in the grand rhetorical manner, 'or the Phrygian master, Dares, who was there and to whom his eyes, a more reliable guide, revealed the truth which fiction (*fabula*) does not know'?[86] Joseph's mind, 'aware of the truth, has banished far from it the poet who plays with fictions', in case 'the unbridled lying of Athens and its falsehoods' should offend his patron, the Archbishop of Canterbury. A similar, but more elaborate, statement is found in Guido's prologue. Certain persons, he complains, have dealt with the story of Troy 'lightly, as poets do, in fanciful inventions by means of certain fictions'.[87] Among them was Homer, who 'turned the pure and simple truth of his story into deceiving paths, inventing many things which did not happen and altering those which did happen'. Hence, he maintained that the gods worshipped by the ancient pagans fought against the Trojans and were defeated with them just like mortal men. But Homer, he continues, was not the only author of falsehoods: Ovid and even Virgil followed his example by writing 'many misleading things in their books'. Guido then explains his personal purpose of preserving 'the true accounts of the reliable writers of this history', so that they may 'endure for all future time hereafter among western peoples, chiefly for the use of those who read Latin, so that they may know how to separate the true from the false'. The norm of historical truth is provided, as one would expect, by Dares and Dictys, who, because they were present at the Trojan War, 'were the most trustworthy recorders of those things which they saw'. Guido, like Joseph of Exeter before him, seems to have believed that his activity as an historian involved the disentangling of historical truth from poetical fiction.

This may throw some light on what Chaucer, in creating *Troilus and Criseyde*, thought he was doing to *Il Filostrato*. Boccaccio was a self-confessed maker of fiction: he had written not as an historian but as a poet who was using an ancient story as 'a cloak for the secret grief' of his own love for a certain Maria d'Aquino.[88] Chaucer, in sharp contrast, assures his readers that he lacks experience of love.

> Forwhi to every lovere I me excuse,
> That of no sentement I this endite,
> But out of Latyn in my tonge it write. . . .
>
> Ek though I speeke of love unfelyngly,
> No wondre is, for it nothyng of newe is;
> A blynd man kan nat juggen wel in hewis.
> (II, 12–21)

Of course, in real life Chaucer did dare to love, as the *Chaucer Life-Records* make quite clear.[89] Maria d'Aquino, to whom *Il Filostrato* is addressed, did not exist. What we are dealing with in each case is not a realistic self-portrait but an imaginative construct which contributes considerably to the distinctive tone and tenor of the poem of which it is part.[90] Boccaccio depicted himself as a pleading lover; Chaucer preferred to depict himself as a Christian historian who approaches pagan antiquity with detachment, and with respect for the historical identity of the pagans. By excising the 'personal' love-interest from the story of Troilus and Criseyde as told by Boccaccio, Chaucer may have been attempting to remove fiction from historical truth.

Chaucer did not mention *Il Filostrato* for the same reason that Guido did not mention Benoît's *Roman de Troie*: these writers were casting themselves in the role of historian (in the sense defined above) and therefore 'modern' works in whatever vernacular would not serve their purpose. Instead, *auctores* had to be cited, 'ancient' writers who had written in Latin, the language of learning in general and historiography in particular. Therefore, Guido repeats Benoît's invocation of Dares and Dictys without referring to Benoît himself. Chaucer, in turn, mentions Dares and Dictys—and Benoît and Guido as well. He may have regarded the *Roman de Troie* and *Historia Destructionis Troiae* as being at a single remove from the eyewitness accounts, and therefore worthy of citation.

Chaucer's references to 'myn auctour called Lollius' in place of Boccaccio is a more complicated issue. The name 'Lollius' may have been created by someone's misreading of a line in one of Horace's *Epistles* as referring to 'Lollius, greatest of writers on the Trojan War'.[91] It is just possible that Chaucer thought that *Il Filostrato* was based on a book by this Lollius: after all, Benoît and Guido (on their own assurances) were following Dares and Dictys, so to who else could this very different work have been indebted? This kind of mistake seems to have been made by Guido in the case of Joseph of Exeter's *De Bello Trojano*, which he probably mistook as the supposedly ancient translation of Dares from Greek into Latin By Cornelius Nepos.[92] But this is to speculate concerning the letter rather than the spirit of what Chaucer was doing. Chaucer did not much care what 'Omer, Dares and Dite' actually had said; he did not bother to verify the existence of his 'auctour Lollius'—he wanted to use the names of the *auctores*, to cash in on their authority.[93] Credit was not given to Boccaccio and Petrarch, therefore, but material from their works was ascribed to writers who were respectable as 'ancients'. For the same reason, *The Knight's Tale*, which conceals its debt to Boccaccio's *Teseida*, contains a grand appeal to the authority of the *Thebiad* of Statius and other 'bookes olde' (I, 2294). By this means, Chaucer applied the authentic finish, as it were the period veneer, to artifacts which were to a large extent of his own making.

Thus far we have been concentrating on the attitudes to history which Chaucer shared with historians of the Trojan War. But the differences are perhaps of greater importance to us, since they illuminate the ways in which Chaucer's individual talent reacted with tradition. A comparison of the ending of *Troilus and Criseyde* with the endings of Guido's *Historia* and Joseph's *De Bello Trojano* is very revealing. Both the Latin writers emphasize their achievement in telling the whole truth and nothing but the truth. Guido justifies his literary activity by dwelling on 'the failure of the great authors, Virgil, Ovid, and Homer, who were very deficient in describing the truth about the fall of Troy, although they composed their works in exceedingly glorious style, whether they treated them according to the stories of the ancients or according to fables'.[94] Joseph of Exeter claims to have 'unravelled the confused abridgement of ancient truth', then looks forward to a more serious enterprise, the composition of a Christian epic about the wars of Antioch.[95] No pagan muse will be of any avail in this case; 'a more glorious Apollo will come down from heaven and fill the void of my trusting heart'. The *De Bello Trojano* ends with an 'envy-postscript' in which Joseph exhorts his book to live 'and flourish free from all detractors'.[96] Similarly, the ending of *Troilus and Criseyde* includes references to previous writers, an address to the 'litel bok', and a variation on the 'envy-postscript', but the total effect is different. Chaucer's contrast between pagan love and Christian love serves to stress the historical position of

his characters and the general pastness of the past, as does his allusion to the
'payens corsed olde rites' as recorded by 'olde clerkis' in poetry (V, 1828-55).
The mention of envy occurs in the context of a comparison of the present poem
with previous ones, but Chaucer, far from pointing to the limitations of the
auctores he cites, expresses the hope that *Troilus and Criseyde* should join the
canon of tragedies:

> Go, litel bok, go, litel myn tragedye . . .
> But litel book, no makyng thow n'envie,
> But subgit be to alle poesye;
> And kis the steppes, where as thow seest pace
> Virgile, Ovide, Omer, Lucan, and Stace.
>
> (V, 1786-92)

Chaucer, in contradistinction to Guido and Joseph, presented his historical
matter in the form of a tragedy; he was the first English master of what in the
Renaissance was called 'tragical history'.

The conception of tragedy which informs *Troilus and Criseyde* and *The
Knight's Tale* was, as has long been recognized, derived from the *De Consolatione Philosophiae* of Boethius.[97] This work, as interpreted by Nicholas Trevet,
seems also to have influenced the theory of tragedy which provides the
thematic principles of *The Monk's Tale*.[98] The ending of the Monk's story of
Croesus, which constitutes the conclusion of the entire work, has no parallel in
Jean de Meun's *Roman de la Rose*, a major source for this 'tragedie'—

> Tragedies noon oother maner thyng
> Ne kan in syngyng crie ne biwaille
> But that Fortune alwey wole assaile
> With unwar strook the regnes that been proude;
> For whan men trusteth hire, thanne wol she faille,
> And covere hire brighte face with a clowde.
>
> (VII, 2761-66)

but there is ample precedent for it in Trevet's commentary on *De Consolatione
Philosophiae* II pr. 2, 29-32. Here Boethius had alluded to the downfalls of two
great historical figures, Croesus and a proud king taken prisoner by the Roman
consul Paulus. Having recounted the story of Croesus, Trevet turns to Paulus,
who was impressed by the contrast between the past prosperity and the present
adversity of his captive: moved by piety, he wept. Trevet then proceeds to gloss
Dame Philosophy's rhetorical question, 'What else is the cry of tragedy but a
lament that happy states are overthrown by the indiscriminate blows of
fortune?' His definition of tragedy is taken from Isidore's *Etymologiae*:

Secundo cum dicit QUID TRAGEDIARUM probat mutabilitatem Fortune diuulgari cotidianis clamoribus, quia clamores poetarum cotidie in
theatro recitancium tragedias nichil aliud continebant quam mutabilitatem Fortune. Et nota quod tragedi dicuntur secundum Ysidorum
Ethymologiarum libro 18, capitulo de ludo scenico, illi qui antiqua gesta
atque facinora sceleratorum regum luctuoso carmine spectante populo
concinebant. Vnde tragedia est carmen de magnis iniquitatibus a prosperitate incipiens et in aduersitate terminans.[99]

26

[In the second place when he says WHAT OF TRAGEDIES he shows that the mutability of fortune is noised abroad in daily clamours, because the clamours of the poets daily reciting their tragedies in the theatres contained nothing else but the mutability of fortune. And note that according to Isidore, *Etymologiae* book 18, the chapter about stage performance, those people are called tragedians who sang about the old deeds and actions of wicked kings in mournful song before the eyes of the people. Hence tragedy is poetry about great iniquities beginning from prosperity and ending in adversity.]

Here we have an instance of a gloss altering the import of the original text by imposing a characteristically medieval interpretation on it. Boethius had been concerned to stress the indiscriminate nature of fortune's blows, and hence of tragic consequences. By contrast, Trevet preferred Isidore's view that sin invited tragedy: a tragedy was a song about great iniquities, with the ancient deeds and criminal actions of kings as its subject-matter. This definition seemed naturally to follow from the cases of the two proud and iniquitous kings, Croesus and the 'most proud king of the Persians', which Trevet had just expounded. Indeed, it is probably due to Trevet's association of Isidore's theory of tragedy with the story of Croesus that Chaucer used both the story and the relevant application of the theory to conclude *The Monk's Tale*.[100]

Moreover, Chaucer may have regarded this conclusion as providing a link with the Monk's prologue, where an expansion of Isidore's theory is to be found:

> Tragedie is to seyn a certeyn storie,
> As olde bookes maken us memorie,
> Of hym that stood in greet prosperitee,
> And is yfallen out of heigh degree
> Into myserie, and endeth wrecchedly.
>
> (VII, 1973–7)

This information could have come from Trevet's gloss (*tragedia est carmen de magnis iniquitatibus a prosperitate incipiens et in aduersitate terminans*), the reference to iniquities having been removed so that the definition could cover all of the Monk's tragic figures, including those who had not deserved their downfalls. In this altered form, Trevet's gloss appears in Chaucer's *Boece* II pr. 2, 70–2: 'Tragedye is to seyn a dite of a prosperite for a tyme, that endeth in wrecchidnesse'. Chaucer's opinion concerning the nature of Boethian tragedy was, in this instance, more true to the letter and spirit of his author than was the opinion of the interpreter whose guidance he usually was prepared to accept.

In *Troilus* and *The Knight's Tale* likewise, there is no suggestion that tragedy has been prompted by criminal or sinful actions, that fortune is exacting retribution for the pride and iniquity of Troilus and Arcite respectively. This provides a considerable contrast with Guido's *Historia* and Joseph of Exeter's *De Bello Trojano*, where a quite different view of the causes and significance of historical events is to be found. In Guido's *Historia* Troy is destroyed not because a basically disinterested Fortune spins her wheel and the city is by chance the loser, but because she deserves to fall through the iniquities of men: the arrogance of Laomedon, the injured pride of Priam, and especially the lust of Paris.[101] Guido and Joseph have harsh things to say about Helen as a cause of the tragic fall of Troy. Her ticklish liver, according to Joseph, was the one part of Helen which 'ruined the whole of her, brought about the clash of kingdoms, and roused the whole world to disaster'.[102] But Chaucer could hardly claim (even if he had wanted to) that Criseyde caused the death of Troilus—whatever else she may be, Criseyde is no Delilah.[103] Ignoring the long descriptions of Troilus's end which Joseph, Benoît and Guido provided, Chaucer devoted a single line to the subject: 'Despitously hym slough the fierse Achille' (V, 1806). This seems to have been unimportant to him, perhaps precisely because Criseyde had nothing to do with it. Neither did Chaucer take up Guido's suggestion that Briseida, like Helen and all women in general, was naturally inclined to lechery, so that Troilus was a young fool to have trusted her.[104] The central focus of *Troilus and Criseyde* is made perfectly clear at the beginning of the poem:

> ye may the double sorwes here
> Of Troilus in lovynge of Criseyde,
> And how that she forsook hym er she deyde.
> (I, 54–6)

Chaucer's interest is in the painful process by which Troilus obtained the love of Criseyde, and the pain he suffered in losing her. The poem charts the rise and fall not of a great man, but of a great love-affair.[105] Fortune is not a retributive agent but an historical fact, a force in which the ancient pagans believed (a point to which we will return in the next chapter). Chaucer, *par excellence* the poet of human love, has created a 'tragical history' of pagan love.

In *The Knight's Tale* also, fortune is treated as an essential part of the pagan world-view, and the theory of tragedy as propounded by Isidore and Trevet is again moderated to suit Chaucer's personal interests. Boccaccio had regarded Arcita as being far superior to Palemone, so that his loss of life and of Emilia was all the more tragic. Arcita's epitaph, with which the poem ends, identifies the cause of his lamentable downfall: 'through devoting my prowess to Emilia I met my death: so shield yourself from love'.[106] By contrast, in *The Knight's Tale* Arcite and Palamon are of equal merit; there is no suggestion that one deserves Emelye more than the other. Moreover, Chaucer's Knight is very aware of the fact of life that one man's downfall is another's opportunity. He ends his tale on a joyful note, with a celebration of the happy marriage of Palamon and Emelye:

> now is Palamon in alle wele,
> Lyvynge in blisse, in richesse, and in heele;
> And Emelye hym loveth so tendrely,
> And he hire serveth al so gentilly,
> That nevere was ther no word hem bitwene
> Of jalousie or any oother teene.
> Thus endeth Palamon and Emelye;
> And God save al this faire compaignye!
> (I, 3101–8)

It is, therefore, most appropriate that the Knight should cut short the Monk's long tale of short tragedies with the protestation that most people can endure only a 'litel hevynesse'. Personally, he is made uncomfortable by hearing of the sudden fall of men who have lived in great wealth and ease, and so he urges the Monk to consider the opposite process:

> the contrarie is joye and greet solas,
> As whan a man hath been in povre estaat,
> And clymbeth up and wexeth fortunat,
> And there abideth in prosperitee.
>
> (VII, 2774–7)

This is precisely what happens to the fortunate Palamon, who moves from the 'povre' (i.e. miserable) position of prisoner and unrequited lover to a state of abiding bliss with Emelye. 'After wo I rede us to be merye', exclaims Duke Theseus (I, 3068). Once again, it is obvious that Chaucer is exploiting the conventions of genre and form in his own inimitable way. *Fabula, historia, tragoedia* . . . he was aware of them all but the servant of none.

'Who knows if all that Chaucer wrote was true'? asks Robert Henryson at the beginning of his sequel to *Troilus, The Testament of Cresseid*.[107] Neither is it clear, Henryson continues, if the 'narratioun' which he describes as the source of *The Testament* is 'authoreist, or fenyeit of the new / Be sum Poeit'. Here are the same elements which (as this chapter has attempted to show) form the basis of Chaucer's approach to pagan antiquity. We recognize the contrast between 'authorised' or *auctor*-based history and inventive fiction, and the principle of appealing to some earlier work to validate personal literary activity (the narration to which Henryson refers having, one presumes, as little foundation in fact as Chaucer's Lollius).

Henryson, however, seems to allow poetic fiction a greater value than Chaucer did. *Troilus and Criseyde*, he is implying, may not be all historically true; his own 'source' may be a fiction—and in this there is, perhaps, the implication that *The Testament* itself may be fictitious. By contrast, Chaucer was not prepared to suggest or imply that there might be a strand of fiction in *Troilus and Criseyde* or in *The Knight's Tale*. One can easily imagine him saying of either of these poems what the Physician said of his tale from Livy, 'this is no fable, / But knowen for historial thyng notable' (VI, 155–6). The traditional superiority of *historia* over *fabula*, and the technique, favoured by late-medieval historians, of emphasizing the truth of one's statements by ostentatious deference to *auctores*, were deeply ingrained in Chaucer's mind, an integral part of his working poetics. This accounts for his concern with the content and form of *historia*. The best writing had to be seen to be true, historically speaking, and therefore it had to employ in some measure the literary procedures characteristic of historiography. By the same token, the best tragedy had to treat of historical personages, and hence we have the emergence of the hybrid genre of tragical history.

Chaucer had 'historical sense' in every sense of the term. He wrote in the literal and historical sense, ignoring all the possibilities of creating allegorical sense. *Troilus and Criseyde* and *The Knight's Tale* are located in historical time and place, not in the timeless land of ethical verities reached by *moralizatio*. The truth-claim of these depictions of classical antiquity relates to historical truth rather than moral truth, Chaucer being concerned with the true-to-life, with verisimilitude, with how actual pagans might have lived, loved and philosophized. The impressive accuracy of his depictions, considered with regard to late-medieval conceptions of paganism, will be intimated in the next chapter and confirmed in Chapters III and IV. For Chaucer was not a (self-styled) historian in the mould of Joseph of Exeter and Guido delle Colonne. He belonged to a later generation, the generation embracing Vincent of Beauvais and Ralph Higden, which is distinguished by a more liberal view of the pagan past. It is this liberal view which is the very essence of Chaucer's historical sense and sensibility.

CHAPTER II

The Shadowy Perfection of the Pagans

'We must see in what consisted the shadowy perfection of these philosophers', declares John of Wales, introducing an account of the achievements of the pagan philosophers.[1] There can be no perfection without divine grace, he continues, yet in many pagans there was perfection after a manner, which 'consisted of the detestation of vice, so far as this was possible without the grace of the faith which illuminates and purges'. Elsewhere, John quotes John of Salisbury's statement that there was in the pagan philosophers 'a venerable image of virtue, though the substance of virtue cannot be found without faith and love'.[2] Would that there were found among us those who have even the image of virtue! For who nowadays puts on 'even the shadow of those virtues, with which the Gentiles flourished, although without Christ they could not grasp the true fruit of blessedness?' In these two passages both the virtues and the failings of the ancient pagans are intimated, but it is abundantly clear that John is determined to give them as much credit as he can as often as he can.

It is the purpose of this chapter to discover what these virtues and failings were supposed to be in Chaucer's day, and especially in Chaucer's sources. First, heathen limitations shall be investigated in respect of their two basic kinds as identified by medieval writers: shortcomings in theology and shortcomings in philosophy. Pagan 'theology' is spoken of in the sense attested by Vincent of Beauvais who, following Augustine, took it to refer to heathen conceptions of the gods, a type of knowledge vastly inferior to Christian theology which had as its subject the one true God.[3] As we shall see, pagan idolatry was a major target for medieval attacks on false notions of deity. The pagan philosophies with which we are concerned are those of greatest interest to Chaucer critics, namely, theories concerning fate, fortune, predestination and the freedom of the will. Secondly, the intellectual and moral achievements of the pagans will be investigated, with special reference to those heathen ideas and actions which approximated most closely to Christian theory and practice. All the good pagans were good, but some were better than others. It will, therefore, be necessary to consider the degrees of perfection which (in the eyes of late-medieval writers) different pagans had attained, and the extent to which prechristian thinkers could be regarded as personally responsible for their shortcomings. This survey will, it is hoped, place us in a good position from which to consider the pagan limitations and achievements delineated in *Troilus and Criseyde* and *The Knight's Tale*.

Let us begin at the beginning, with medieval descriptions of who and what the pagans were, and how their gods originated. Isidore of Seville had claimed that *pagani* were so named from the country regions (*pagi*) around Athens, in which places the gentiles set up lights and idols.[4] The gentiles, according to Isidore, are those who are without the law (i.e. the law of Christ), because they did not yet believe.[5] They are called *gentiles* because they are just as they were generated or born (*geniti*), 'that is, just as they descended into the flesh in sin, namely serving idols and not yet regenerated' in Christ. A version of this explanation is found in Guido's *Historia Destructionis Troiae*: 'They are called gentiles because they were always without the law, and were always thus, so that they are stated to have been born serving idols from the first'.[6] Isidore also remarked that since the advent of the Christian faith the term 'gentiles' refers to unbelievers, whereas 'apostates' designates those who, having received baptism, revert to the cult of idols and the contagion of sacrifices.[7] Hugutio of Pisa and William Brito, who repeated Isidore's definition of *pagani*, add that the term describes all those who do not dwell in the city of god, that is, the Church.[8] All these accounts stress the contrast between the pagan past and the Christian present, and identify idol-worship as an essential feature of paganism.

The most generally accepted explanation of the origin of the pagan gods, and hence of idol-worship, was the euhemeristic theory that these deities originally were mortal men who, through misplaced reverence or fear, had become falsely worshipped as gods.[9] In his *Speculum Historiale* Vincent of Beauvais quotes Isidore verbatim on this subject: 'Those whom the pagans claim to be gods can be shown to have once been men; they began to be worshipped among their own people after their death, on account of the life or merits of each one: for example, Isis in Egypt, Jove in Crete, Juba among the Moors, Faunus among the Latins, and Quirinus among the Romans'.[10] This error had been compounded by ancient poets and mythmakers, who sung their praises and by composing odes elevated them to heaven. Of course, some poets did attempt to reduce the gods to physical causes, suggesting that they were to be understood in terms of the elements.[12] Robert Holcot, expounding Wisdom 13.2, recounts that the Chaldeans worshipped fire, named Vulcan by the gentiles; others worshipped the ether, which the gentiles named Jove; the sun was supposed to be Phoebus, the first son of Jove, and so on.[13] For Isidore of Seville this kind of argument was a vain attempt to confer respectability on lying fictions about the gods by interpreting them naturalistically;[14] Holcot, Vincent and other late-medieval writers were more charitable, attempting as they were to bring out the praiseworthy aspects of classical antiquity.

On the other hand, the pagan gods were associated with the planets which bore the same names. Isidore claimed that the Romans consecrated the planets with the names of the gods, 'that is, of Jupiter, Saturn, Mars, Venus and Mercury'.[15] Guido's *Historia* takes a different view. 'Jupiter or Jove acquired the name of the planet Jupiter, and the pagans worshipped him by the name of the highest god'; Mercury was named after the planet Mercury, and so on.[16] Such thinking seems to be circular. Isidore believes that the planets were named after the gods, who originally were mere mortals; Guido believes that certain men, who eventually were worshipped as gods, were named after the planets. At any rate, it is clear that the importance of the link between the gods and the planets was sustained by the commonplace medieval belief that heavenly bodies had real power over human lives. But how could dead men continue to be the objects of worship? The reason usually offered was that this was due to the intervention of demons or devils, who sought to lead mankind astray.[17] Therefore, the real objects of much pagan worship were devils, those angels who had been banished to Hell because of the great pride of Lucifer.

This is made very clear in the learned digression on the origins of idolatry which constitutes Guido's major addition to the material he found in the *Roman de Troie*.[18] There is a lack of agreement, he explains, concerning the identity of the first person to make an idol. According to the Jews Ishmael fashioned the first image from clay, but the pagans say that it was Prometheus, and that from him developed the art of making images and statues. An Assyrian king called Ninus, the son of Belus, was the instigator of the worship of such idols. When Belus died Ninus 'ordered an image constructed of gold which was amazingly like his father, so that for his comfort and in memory of his father he could imagine by the sight of the image that he was seeing his father'. Accordingly, King Ninus worshipped this gold image as if it were a god and ordered his people to worship it too, 'and he handed it down to be believed by all Assyrians' that Belus was deified in Heaven. A demon encouraged this error by entering into the idol of Belus and answering the questions of those who sought its advice:

Et sic, non multo postmodum tempore procedente, spiritus immundus in hoc ydolum Belli regis ingressus responsa petentibus exhibebat. Vnde apud Assyrios illud ydolum dictum est Bellus. Alii dixerunt Bel, alii Beel, alii Baal, alii Belphegor, alii Belzabuch, alii Belzebub. Et huius ydoli exemplo gentiles processerunt ad ydolorum cultum, fingentes homines mortuos esse deos et pro diis adorabant eos. Vnde dixerunt primum deum fuisse Saturnum. Qui Saturnus fuit rex Crete, nato nomine ab illo planeta qui dicitur Saturnus. Quo mortuo deum esse dixerunt, non habentem neque patrem neque matrem.

[And so, after not much time had gone by, an unclean spirit entered into this idol of King Belus and gave answers to those who sought them. This is why this idol was called Belus among the Assyrians. Some say Bel, some Beel, some Baal, some Beelphegor, some Belzabuch, some Beelzebub. From the example of this idol, the pagans proceeded to the worship of idols, imagining that dead men were gods and adoring them as gods. This is why they said the first god was Saturn. This Saturn was the king of Crete, his name being taken from that planet which is called Saturn. When he was dead he was said to be a god, having neither father nor mother.]

From Guido's subsequent account of the origin of devils it is clear that this unclean spirit is one of those who fell from heaven with Satan, the Leviathan or Prince of Devils who 'with his cunning temptations cast our miserable parents and their descendants into perpetual ruin'.[19] Through the malevolent influence of Satan, it would seem, idolatry spread, and in different nations pagans worshipped different gods. Idolatry and polytheism were, therefore, supposed to have been propagated by the forces of evil.

According to a common medieval etymology, the name *daemonas* ('demons') came from a Greek word meaning 'experts' or 'those who know things', for demons have foreknowledge of many future things, whence they can make predictions.[20] In his *Speculum Doctrinale* Vincent of Beauvais quotes St Augustine's version of this etymology, then repeats Peter Lombard's statement that, although the evil angels may be inflexible through malice, they have not lost their lively perception.[21] As Isidore says, demons are knowledgeable partly on account of the subtlety of their sense, partly because of the experience which they have gained during their long lives, and partly because they retain (by divine permission) some of their angelic powers of revelation.[22] In Vincent's *Speculum Historiale* the process by which the worshippers of idols are deceived by false images is included in a list of the ways in which devils can provoke men to sin.[23] The relationship between pagan images and demons is described comprehensively in the apocryphal *Speculum Morale*, through a distinction between the initiating or forming cause (*causa dispositiua*) and the completing cause (*causa consummatiua*) of idolatry.[24] The *causa dispositiua* is itself threefold, declares the anonymous compiler with his usual scholastic precision. First, it proceeded from inordinate affection: not being content to honour someone as a man, people revered him as a god. This reason is intimated in the Book of Wisdom 14.15: 'For a father being afflicted with bitter grief, made to himself the image of his son who was quickly taken away: and him who had then died as a man, he began to worship as a god'. The same authority adds that men, serving either their affection, or their kings, imposed the incommunicable name of deity on mere pieces of wood and stone (Wisdom 14.21). The second reason, our compiler continues, was the great delight in representation which is a facet of human nature. In Wisdom 13.11–19 we are told how an artist or carpenter might, by the skill of his craft, fashion a piece of wood into the image of a man, and then proceed to worship it, inquiring of it concerning his substance, his children, or his marriage. The third reason was the inability of men to see the Creator in His creation. Preoccupied with the beauty or power of creatures, vain men failed 'by attending to the works' to acknowledge who was the workman, but instead 'imagined either the fire, or the wind, or the swift air, or the circle of the stars, or the great water, or the sun and the moon, to be the gods that rule the world' (Wisdom 13.1–2). All three reasons, it would seem, were due to men, either through ignorance of the intellect or disorder of the affection. The compiler then proceeds to the *causa consummatiua*, which was due to demons, who in order to make erring men worship them presented themselves in idols by giving responses and doing things which seemed marvellous to mortals. Whence it is stated in Psalm 95.5, 'all the gentile gods are demons'. This information helps us to grasp how medieval writers could envisage certain pagan oracles as being at once true and full of falsehood. Those demons who inhabited heathen images could indeed foresee the future, but, since they were of the race of 'prevaricating angels whose prince was the devil'[25] their answers were not to be trusted.

One of the best-known cases of a deceptive pagan prophecy concerned the proud king Croesus, to whom Boethius had referred in *De Consolatione Philosophiae* II pr. 2. Explaining this allusion, Nicholas Trevet tells of how Croesus consulted the Delphic oracle about his projected war against Persia.[26]

Apollo's answer was ambiguous: 'If Croesus crosses the Alys, a great kingdom will fall'. Croesus, reassured by this prediction, crossed the river Alys, and a great kingdom did fall—his own. Apollo was notorious for his misleading answers, as is made clear by Isidore of Seville's discussion of *amphibolia* as a form of speech. His first example of ambiguity is the response of Apollo to Pyrrhus: 'I say that you, O man sprung from Aeacus, the Romans can defeat'.[27] Here it is uncertain who will be the victor, the Romans or Pyrrhus. It is little wonder, then, that Chaucer's Criseyde, with her father's devotion to Apollo in mind, should protest that

> '. . . goddes speken in amphibologies,
> And, for a sooth, they tellen twenty lyes'.
> (IV, 1406–7)

Stories of demons deceiving men through the agency of oracles, false prophets or speaking images, were legion in the late Middle Ages.[28] For example, in the *Polychronicon* Ralph Higden relates how one Stephen, Proctor of Gascoigne, consulted a spirit which animated a head of brass.[29] First he asked, would he see King Richard again (on the King's return from the Holy Land)?, to which the spirit answered in the negative. Then he asked, how long would his administration endure? The spirit answered, until his death. Finally Stephen asked, where would he die? to which the spirit answered 'in plume'. Thereafter, Stephen commanded that no plumes or feathers should be put near him, and felt free to oppress his people. But this wicked man eventually was killed in a castle called 'Plume', 'and so the decepcion of the spiritte was expressede'. Higden then tells a similar story of how a man was told by a spirit that he should possess Greece. To his surprise, the Greeks refused to have him as their ruler. All was revealed when he married a woman called 'Greece', thereby possessing Greece.

More complicated, and certainly more serious, is Guido delle Colonne's account of how Achilles and Patroclus went to Delphos to seek an answer from Apollo concerning the outcome of their expedition to Troy.[30] In the temple of Apollo there was a very great image, all made of gold, in honour of the god. This idol, a deaf and dumb object made in the similitude of a mortal man, had been entered by an unclean spirit who sought to keep his worshippers in a state of error:

Que licet fuisset ex auro composita et in ueritate fuisset surda et muta, tamen secundum gentilium errores colencium ydolatriam (que principaliter apud ipsos inualuit, cum omisissent uerum cultum Dei ueri, qui in sapientia, id est in filio Dei, domino nostro Ihesu Christo, ex nichilo cuncta creauit) adheserunt diis surdis et mutis, qui pro certo homines mortales fuerunt, credentes et putantes eos esse deos, quorum potencia nulla erat. Sed responsa que dabantur ab eis non ipsi sed qui ingrediebantur in eorum ymagines dabant, qui spiritus immundi pro certo erant, ut per eorum responsa homines in perpetuis errorum cecitatibus conseruarent.

[Although it was made of gold, and in truth was deaf and dumb, still, the pagans, according to their error, embracing idolatry (which chiefly prevailed among them because they lacked the true worship of the true God, who in His Wisdom, that is, in the Son of God, Our Lord Jesus Christ, created all things of nothing), clung to the worship of deaf and dumb gods, who assuredly had been mortal men, believing and considering that those who had no power were gods. But the answers which were given by them were given not by them but by those who entered into their images, who were surely unclean spirits, so that through their answers men were kept in the perpetual blindness of error.]

After providing the account of the origins of idolatry and of demons which was described above, Guido returns to Delphos and Apollo's answer.[31] Speaking in a low voice, the spirit tells Achilles that in ten years Troy will fall to the Greeks. This prediction is then confirmed by Calchas, a Trojan priest and the father of Briseida (the antecedent of Boccaccio's Criseida and Chaucer's Criseyde), who has decided to throw in his lot with the enemy in the light of a warning from Apollo. There is no need for Guido explicitly to make the point that the responses received by these men are deceptive, even though true.[32] The implication is too strong to miss; the import of Guido's thorough analysis of dumb images and their unclean inhabitants is abundantly clear. Of course, the Greeks did win the war after ten years, just as Apollo had promised, but their loss both during and after the siege of Troy was a terrible price to pay. Had Achilles been told the whole truth, he might have thought twice about embarking on a course of action which would result in his own death and those of many comrades-in-arms. But as a devil in disguise, Apollo was careful to provide just the right amount of accurate information required to bring his worshipper to grief. 'Demons greatly delight in the shedding of human blood', to quote Robert Holcot.[33]

Also implicit in Guido's narrative is a criticism of the inordinate extent to which the heathen relied on their ungodly gods. This is quite explicit in Joseph of Exeter's version of the episode, where the 'amazing faith' of the Greeks is ridiculed.[34] The same warriors 'whom passion dragged headlong into battle and who chafed at every delay, gladly idled their time away in peaceful prayer and calmly sought the oracles. Grief put aside its pitiful sighs, glory its laurels, anger its threats, the army stayed rooted to the spot, its wars suspended, and Mars himself waited on the permission of that loquacious cave', that is, the cave of the Delphic oracle. For Joseph such an excess of misplaced reverence is but one instance of the 'credulous blindness of pagan superstition'. Another case in point is the way in which certain heathen worshipped animals and other natural things. Hence Joseph does not know whether to 'lament the idols of the Egyptians with laughter, or tears, or a mixture of both'. For in Egypt 'they worshipped crops, trees, vegetables, serpents that crept, and birds that flew'. Indeed, Joseph complains, such stupidity has by no means ceased in our own age. Fortune-tellers in Spain 'classify the birds of their country by song, or flight, or taste, considering these as omens of things to come'. Elsewhere, old women 'hate to dream of laughter and fear the loss of teeth'; they foretell future events 'by the prophetic chattering of their magpies or the itching of their ears'. But Joseph's most pungent sarcasm is reserved for the Delphic oracle: 'More in error, however, were those answers and that wind of Delphi, which wretched souls used to call on, and which because of its glorious reputation they wrongly thought was God'. 'He whom His universe proclaims as its Creator', Joseph exclaims, 'does not bellow in a cave'.

The fact that men had stooped to worship material things struck many medieval writers as absurd. This attitude is conveyed in the attack on idolatry found in the prose *Roman de Troie*, a revision of Benoît's work made around the middle of the thirteenth century. The anonymous writer ridicules idols by indicating the 'wood, copper or other metal' of which they are made.[35] Guido's reference to the deafness and dumbness of the golden image of Apollo has already been mentioned. Elsewhere the emphasis is placed on the fact that pagans worshipped objects of their own making. According to Holcot, in Wisdom 13.11–16 idols are derided on three counts: because of the material from which they are made, because of the manner in which they are made, and because of the place in which they are put.[36] Reading his passage from Wisdom in the light of Isaiah 44.13–17, he tells the story of the artificer or carpenter who, having cut down a large tree in a wood, divides it in three parts. From the first part he makes a vessel, or an instrument necessary for life such as a cart, a ship, or a plough. From the second part, which consists of the fragments left over from the vessel, he makes a fire on which to cook his food. From the third part, which is full of humps and knots, and from which nothing necessary for human life can be made, he makes an idol. It is most fatuous, therefore, to believe this to be a god, since it is of the same substance as the material which he burnt and the material from which he made his plough. Moreover, Solomon states that the carpenter carves his idol diligently 'when he has nothing else to do', thereby deriding idols in respect of the manner in which they are made. By the knowledge of his craft he shapes a statue from the wood, not creating any new thing, but removing pieces of wood one after the other, thereby obtaining the likeness of a man. Alternatively, he may carve the wood after 'the resemblance of some beast', just as the Egyptians depicted Arpis in the form of an ox, Hammon as a ram, and Anubis as a dog. Then the image is covered over with red paint and dye. Holcot regards this red dye as a false colour, since it conceals the natural colour of the wood and gives it the appearance of something which it is not, every flaw in the image being hidden. Finally, idols are derided by reason of their location, when we are told that the carpenter makes a worthy dwelling-place for his image. The pagans placed their images in the most beautiful temples, declares Holcot, revealing his aesthetic sense. An idol must be fixed firmly lest it should fall—but the statue of Dagon fell before the ark of God (I Kings 5.1–5). What the carpenter has made is an image of a man and not a man; it needs the help of a man and by no means can help a man.

The silliness and fatuity of the pagans in making vows, prayers and supplications to such artifacts is the subject of Holcot's next lecture.[37] The carpenter is 'not ashamed to speak to that which has no life' even though he ought to be, since he himself is a rational creature whereas the idol, lacking a soul, is not. Although his idol is 'weak', that is, powerless to confer health, 'for health he makes supplication and for life prays to that which is dead', an object made either of dry wood or lifeless stone (Wisdom 13.18). For help this fool 'calls on that which is unprofitable', just as the priests of Baal called on their god in vain, as we read in III Kings 18: 'There was no voice, nor any that answered: and they leaped over the altar that they had made; . . . and they cut themselves after their manner with knives and lancets, till they were all covered with blood' (verses 26 and 28). Then Elias with good reason mocked these priests, saying that perhaps Baal was talking, or in an inn, or on a journey, or asleep and in need of awakening. This chimes with Wisdom 13.19, where Solomon ridicules the foolishness of those who 'for a good journey' pray to an idol that cannot walk, and in general appeal to the very thing that is unable to do anything.

But in view of all these criticisms of pagan images, what ought we to think of Christian images? Should Christians adore images of Christ and of the Saints? Holcot confronted this problem at the very beginning of his treatment of idolatry.[38] It would appear that we should not make images, because it is stated in Exodus 22.4, 'Thou shalt not make to thyself an image nor any likeness'. If it is not right to make them, surely it is worse to adore them. When idolatry is reprehended in Scripture it is always spoken of with reference to images made by human hands, as Wisdom 13.10 makes clear. And Christian artifacts are, after all, objects made of gold and silver, wood and stone. Since it is written in Scripture that such things are not allowed, it would seem to follow that it is superstitious to employ images.

Holcot demolishes this argument by citing the traditional practice of the Church, St John Damascene, and his fellow-Dominican St Thomas Aquinas. According to Aquinas's commentary on the *Sentences* of Peter Lombard, an image can be considered in two ways, either with regard to what it is in itself or with regard to what it signifies.[39] The spiritual realities signified by images are the proper objects of Christian reverence. Holcot proceeds to quote Aquinas's account of the threefold cause of the institution of images: for the instruction of laymen (for whom images take the place of books), in order that the mystery of the incarnation and the examples of the Saints may be the more firmly and directly imprinted on the memory, and in order to excite the affection of devotion, which is caused more readily by things seen than by things heard.[40] Then Holcot emphasises the point that Christian images are quite different in nature and in usage from pagan similitudes, the latter having originated through affection for the dead and having been sustained by demons who entered into the effigies or images of the departed.[41]

A basically similar pattern of thought informs the portrayal of Dame Idolatry provided in the second recension (1335) of Guillaume de Deguileville's popular poem *Le Pélerinage de la vie humaine*. This is hardly surprising, since Deguileville is imaginatively elaborating on the carpenter episode of Wisdom 13.11–19, the focus of Holcot's comments on idolatry and the pagan gods which have been outlined above. *Le Pélerinage* will be cited as an example of the way in which a poet could powerfully dramatize the doctrinal common-places which thus far have been the subject of this chapter. The following paraphrase follows the Middle English translation of 1426 which is usually attributed to John Lydgate.[42]

Deguileville's pilgrim moves from the island where he has encountered Astrology and Geomancy to another island, which is inhabited by an ugly old hag named Idolatry, who whinnies like a horse. In her house is found a foul image of a man crowned like a king, holding a sword in his hand and bearing on his shoulders a shield which is painted with black flies and spiders. A devotee—apparently a mason or carpenter—kneels before this idol, making his sacrifice. Idolatry, who delights in this sight, reveals that she is the friend and daughter of Satan, who is enclosed in the image, and always gives ambiguous answers to infect the carpenter's soul with sin and to trouble his wits. The fool asks the idol for a response, but it itself does not hear, being as dumb as a stone. It has eyes but cannot see; feet, but it cannot walk a foot away from its chair; its sword and shield are of no avail in battle (cf. Wisdom 13.18–19). What is especially absurd is that the carpenter made the idol himself, and therefore knows that it cannot help him—a clear echo of Wisdom 13.15–16.

> The same sylue carpenter
> Dyde a-forn hys bysy peyne
> To forge hym, wyth hys handys tweyne,
> And made hym ffyrst off swych entaylle,
> And wot he may nothyng avaylle
> To helpe hym, whan that al ys do.
> They ben A-coursyd, bothe two.
>
> (20934–40)

The carpenter, refusing the pilgrim's advice to repent, accuses him and Christians in general of revering idols which are equally useless. The reply is twofold: images of the Saints are mere 'spectacles' and 'merours' of the spiritual realities which they represent, and they serve as books for the unlearned.[43] This type of defence is utterly predictable, but it should be remembered that it was of far greater significance in Lydgate's day than in the time of Deguileville or Holcot, in view of the Wycliffite rejection of the traditional role of images in worship. Wyclif himself had opposed the veneration of religious *objets d'art* with moderation, but by the late 1380's a strong distrust of them had become one of the distinguishing marks of a Lollard.[44] This was the period in which Chaucer composed his great poems about pagan idolaters, *Troilus and Criseyde* and the final version of the tale of Palamon and Arcite.

But let us return, for the moment, to *The Pilgrimage of the Life of Man*. Why, the pilgrim asks the carpenter, should he persist in worshipping an idol which contains Satan and will therefore hurt him mortally? But the 'vyleyn' refuses to argue any more, and threatens to cut off his opponent's head if he does not worship his idol, whereupon the pilgrim departs in great fear. This attempt at coercion is consonant with one of the reasons for the continuance of idolatry offered in Wisdom 14.16: men had to maintain the wicked custom of pagan rites and sacrifices to idols for fear of offending the tyrants who enforced error as law. Robert Holcot interpreted this passage with the aid of the tale of King Syrophanes of Egypt, drawn from Fulgentius (as expounded by Ridevall) and Alexander Nequam.[45] Out of inordinate corporeal affection Syrophanes set up an image of his dead son: in seeking a remedy for sorrow he founded a nursery of sadness. The king's retainers made offerings to this idol in order to please their ruler, and those who fled to it obtained pardon from their misdeeds. Clearly, such reverence stemmed from fear rather than love. Whence Petronius says, *Primus in orbe deos fecit inesse timor* ('Fear first caused the gods to exist in the world').[46] This statement, as quoted by Holcot, may be the source of the remark of Chaucer's Criseyde that 'drede fond first goddes' (IV, 1408). It is possible to argue that, in the pagan world of *Troilus and Criseyde*, fear is as important an emotion as is love.

This completes our brief review of the major limitations inherent in heathen conceptions of deity, in what may be called (with ample medieval precedent) pagan theology. We shall now proceed to describe some of the limitations of pagan philosophy, paying special attention to doctrines of fate and fortune.

II   IMPERFECT PAGAN PHILOSOPHY

Since late-medieval scholars generally believed that many of the ancient pagans had been fatalists, it is necessary to investigate their understanding of the term *fatum* ('fate') in this context. Vincent of Beauvais repeated Isidore of Seville's definition of fate as whatever is spoken by the gods, or whatever is decreed by Jupiter, the supreme pagan deity.[47] Drawing on the description of pagan antiquity in St Augustine's *De Civitate Dei*, Isidore had stated that *fatum* is derived from *fari* ('to speak'), but this must be understood in a special sense.[48] We Christians cannot deny that it is written in Scripture, 'God hath spoken once . . .' (Psalm 61.12), which is to be interpreted as God speaking immovably and unchangeably, so that all things must befall just as He said they would, and meant to have them. In other words, the notion of fate can be accepted by a Christian if it is reduced to the decrees of the one true God. Isidore proceeds to explain that fortune takes its name from 'fortuitous things', and was imagined as a goddess sporting with human cases and fortunes. Fate and fortune differ in so far as fortune consists in those things which occur by chance and apparently without reason, whereas fate is fixed and ordered with regard to individuals.

Elaborate versions of these definitions and distinctions were provided in the early fourteenth century by Nicholas Trevet and Thomas Bradwardine. Expounding Boethius's treatment of the relationship of fate and providence in *De Consolatione Philosophiae* IV pr. 6, Trevet says that fate can be taken in two ways, as may be gathered from the words of Augustine in *De Civitate Dei*.[49] First, it may be understood as the power or position of the stars when one is born or conceived. Taken this way, fate is nothing, by which Trevet means that it does not determine the lives of men. The Saints, he explains, understood *fatum* in this sense when they absolutely denied that it existed. For example, in his Epiphany homily St Gregory states that the notion that there is such a thing as fate should be dismissed from the hearts of the faithful. The second sense of *fatum* is defined by Augustine in *De Civitate Dei* V.9: 'we neither deny an order of causes wherein the will of God is all in all; neither do we call it by the name of fate, unless fate be derived of *fari*, "to speak"'. Although this sense is employed less often by the Saints than the first it seems to be the more ancient of the two, Trevet explains, and certainly it is in this second sense that Boethius is using the term when he speaks of 'the manifold manner in which all things behave' as follows: 'this manner, when it is contemplated in the utter purity of the divine intelligence, is called providence; but when related to those things it moves and disposes, it was by the ancients called fate'. Indeed, the poets feigned three fates, called Clotho, Lachesis and Atropos, on account of the threefold manner in which mutable things are disposed.[50] For mutable things either move from non-being to being, or continue in existence by duration of time, or pass from being to non-being. The first of these events is attributed to Clotho, to be interpreted as evocation or generation, who is said to carry a distaff because she provides the beginning of existence. The second is attributed to Lachesis, to be interpreted as 'lot' and 'fortune', who is supposed to pull the thread because she produces the existence of things. The third and last is attributed to Atropos, who is interpreted as 'without turning' because after something ceases to exist it cannot return to its former existence. She cuts the thread, because she ends the space of existence. Considering these three types of event together, fate is, as Boethius says, 'a disposition inherent in changing things'. Through it 'providence binds all things together, each in its own proper ordering'.

But if fate is an ever-changing nexus, namely the 'movable interlacing and temporal ordering' of the divine disposition, how can Boethius say that the fatal course 'moves the heaven and the stars' and 'binds the acts and fortunes of men in an unbreakable chain of causes'? Trevet points out that, although the sky and stars are, in terms of substance, immediately from the God who created them, yet their movements and the phenomena proceeding from them (such as eclipses, conjunctions, oppositions and the like) are from God through the agency of mediating secondary causes, and hence they are subject to fate. Thus, when Boethius speaks of the way in which the indissoluble chain of causes binds the acts of men, this may not be regarded as a contradiction of his statement about fate's moving nature. Trevet resolves the difficulty by distinguishing between two ways in which the fatal course may be considered. First, it may be considered in so far as it consists in the secondary causes themselves, which order and disposition is called fate. Secondly, it may be considered in so far as it is subordinate to and dependent on the divine providence itself, and in this way immobility is obtained. This lack of change, however, is not absolute but conditional—in accordance with which we speak of conditional necessity thus: 'if God saw this, this will be'.

Boethius, Trevet continues, proves that the fact that fate is immobile in this way, is perfectly congenial. At the outset he shows the divine rule to be fitting and appropriate, saying that 'things are governed in the best way if the simplicity which rests in the divine mind produces an inflexible order of causes', because if someone could deflect the order of divine providence the impotence of the ruler would be manifest. But from this it cannot simply be concluded that all things come about by necessity, for the following reason. Being precedes necessity and contingents; necessity and contingents follow being as its proper manners. Since God is the provider of all being, consequently these manners of being come under His provision also. Therefore, He sees to it that things result necessarily only to the extent that these things have proximate causes which are contingently necessary. Causes, although they are changeable in so far as they are contingent, can yet be disposed in a fixed order by divine providence. Such immobility will not be absolute immobility but conditional immobility, depending on the divine providence. And so, the freedom of the human will is assured; we are not 'fated' in the sense of being rigidly determined in all our acts by absolute or 'simple' necessity.

This distinction between absolute and conditional necessity is echoed in Chaucer's *Nun's Priest's Tale* in a famous passage which links Thomas

Bradwardine with St Augustine and Boethius as experts on the subject of divine foreknowledge and predestination:

> But I ne kan nat bulte it to the bren
> As kan the hooly doctour Augustyn,
> Or Boece, or the Bisshop Bradwardyn,
> Wheither that Goddes worthy forwityng
> Streyneth me nedely for to doon a thyng,—
> 'Nedely' clepe I symple necessitee;
> Or elles, if free choys be graunted me
> To do that same thyng, or do it noght,
> Though God forwoot it er that was wrought;
> Or if his wityng streyneth never a deel
> But by necessitee condicioneel.
>
> (VII, 3240–50)

Bradwardine sifts this matter 'to the bren' in both the *Sermo Epinicius* and *De Causa Dei*, where the notion that secondary causes (such as fate, fortune or the stars) have some independence in causation is systematically refuted. These causes are, he argues vehemently, obedient instruments of the divine will. Very much in Bradwardine's mind were the erroneous views on necessity and fate which had been condemned in 1270 and 1277 by the Bishop of Paris.[51] The main object of Stephen Tempier's attack were the so-called 'Latin Averroists', who seem to have included Siger of Brabant and Boethius of Dacia. The influence of Arabian commentaries on Aristotle had encouraged the formulation of philosophies which denied freedom of choice to both God and man. For example, God was supposed to necessitate earthly events by the medium of heavenly bodies (1270, condemned proposition 4).[52] The divine artificer has set in motion a vast machine which He cannot stop and with which He cannot interfere. Consequently, human acts cannot be said to be ruled by the divine providence (1270, condemned proposition 12): God is subject to His own determinism. Freedom is thus denied to God, and also to man, in whom freedom is a passive power which is moved with necessity by the desired object (1270, condemned proposition 9). The nominalistic theory of the absolute power of God, as held by such thinkers as William of Ockham and Robert Holcot, may be regarded as an attempt to counter these errors with an affirmation of the divine freedom,[53] as may their formulation of a relatively optimistic view of man's natural abilities, which Bradwardine castigated as a new form of pelagianism.[54] Bradwardine was equally concerned to curtail the power allowed to secondary causes, but his solution was very different.[55] In the fashion of 'Boece' and 'the hooly doctour Augustyn' he asserted the sovereignty of the first and primary cause over all secondary and inferior causes.

The influence of *De Consolatione Philosophiae* and *De Civitate Dei* is writ large in the three semantic analyses of the term *fatum* provided in *De Causa Dei* I.28, which shall be summarized in turn.[56] According to the first analysis, one may distinguish between the common power of the stars which, God willing, *generally* regulates all earthly things, and that particular power which *specially* consists in a certain conjunction of heavenly bodies which is supposed to determine what the future will bring to a man born under it.[57] The former may be accepted but the latter must be denied.

According to Bradwardine's second analysis, *fatum* may be understood to refer to divine dictates, an interpretation already familiar to us from the statements of Isidore and Trevet cited above. Following Augustine, Bradwardine explains that the Stoics and other pagan moral philosophers believed that *fatum* was derived from *fari*, meaning 'to speak', and so they identified fate with the dictates of Jove, their greatest God. *Fatum* was the name given to the will of that great and all-disposing god whom they called Jove, whose power was insurmountably extended through the series of secondary causes. Christians hold the same belief, Bradwardine continues, but of course they substitute the true God for Jove in this causal scheme. As Augustine says, we regard as vain and frivolous the notion of fate as a position of stars in nativities and conceptions; neither do we call an order of causes by the name of fate, unless *fatum* is understood to be derived from *fari*.

According to Bradwardine's third analysis, *fatum* may be taken either as the active will of God in so far as it disposes all earthly things, or as the passive disposition inherent in creatures. The first of these senses is attested by Augustine, when he quotes from Seneca and Homer verses which identify fate with the will of Jove. The Stoics found in Homer a description of Jove, whom they held to be that great god who caused light and heat to fill the earth:

> Tales sunt hominum mentes qualis pater ipse,
> Jupiter auctiferas lustravit lumine terras.
>
> [Such are the minds of men as Jove the great
> Vouchsafes, that fills the earth with light, and heat.]

Bradwardine, anxious to secure Homer as a good pagan, criticizes Aristotle for having misunderstood him. Aristotle thought Homer's phrase 'father of men and of gods' referred to the sun: in fact, says Bradwardine, it refers to Jove. The second sense of fate in this analysis, that is, as the passive disposition inherent in creatures, is attested by Boethius in *De Consolatione Philosophiae* IV pr. 6. Here, recounts Bradwardine, providence is described as the divine reason itself, which disposes all things, whereas fate is a disposition inherent in changing things, by which providence connects all things in their due order (cf. p. 41 above). Providence connects all things together, but fate puts every particular thing into motion, being distributed by places, forms and time: this unfolding of temporal order being united into the foresight of God's mind is providence, and the same uniting being digested and unfolded in time is called fate. Bradwardine explains that Boethius takes fate *secundum effectum* ('as effect') and not *secundum efficientiam voluntatis divinae* ('according to the effecting of the divine will'), which he understands as providence. By contrast, Seneca, Homer and the Stoics take fate 'according to the effecting of the divine will', because they had a single word, *fatum*, for what Boethius described with the two terms *fatum* and *providentia*. Thus the good pagans are free from error, their fault being merely one of expression. Bradwardine sums up with another quotation from *De Civitate Dei*, which indicates the limitations of pagan philosophies. Let Cicero, who denied divine prescience, wrangle, together with the Stoics who said that the order of causes is fated, or is fate itself! Cicero could not accept that God knows assuredly the set order of causes: we Christians detest this error even more than the Stoics did. Bradwardine, it would seem, shares Augustine's preference for the Stoics, whose main fault was their use of the term *fatum* in a false sense. This chapter of *De Causa Dei* ends with the attribution to God of a controlling power so total that one may suspect that Bradwardine has rejected all rival forms of necessity in order to substitute a strict divine predestination.

In the next chapter of *De Causa Dei* Bradwardine argues that all *fortuna* ('fortune') is reducible to God, and here the Stoics, together with Aristotle and his Arabian interpreters, are upheld as the best of the pagan authorities on that subject.[58] Many pagans, including Sallust, Democritus, Epicurus and Ovid, believed in mere chance (*casus*), but the Stoics affirmed that all is governed by divine providence. From their differing positions Bradwardine extracts the common belief that fortune and chance exist when something occurs which is beyond the intention of the agent. Then he turns to Boethius, who argued that the opinion that certain things happen in a purely fortuitous and casual manner is to be denied, because everything that occurs occurs in accordance with the intention of some agent. The question is, which agent? Astrologers claim that it is the power of the stars, in which case all apparently fortuitous events would be produced by the determinate causation of many heavenly bodies. But heavenly bodies are in turn controlled by God, and hence have no independence in causation. Others, Bradwardine continues, speak of the goddess Fortuna, who is portrayed as a blind woman distributing good and evil irrationally. But Isaiah 65.11 speaks contemptuously of those who spread a table for the god Fortune and pour libations in his honour. Bradwardine quotes Aristotle as saying that *casus* and *fortuna* are causes *per accidens*: therefore they are reducible to some cause *per se*, and every cause *per se* is reducible to the final cause and unmoved mover, God. In *De Bona Fortuna* Aristotle argues that good fortune comes from God, in his *Rhetorica* he calls God the author of fortune, and in his *Ethics* he says that men are good not merely by their personal power but by a divine cause, and it is in this that the real 'good fortune' consists. Highly selective quotations from Arab commentators on Aristotle, together with citations of Augustine, Boethius, the Stoics and Holy Scripture are used to define a single authoritative view of fortune. According to Bradwardine, Christians and the most enlightened of the pagans share the conviction that there is no such thing as mere chance, that fortune in the sense of an arbitrary force simply does not exist.

Bradwardine's main conclusions on the subject of astral determinism are advanced with impressive rhetoric in the *Sermo Epinicius* and with full intellectual rigour in *De Causa Dei* II.3. It appears from the *Sermo Epinicius* that, on the eve of the battle of Crécy some of Edward III's soldiers had tried to predict the outcome of the battle. Such men, Bradwardine complains, are not worthy of the name 'Christian'.[59] In emulating those misguided pagans who worshipped the sun, moon and stars as gods, and certain ancient Jews who fell into the same error, they deny their faith and brand themselves as antichristians and apostates. Since the birth of Christ there has been no excuse for such practices. According to Christian tradition the entire heavens were created in the beginning by God, and so they cannot do anything other than serve His will. This is attested by Baruch 3.34–5, 'joyfully the stars shine out, keeping the watches he has appointed, answer when he calls their muster-roll, and offer their glad radiance to him who fashioned them'. God is perfectly entitled to intervene in the normal operations of His universe, thereby proving the point

44

that He is more powerful than the stars. In Exodus 10.22–3 we read how Moses stretched out his hand towards the sky, and it became dark throughout the land of Egypt for three days, but there was light in the homes of the Israelites. Similarly, Joshua spoke with the Lord, and the sun and moon stood still until his armies had defeated the Amorites (Joshua 10.13). What astrologer could have prognosticated this? Truly, Bradwardine exclaims, behold one prognostication which cannot fail: whatever God wishes to do or be done, that will be done! The obvious moral is that we should not displease God lest He deny us victory. Isaiah tells us how astrological lore let down the Babylonians, who were unable to foretell their own ruin, or to charm away disaster. One cannot see in the constellations a presentiment of victory or defeat, for a day which is victorious for one side is simultaneously a day of defeat for the other. Bradwardine cites the Church's condemnation of the judicial art of predicting particular events, thereby enforcing the theme of his sermon, that God alone, and not any secondary cause like the stars, is to be thanked for the victory, which was granted as a reward for virtue and because the English cause was just.

In *De Causa Dei* II.3 Bradwardine stresses the point that no secondary and inferior cause can necessitate the created will to act rationally and freely in a meritorious way, or to sin.[60] A rational creature is free of will, and naturally free: this is what distinguishes man from the beasts. If the human will could be necessitated by some secondary cause, it would surely be by astral influences, which seem to have the maximum effect on subjects, to such an extent that astrologers often appear to foretell the mores and actions of men. But this notion, Bradwardine declares firmly, does not withstand rational analysis. Stars and stellar virtues are material and irrational things, whereas the human rational soul is immaterial, more perfect, and naturally superior. As Augustine says in *De Libero Arbitrio*, nothing can move the genuinely virtuous soul to act in a contrary way. Ptolemy rightly says that the wise man will build on what the stars have given him by way of natural virtue.

The value of a good moral education is pointed out. Experience shows us that any opinions or acts to which a child may be disposed at birth can be altered by teaching, by the child's being brought into contact with the views of its parents, friends and tutors: thus, the child may become settled in better ways. Hermes Trismegistis says that one should study the natural dispositions fostered in us by the heavens, then encourage the good ones and conquer the bad. Ptolemy compares the wise man to a true husbandman, who will make the most of stellar assistance, and fortify himself against future mishap. Bradwardine provides the *exemplum* of a rich merchant he once met who confessed that the stars had predisposed him to homosexuality, yet, through constant struggle and the guidance of the divine law, he was managing to repress these tendencies.

All the catholic doctors condemn astral fatalism, Bradwardine affirms, especially if it implies necessity. If the human will was being necessitated in its action by some external cause, this would take the form of a strong temptation, but a temptation, however strong, can always be rejected. While one cannot deny the power of the stars in *inclining* someone to perform certain actions, this is not necessitation because the person retains his option of contradiction and refusal, his free will.[61] Bradwardine supports this view with the *exemplum* of Hippocrates and Philimon from the *Secreta Secretorum*, which (in common with all the scholars of his day) he believed to be a genuine work of Aristotle.[62] The disciples of Hippocrates were shocked when Philimon, having examined a painting of the philosopher's figure, said that it was the figure of a covetous, deceptive and lecherous man. Yet Hippocrates confirmed Philimon's judgment, admitting that he had indeed inclined to all these vices but, having made his soul a king to itself, had managed to control them. According to Bradwardine, Plato, Socrates, Seneca and all the other moral philosophers frequently teach, and more frequently assume, that the virtues and vices are in the power of the human will. He quotes Augustine as saying that only those who are the slaves of cupidity lose their free will.

Bradwardine's Christian and pagan authorities have proved, to his satisfaction at least, that no temptation can overcome a freely-disposed virtuous will. All doubts are swept aside with a confident assertion of the freedom of the will from astral determinism. Anyone born under an unfortunate disposition of stars may refuse to perform the corresponding evil actions. This may not be easy, and the person in question may never become securely settled in the apposite virtues, but it certainly is possible. We are responsible for our own actions, and cannot blame our faults on the stars. Yet, because stellar influences do at least incline men to perform certain actions, the theologian should know something of the science of astrology. The importance of a sane astrology for ethics and medicine cannot be doubted either. Bradwardine, a pioneer of experimental science at Oxford, recommends the study of mathematics, astronomy, and the genuine science of astrology which operates in accordance with firm guidelines.

Similar affirmations of the power of the will to withstand stellar influence are found in the writings of, for example, Albert the Great and Thomas Aquinas. In a passage incorporated in Vincent's *Speculum Naturale*, Albert explains that the stars necessarily govern the 'vegetative spirit' of plants and the 'sensible spirit' of animals, because these things are absolutely dependent on matter.[63] The human soul, on the other hand, is dependent on matter only in a certain respect (*secundum quid*), and hence the stars may influence a man's will through his body, but this is not necessitation. 'The effect does not always follow necessarily from the constellation'. In his opuscule *De Iudiciis Astrorum*, Aquinas distinguishes between those things that depend on the stars directly (such as the weather, physical health, and agriculture) and activities that depend on free will, which in no way is determined by the stars.[64] His conclusion is that, while doctors of medicine and farmers may benefit from predictions relating to the first category, it is a grave sin to consult the stars about the fate of individuals, for the devil can make use of such superstition for his own evil purposes.

The practice of making 'particular' predictions, i.e. predictions concerning the destinies of individuals from the configuration of the stars at their births, was usually termed 'judicial astrology' and regarded as a pagan practice which was as uncertain as it was unlawful.[65] By contrast, 'general' predictions of such major and universal events as famines, pestilences, and the falls of cities, which involved a large number of people, were supposed to have a high degree of accuracy and could legitimately be made by Christian scholars. An especially interesting application of this distinction is found in the *Summa Iudicialis de Accidentibus Mundi* of John Ashenden, who, like Bradwardine, was a fellow of Merton College, Oxford. John's famous reference-book was completed in

1348, four years after *De Causa Dei* had been published, at a time when 'Bradwardine's upbraiding of the fellows of their college . . . and a theological reaction against natural philosophy' were probably making themselves felt.[66] This may to some extent account for the care with which Ashenden delimits the scope of his treatise: the judicial astrology which is his main interest comprises general rather than particular predictions. Ptolemy, he explains, divided astrology into two principal parts, the first and the greatest of which is the 'universal part', which concerns what will happen in entire regions and lands.[67] This is the subject of the second book of the *Summa Iudicialis*, wherein Ashenden refuses to discuss births, because of the difficulty of prognosticating in this area and the great precision required. We will return to the distinction between general and particular predictions in our next chapter, since it has considerable bearing on Chaucer's attitude to, and deployment of, fatalistic philosophy in *Troilus and Criseyde*.

What emerges very clearly from these discussions of fate, predestination and human freedom by Trevet, Bradwardine and the rest is a firm refusal to lump together all pagan views on such subjects and reject them indiscriminately. In particular, Bradwardine is consistent in distinguishing between the faults of fatalists and 'vain astrologers' and the virtues of those noble Stoics and other good pagans who to some extent anticipated Christian conceptions of the workings of divine providence. The desire to harmonize Christian and pagan opinions on common intellectual problems is one of the most characteristic features of late-medieval scholastic procedure, but it takes on a special significance in *De Causa Dei*. Bradwardine was determined to obtain a consensus of opinion on the sovereignty of God,[68] who wields supreme power over all the instrumental causes which enact His will and who gives grace freely and without obligation to mankind. From our point of view the most interesting facet of this consensus concerns the heathen testimonies to, and prophecies of, Christ and Christian truths, which Bradwardine and his fellow-schoolmen so loved to cite. This is, as it were, the other side of the coin from the untrustworthy pagan prophecies which we have investigated already, those ambiguous answers made by deceptive demons who sought to sustain soul-destroying error.

III   PAGAN FORERUNNERS AND 'FRIENDS OF GOD'

There is, Bradwardine claims, no substantial article of the Christian faith which God did not reveal many times, through venerable prophets or various foretellings, before the advent of the Christian faith.[69] This statement is substantiated with an abundance of Christian and pagan prophecies. Bradwardine begins by defending prophetic passages in the Old Testament against the charge of interpolation, and then proceeds to defend the prophets themselves. They cannot be regarded as charlatans because of the obvious goodness of their lives and their ability to work miracles in life and in death. Moreover, the fact that their prophecies came true is surely a good argument for their integrity.

Who can doubt the power of God to illuminate and inspire a man, so that he becomes a prophet? Certainly, all the great philosophers concede the existence of true prophets. In his *Secreta Secretorum* Aristotle takes it as proved that prophets are most pure in intellect and most true in vision. The sibylline prophecies rightly are held in great reverence. Bradwardine then quotes two prophecies which reveal the existence of good pagans who anticipated the coming of Christ. When the tomb of Balaam was opened by the Emperor Constantine, a golden blade was found lying by the corpse. On it was written, 'Christ will be born of the Virgin Mary, and I believe in Him'. (Nicholas of Lyre's use of this story has already been discussed, on p. 2 above.) Secondly, in the reign of King Ferrandus of Castile a book was discovered, about the size of a Psalter and written in three languages, which told the history of the Jews, the Greeks and the Romans. This book prophesied the coming of Christ, and even managed to foretell the time in which it would be recovered.

Bradwardine then cites the case of the three wise men from the East, well instructed in the doctrine of the abovementioned Balaam, who correctly interpreted the star of Bethlehem as a sign of Christ's birth. Historical confirmation of the existence of this star may be obtained from Pliny and Plato, and from Roman and Egyptian iconography. God has complete control over His creation, including all heavenly bodies, as is manifest by the eclipse of the sun at the time of Christ's death, in the middle of the lunar month when no such event could occur naturally. On seeing this sight, the great gentile philosopher Dionysius the Areopagite exclaimed, 'Either the god of nature suffers, or the mechanism of the universe is dissolved'. When St Paul came to tell the Athenians that Christ was the 'unknown God' in whom they believed already, Dionysius received the faith. Here Bradwardine may have been influenced by another work which, incidentally, was probably known to Chaucer, the *Tractatus de Sphera* written in the early thirteenth century by John of Holywood (Johannes de Sacrobosco).[70] At the end of his explanation of the causes of eclipses, John states that the solar eclipse which accompanied the Passion was not natural but 'miraculous and contrary to nature, since a solar eclipse ought to occur at new moon or thereabouts'.[71] On this account Dionysius is reported to have made his remark about the suffering God of nature. This discussion by John of Holywood seems to be the source of one of Guido delle Colonne's personal contributions to the matter of Troy, an elaboration of Benoît's treatment of the magical powers possessed by Medea.[72] The pagans of antiquity were willing to believe that she could force the sun and moon to go into eclipse against the natural order. Guido's rejoinder is that the high and eternal God imposed on the heavenly bodies for all eternity laws which they will not disregard. The only occasion on which a solar eclipse took place contrary to the laws of nature was when the incarnate Sun of God gave up His spirit on the tree of the Cross. Hence Dionysius, 'the most eminent gentile philosopher, who lived in Athens and was very active in the schools', said in stupefaction that either the mechanism of the world was dissolved or the God of nature was suffering. But Guido cannot resist making the point that, despite his great learning, Dionysius was 'tainted by the error of the pagans'.

That comment is absolutely characteristic of Guido, who misses no opportunity to criticize the pagans. By contrast, those writers who helped to inform Chaucer's view of pagan antiquity, including Vincent of Beauvais, John of Wales, Trevet, Holcot and Bradwardine, missed no opportunity to point out their intellectual and moral achievements.[73] Bradwardine's Dionysius is a good pagan who is ripe for conversion. By means of an apparent disruption in the mechanics of the universe he has inferred the existence of a suffering deity, so that when St Paul identifies the 'unknown God' of the Athenians with Christ, he can believe in Him immediately and without question. This portrait is typical of the depictions of pagan forerunners and 'friends of God' provided by the classicizing clerics of the later Middle Ages. We shall now consider other examples.

Those pagan prophets who had managed to predict the coming of Christ were among the most enlightened of the good pagans. The commonplace belief that Virgil's fourth eclogue was a Messianic prophecy of Christ is reiterated by Vincent of Beauvais.[74] Bradwardine makes much of two sibylline prophecies: one takes the form of 27 Greek verses which is an acrostic spell out the name of 'Jesus Christ the Son of God, Saviour'; the other is the popular tale of Octavian and the sibyl.[75] The story of how the Roman Emperor Octavian was saved from the common pagan sin of deifying what was human is told in some detail in Jacob of Voragine's *Legenda Aurea* (written between 1255 and 1266).[76] Caxton englishes the relevant passage as follows:

> Octavian the Emperor, like as Innocent recordeth, that he was much desired of his council and of his people, that he should do men worship him as God. For never before had there been before him so great a master and lord of the world as he was. Then the Emperor sent for a prophetess named Sibyl, for to demand of her if there were any so great and like him in the earth, or if any should come after him. Thus at the hour of mid-day she beheld the heaven, and saw a circle of gold about the sun, and in the middle of the circle a maid holding a child in her arms. Then she called the Emperor and shewed it to him. When Octavian saw that he marvelled over much, whereof Sibyl said to him Hic puer major te est, ipsum adorara. This child is greater lord than thou art, worship him. Then when the Emperor understood that this child was a greater lord than he was, he would not be worshipped as God, but worshipped this child that should be born. Wherefore the christian men made a church of the same chamber of the Emperor, and named it Ara cœli.[77]

Octavian's wise and humble acceptance of his own humanity provides a striking contrast with the fatuous practice of those tyrants who, according to the Book of Wisdom, had enforced idolatrous error as law. Indeed, in the same section of the *Legenda Aurea* Jacob gives an example of a deceptive pagan prophecy. Because the world was then in so great peace, the Romans had made a temple named the Temple of Peace, filled with many marvellous images.[78] When Apollo was asked how long this edifice would stand, he answered that it would endure until a virgin gave birth to a child. Believing that this was an utter impossibility, the pagans wrote in the portal of the temple that it would endure for ever. But when Christ was born of the Virgin Mary it all fell down. The birth of Christ, therefore, marked the end of idolatry.

Some pagans, it would seem, were so mentally well-prepared for Christianity that they believed in Christ the minute they heard of Him; some had been granted glimmerings of the coming dispensation in reliable prophecies. Others had not been so gifted, having been born in the wrong place at the wrong time, and/or lacking the divine grace to anticipate the incarnation. But certain of the virtuous heathen who fell into this large category had at least reached an intellectual position in which they confidently could abjure the gods and embrace a monotheistic view of deity.

Vincent of Beauvais, following Augustine's *De Civitate Dei*, emphasizes the fact that many pagans had affirmed their multitude of Gods to be but one and the same Jupiter, of whom the famous poet Virgil was thought to say in his fourth eclogue, 'God His spirit imparts / To the earth's, the sea's, and heaven's profoundest parts'.[79] What, then, should the pagans lose by taking the shorter course, and instead of worshipping all His parts adore but one God? Vincent collects together *auctoritates* from Isidore, Clement and Augustine to prove that the Platonists had attained an impressive measure of truth, and that Abraham and many gentile philosophers had reached the knowledge of the one God.[80] Among all the heathen thinkers the Platonists were supreme in both practical and contemplative philosophy. They say that no mutable thing was God, and therefore went further than all mutable spirits and souls to seek for Him. What they knew of God, Augustine explained, 'He did manifest unto them by teaching them the gradual contemplation of His parts invisible by His works visible'. This is a clear allusion to Romans 1.20, 'For the invisible things of Him, from the creation of the world, are clearly seen, being understood by the things that are made'. Vincent also includes a statement by Clement to the effect that Abraham inferred from his study of the stars the existence of a Creator whose providence ruled everything, whereupon an angel appeared in a vision to teach him more plainly those things which he had perceived. From this grouping together of extracts, as from several of Bradwardine's discussions as paraphrased above, it would appear that the Old Testament patriarchs and prophets were believed to be on a par, historically speaking, with certain pagan philosophers, since they had all lived long before the time of Christ. One consequence of this was that they operated on the same intellectual level, relying on their native wit for the most part, and being encouraged by the occasional divine revelation.

Tales of how the virtues of monotheistic pagans had been tried and tested in circumstances of exceptional adversity are provided by Vincent of Beauvais and by many of the classicizing clerics who scanned his vast compilation for information about antiquity. For example, in the *Speculum Historiale* and Higden's *Polychronicon* a story is told about the monotheistic and ascetic Brahmans winning a moral victory over King Alexander the Great, the most powerful of all pagan conquerors.[81] When Alexander prepares to attack the Brahmans, they send him a letter pointing out that he has nothing to gain from them. Their God is the God of all, who is pleased with good works rather than with worldly riches, and so they live in communal poverty. Since their desires are restrained by nature they need no artificial laws; neither do they need to cultivate the earth to produce their food nor to indulge in plays and entertainments, preferring the pleasures of contemplating the heavens. Eventually Alexander, having had all his philosophical arguments against this way of life crushingly refuted, gives in and confesses to the Brahman king that he lives in a state of perpetual fear.

Because the *De Consolatione Philosophiae* was written by a noble philosopher who had been put to death by a tyrant, the medieval scholars who produced commentaries on this work regarded it as, among other things, a repository of *exempla* of martyred philosophers (using the term 'martyred' in the strict sense). In *De Consolatione Philosophiae* I pr. 3, 19–21 Boethius had alluded to the death of Socrates. Expounding this passage, William of Conches declared that Plato's master Socrates refused to swear by Jove, Apollo and the rest, believing that there was one God alone.[82] Because of this, he was expelled from Athens and forced to drink a poisonous fluid, wherefore he died. William of Conches then proceeds to speculate concerning the fate of the soul of Socrates. Since he was killed on account of his wisdom he merited a 'crown' and reward of some kind. Had he not believed in a redeeming God, he would have suffered less pain in the afterlife due to the unjust way in which he was put to death; had he believed, he would have been saved, like the gentile Job. Writing in the late thirteenth century, William of Aragon provided a more elaborate gloss.[83] Socrates, one of 'God's friends', composed a book on the unity of God in which he taught that not the gods but God should be revered. Consequently, the pagan priests forced him to drink poison. When Socrates drank a cupful of poison in the name of the one true God he was unharmed, but when he drank another cupful in the name of the pagan deities he died instantly. This miracle moved a multitude of the people to kill the priests, and Socrates was buried with honour in the temple, 'as a friend of the true God' (an echo of Wisdom 7.27). Nicholas Trevet was more restrained, being content to reiterate Augustine's statement that Socrates, having revealed in his moral disputations the ignorance of his fellow Athenians, had a caluminous accusation made against him and eventually was executed.[84]

The short account of the death of Socrates found in Jean de Meun's *Roman de la Rose* seems to be an amplification of the William of Conches gloss.[85] Jean claims that, whatever happened, Socrates was always calm, regarding good and ill fortune alike. He believed in one God and rejected polytheism, and therefore was forced to drink poison.[86] The *Roman* proceeds to recount another *exemplum* of persecuted pagan virtue, of how the noble philosopher Seneca was forced to commit suicide also, and here again one may detect the influence of a Boethius commentary.[87] Jean says that Nero made a martyr of his good teacher ('Seneque mist il a martire, / Son bon maistre'), which is in keeping with the common tendency of the commentators to regard the virtuous philosophers named by Boethius as something like pagan saints. This pervasive attitude accounts for the hagiographic tone of the subsequent narrative. Jean recounts how Nero ordered Seneca to discharge his veins into a warm bath. The noble pagan—clearly a monotheist—prays that his soul might return to the God who made it:

> li fist eslire
> De quel mort mourir il vourrait;
> Cil vit qu'eschaper ne pourrait,
> Tant iere poissanz li maufez:
> 'Donc seit', dist il, 'uns bainz chaufez,
> Puis que d'eschaper est neienz,
> E me faites saignier laienz
> Tant que je muire en l'eve chaude,
> E que m'ame joieuse e baude
> A Deu qui la fourma se rende,
> Qui d'autres tormenz la defende'.

(6212–22)[88]

51

[He made him choose the death by which he wanted to die. Seneca saw that the devil was so powerful that he could not escape. 'Then', he said, 'since it is impossible to escape, let a bath be heated and have me bled therein so that I may die in warm water and that my joyous, happy soul may return to God, who formed it and who forbids it any further torments'.]

Nero has the death-sentence carried out without delay. The only reason for his crime was that, according to the custom, from his youth he had borne Seneca that reverence which pupils should do to their master, but as emperor Nero believed he should do reverence to no man, whether senator or teacher.

The inspiration for this account could have come from Jean's reading of either William of Conches on *De Consolatione Philosophiae* III pr. 5.25–6, or William of Aragon on I pr. 3.28.[89] According to William of Conches, when Nero was made emperor he pretended that he feared Seneca as he had done when the philosopher had been his teacher. When the occasion arose, he ordered Seneca to choose the kind of death he wanted, because he could live no longer. Satiated with food and drink, Seneca entered a bath, had a vein in each arm cut and, drinking poison, he died. William of Aragon explains how Seneca was killed by Nero, whom he had taught as a child. At a palace banquet Nero, seated in his regal majesty, caught sight of Seneca and remembered that, once when teaching him, Seneca had struck him. Moved by fury, Nero called on Seneca to choose the manner of his death. Seneca decided to be bled in both arms, in a bath. Thus Seneca nourished the heart of the man who took away his life. These glosses clearly reveal Jean de Meun's original touches: Nero being irked by having had to stand in the presence of his schoolteacher, as is the custom; Seneca praying to his Creator. Perhaps the description of the monotheism of Socrates which Jean found in his Boethius commentary encouraged him to credit Seneca with a similar degree of enlightenment.

Trevet's gloss on the death of Seneca follows that of William of Conches, although the detail that Seneca died in a bath is omitted—perhaps Trevet regarded this as too ridiculous a detail to include in such a serious and edifying tale of pagan virtue.[90] The short tragedy of Nero included in Chaucer's *Monk's Tale* follows Jean's *Roman* closely, with one detail, Nero's fear of Seneca when he was his pupil, probably coming from Trevet's gloss. Chaucer concentrates not on Seneca's monotheism but on his moral virtue, and the impressive way in which he had educated the future emperor:

> In yowthe a maister hadde this emperour
> To teche hym letterure and curteisye,
> For of moralitee he was the flour,
> As in his tyme, but if books lye;
> And whil this maister hadde of hym maistrye,
> He maked hym so konnyng and so sowple
> That longe tyme it was er tirannye
> Or any vice dorste on hym uncowple.
>
> This Seneca, of which that I devyse,
> By cause Nero hadde of hym swich drede,
> For he fro vices wolde hym ay chastise

Discreetly, as by word and nat by dede,—
'Sire,' wolde he seyn, 'an emperour moot nede
Be vertuous and hate tirannye' . . .

(VII, 2495–2508)

Unfortunately, when Nero grows up he becomes a tyrant, and forces his teacher to bleed to death in a bath: 'thus hath Nero slayn his maister deere' (2518).[91]

The best medieval example of all the good pagans who, although not necessarily or obviously monotheistic, had attained a standard of virtue which would put many a Christian to shame, was undoubtedly Trajan. John of Salisbury did not hesitate to prefer Trajan before all the other Roman emperors, including Julius Caesar and Augustus, because he founded the greatness of his reign solely on the practice of virtue.[92] In the thirteenth and fourteenth centuries the destiny of Trajan's soul became a test-case for medieval theories concerning the relative importance of divine grace and human merit in attaining salvation.[93]

The tale of Trajan included in John of Wales's *Communiloquium* follows the version in John of Salisbury's *Policraticus*.[94] Being an exemplary ruler, Trajan listened to a widow who came to him lamenting, begging him to bring to justice the men who had murdered her innocent son:

'Tu', inquit, 'Auguste, imperas, et ego tam atrocem iniuriam patior'. Qui licet equum ascendisset ad bellum profecturus, respondit ille, 'Ego tibi satisfaciam cum rediero'. 'Quid', inquit illa, 'si non redieris'? 'Successor', inquit, 'meus satisfaciet tibi'. Et illa, 'Quid tibi proderit si alius benefecerit? Tu mihi debitor es secundum opera mercedem recepturus. Fraus utique est nolle reddere quod debetur. Successor tuus iniuriam patientibus pro se tenebitur. Te vero non liberabit iustitia aliena. Bene agetur cum successore tuo, si liberauerit seipsum'. Quibus verbis motus, imperator de equo descendit et causam presentialiter examinans condigna satisfactione viduam consolatus est.

[She said, 'You govern, O emperor, and yet I suffer such a dreadful injury'. Although he had mounted his horse to go off to war, he answered her, 'I will satisfy you when I return'. 'But what', she replied, 'if you do not return'? 'My successor will satisfy you', he said. And she replied, 'What will it avail you if another should perform a good action? You are my debtor and you will be rewarded according to your deeds. It is fraudulent not to give what is owed. Your successor will be responsible on his own account for those who have suffered injury. The justice done by another will not exonerate you; your successor will do well if he exonerates himself'. Moved by these words, the emperor got off his horse and, the case being examined presently, the widow was consoled with appropriate satisfaction.]

The similar version of this story found in Vincent's *Speculum Historiale* is the direct source of the account in Higden's *Polychronicon*.[95] On another occasion, Higden adds, when Trajan's son accidentally killed a widow's son, Trajan gave the widow the son who had done this deed in place of her own.

53

A comprehensive theological treatment of Trajan's life and afterlife is provided in Jacob of Voragine's *Legenda Aurea*.[96] Having recounted how Trajan dealt justly with the widow, Jacob tells how, much later in time, on a certain day St Gregory passed through Trajan's forum, remembered the emperor's just actions, and in St Peter's basilica wept most bitterly because this good man had died a pagan. God responded by telling the Pope that He had granted his petition, but warned him against making entreaties on behalf of any other damned soul. Jacob then offers several possible explanations of what actually happened. According to John Damascene the divine answer was as follows: 'I have heard your prayer and I grant Trajan mercy'. Concerning this some say that Trajan was briefly recalled to life, where with consequent grace he merited mercy and thus was saved: therefore, he had not been condemned to hell finally nor damned definitely. Others claim that the soul of Trajan was not absolved absolutely from the penalty of eternal pain, but that it was suspended for a time, until the day of judgment. Others say that only the place or manner of his pain was changed by the grace of Christ. Others, like John the Deacon who compiled this legend, believe that it should be understood in this way: Gregory shed tears on account of Trajan rather than prayed for him, and God frequently grants that which a man wishes to pray for though he does not presume to do so.[97] Trajan's soul was not liberated from hell and placed in paradise, but simply freed from the torments of hell. It is possible, as John says, for a soul to be in hell and not to feel its torments, by divine mercy. Others say that eternal pain consists in two things, namely, in the feeling of pain and in that pain of being damned which is the absence of vision of God. Therefore, eternal pain in the first sense was taken away from Trajan, but in the second sense was retained, the emperor's soul being denied the sight of God.

The short account of Trajan in *Piers Plowman* seems to have been derived from the *Legenda Aurea*, although Langland seems to incline (especially in the B-text) to the opinion that the emperor's merit was the main factor which moved God to save him, though of course the Pope's prayer did play an important part.[98] Langland also emphasizes that there are three kinds of baptism: by water, by shedding of blood, and by fire (i.e. by steadfast faith, what Langland calls 'ferme bileue').[99] Trajan's 'bileue' was great: the implication is that he may have been baptised by fire, human merit and divine grace operating together to effect his salvation.

> 'Ne wolde neuere trewe god but trewe truþe were allowed.
> And wheiþer it worþ of truþe or no3t, þe worþ of bileue is gret,
> And an hope hangynge þerinne to haue a mede for his truþe . . .'
> (B-text, XII, 290–2)

This fideistic argument is persuasive, if not provable either by reason or written authority. It is crucial to realise that it is being delivered by the character Ymaginatif. According to late-medieval theory of imagination, imaginative thinking produces not certainties but possibilities, often in areas of thought where a mere mortal cannot expect to reach absolute certainty. We cannot *prove* that Aristotle and the other good pagans are saved, but, since we believe by faith in the goodness and grace of God, we can *hope* that he will give their souls rest.

'And wheiþer he [i.e. Aristotle] be saaf or noȝt saaf, þe soþe woot no clergie,
Ne of Sortes ne of Salamon no scripture kan telle.
Ac god is so good, I hope þat siþþe he gaf hem wittes
To wissen vs wyes þerwiþ þat wisshen to be saued . . .
That god for his grace gyue hir soules reste . . .'

(B-text, XII, 270–5)

Langland is relying on faith, hope and love, on belief in God's goodness and truth; there is no suggestion that we are being offered certain knowledge or indubitable wisdom. Such moderation contrasts strikingly with the dogmatic outburst of John Trevisa who, having translated Ralph Higden's version of the story of Trajan, exclaims that anybody who believes that Gregory won Trajan's soul from hell is worse than mad and far away from correct belief.

For so greet riȝtwisnesse it semeþ þat Seint Gregorie
wan his soule out of helle. *Trevisa.* So it myȝte seme
to a man þat were worse þan wood, and out of riȝt bileve.

These considerable differences of opinion will serve to remind us that the problem of the salvation of the heathen was very much a live issue in Chaucer's day. One of the possible explanations of Trajan's destiny collected by Jacob of Voragine was that the pagan was restored to life long enough for the normal process of salvation to operate.[101] A similar solution—if indeed it can be called that—is offered in a fascinating alliterative poem of the late fourteenth century, *St Erkenwald*, which obviously is based on some form of the Trajan legend.[102] Here the corpse of an unnamed pagan judge is miraculously preserved until it can be baptised by the saint. However, the blatant legalism of this procedure is mitigated somewhat when the poet has St Erkenwald weep over the body of the pagan and anticipate the words he will say when he baptises him formally. But there is no need to send for water to effect the baptism: the saint's tear constitutes holy water of indubitable efficacy, and he actually has said the right words. Therefore, the soul of the pagan judge can ascend to heaven while his body crumbles to dust.

The solution offered by the nominalist theologians of the early fourteenth century swept away all legalism of this kind, with an affirmation of what men can achieve *ex puris naturalibus*, that is, under purely natural conditions, without the aid of external grace. Bradwardine, however, felt that they had espoused a different kind of legalism, by binding God to reward human merit and therefore placing restrictions on the divine freedom to bestow grace when and where He wished. Among the 'modern Pelagians' castigated in *De Causa Dei* seem to have been William of Ockham, Thomas Buckingham, Adam Woodham—and Robert Holcot.[104] Our discussion of Holcot's attitudes to the virtuous heathen will concentrate on his Wisdom commentary, since it is an acknowledged Chaucer source. The unusual nature of this work should be appreciated, since controversial opinions of the type expressed therein were normally reserved for quodlibetal questions, *summae*, and commentaries on the *Sentences* of Peter Lombard, works written by and for academics within the intellectual confines and sanctuary of the schools. Bible commentaries, on the other hand, always had a wider readership, and Holcot on Wisdom became a best-seller of its day—which is hardly surprising, since he treated his text as a

Biblical 'Mirror for Princes'.[105] Consequently, Holcot's allegedly 'Pelagian' views reached a wider audience, which seems to have included Chaucer, Thomas Hoccleve, and perhaps John Gower.[106]

In a quodlibet on the Mosaic Law, Holcot investigates the lot of the good Jews who, living before the advent of Christ, diligently observed such laws as they had.[107] His conclusion is that observance of the Mosaic Law did indeed merit eternal life, because such observance could not be without grace and justice. The point is summed up in a syllogism:

Every man who is just before God is worthy of eternal life.
Every observer of the Mosaic Law is just before God.
Therefore, every observer of the Mosaic Law is worthy of eternal life.

Examples of such observers include Moses, Joshua, Samuel, David, Ezechiel, Josia and Judas Machabaeis: the Church venerates them as if they were saints, and believes that they merited eternal life, although they lacked the revelation of Christ.

Holcot's major premiss here refers to all men who are just before God, and it is clear from the full context of the quodlibet that he is thinking also of those good pagans who shared with the good Jews the problems resulting from having been born too soon. This is made perfectly explicit by a passage in Holcot's *Sentences* commentary in which he discusses Romans 2.14, 'When gentiles who have not the law do by nature what the law requires, they are a law unto themselves'.[108] Those gentiles, he argues, who lived in accordance with the principles of natural law, even though they lacked the Mosaic Law, received faith and grace from God, and observed the law, and loved God above all else.[109] This statement might be construed as an instance of that 'modern Pelagianism' attacked by Bradwardine. Yet Holcot was convinced of the importance of grace. As he puts it in his Wisdom commentary, no-one can become just before God without the influence of the holy Spirit.[110] The necessity of grace is stressed also in the final section of Holcot's quodlibet on the Mosaic Law.[111] A colleague (*socius*) had suggested that, as things now stand, a person can be saved without baptism or grace. Holcot is prepared to be liberal about baptism but not about grace. If the colleague was thinking of baptism by water, it may be pointed out that no catholic believes such baptism to be necessary for salvation in the sense that without it a man cannot be saved[112]— one wonders what the *Erkenwald*-poet would have made of that! When Peter Lombard said in his *Sentences* that a man can be justified and saved without baptism, he was thinking solely of baptism by water. But there are two other kinds of baptism, which are equally efficacious: by the shedding of blood (in the case of a martyr) and by fire (that is, by the holy Ghost). One is reminded of the passage in *Piers Plowman* where Ymaginatif makes the same distinction. Regarding grace, however, Holcot is unequivocal: there is no doubt that a man without grace is damned.[113]

This insistence on grace might appear to clear Holcot from the charge of Pelagianism which has been laid against him. Indeed, Meissner can claim that Holcot does not deviate from the Thomistic doctrine of grace and predestination.[114] But when Holcot discusses the ways in which grace can be earned by human merit his originality becomes apparent, as Oberman has demonstrated so well:

God is committed to give his grace to all who do what is in them. This does not detract from His sovereignty, since in eternity God was free to establish totally different laws; he was free to act with absolute power, the *potentia absoluta*, subject only to the law of noncontradiction or the law of consistency. Out of sheer mercy and grace, he freely decided in eternity to establish the law that he would convey grace to all who make full use of their natural capacities. Though the law as such is freely given, and therefore an expression of God's *potentia absoluta*, God is now committed to it, in the order chosen by him, the order of his *potentia ordinata*, and he therefore gives his grace 'necessarily'.[115]

These beliefs are manifest in Holcot's Wisdom commentary. For instance, there we find the argument that works done out of natural goodness merit eternal life *de congruo*, that is, they meet the standard of God's generosity.[116] By this Holcot means that if a man 'does what is in him' (the *facere quod in se est*) God will reciprocate by doing what is in Him.[117] In other words, if a good pagan walks by the best light he has, he will merit, and receive, his eternal reward.

Holcot is obliged to face the question, can a man acquire by natural reason that knowledge which is necessary for salvation, or is it essential that certain supernatural truths should be bestowed on him by divine revelation? His basic answer is that it is God who ordains all natural things according to the goodness of His will, and God is no niggard. If a man 'does what is in him' he will be sufficiently informed concerning those things which are necessary for salvation.[118] The human reason cannot by its own powers reach such truths: as a nominalist, Holcot believes that very little can be proved by reason alone.[119] The human reason is defective, as every man knows from experience. Therefore it is fitting that men should be regulated in accordance with a superior reason, namely God's, in which reason men should have faith.[120] On the other hand, without the discourse of reason and the voluntary perception of truth, faith is not possible. Reason is required for belief and faith, and is not repugnant to them. In sum, faith and reason are not opposed but complementary. Attitudes such as these might warn us against making facile generalisations about the supposed disjunction of faith and reason in fourteenth-century thought.[121] Holcot visualises a partnership between God and man: if a man 'does what is in him' and develops his natural capacities, God will ensure that he has faith, that he knows what he must know in order to merit salvation. In this way, the good pagan can be saved *de potentia Dei ordinata*.

It is, therefore, crucial to realise precisely why and how certain gentiles were criticized in the Book of Wisdom. In Wisdom 13.1 we read that all men are vain 'who by these good things that are seen, could not understand him that is, neither by attending to the works have acknowledged who was the workman'. Here, Holcot claims, the inspired author reprehends the obtuseness of those gentiles who studied natural phenomena with their utmost labours, and yet lacked knowledge of God. So concerned were they with investigating the causes of things that they did not properly investigate the first cause, God.[122] This failure to address themselves to the most important issues is the reason why the gentile philosophers in question are being reprehended, not because of their failure to demonstrate that God is the rewarder of goodness. Even Christians, who alone have knowledge of the true God, cannot do this; no-one can prove by reason that God exists or that He created the world.[123] However, those who dispose themselves innocently towards God, and studiously exercise their natural reason, will receive such knowledge of God as will suffice for their salvation. A good example of such a man, Holcot claims, was Cornelius the Centurion, referred to in Acts 10. Though a gentile, he was a godly man who was well spoken of by the whole Jewish nation. As St Peter observed, in every nation anyone who fears God and does what is right is acceptable to Him. Cornelius received a vision in which an angel told him to meet St Peter, whereupon he learned all that was necessary for his salvation. Similarly, Ananias was sent to St Paul (Acts 9.10–20). Holcot concludes that if men employ their reason correctly, and if human guilt does not intervene, with the help of divine revelation or inspiration they will come to have knowledge of a kind which is beyond mere philosophical wisdom.

This principle underlies Holcot's exegesis of Wisdom 7.27, where it is stated that Wisdom 'reneweth all things, and through nations conveyeth herself into holy souls', making 'the friends of God and prophets'.[124] God, who is 'not a respecter of persons', did not confine His favours to the circumcised. St Peter stated that any just man in any nation is acceptable to God (Acts 10.34), after having been sent by God to teach the good pagan Cornelius all that was necessary for his salvation. Wisdom, therefore, which is a gift of God, conveys herself into holy souls in so far as she inspires them with divine reverence and with those things which are necessary for salvation. The souls in question are 'holy' not in the sense of having been holy before Wisdom came to them, but inasmuch as they were made holy by this operation of Wisdom.

Again and again Holcot returns to the issue of the quality of the pagans' knowledge and the precise nature of their faults. He had to attempt to reconcile two apparently conflicting statements concerning the common gentile failure to know the one true God: Wisdom 13.6 claims that 'their fault is little' but Wisdom 13.8 states that 'Excuse them we may not'. Holcot concedes that those gentiles who explored 'the world around them' are less culpable than those who worshipped idols, and then proceeds with his main argument, which is that certain gentiles are indeed culpable because they had a firm basis for acquiring knowledge of God but refused to act on it.[125] This knowledge was obtained not through reason—which Holcot believes to be impossible—but through revelation. According to the intention of Augustine in *De Civitate Dei*, the fact of God's existence was originally preached by Adam and his sons, and this knowledge was transmitted by holy prophets who lived before the time of the Greek and Barbarian philosophers.[126] Therefore, the gentile philosophers reprehended in the Book of Wisdom could, on hearing of God's existence from His followers, have added faith to their reasonings about the empirical world: they would then have been in a position to affirm the existence of God. Because they did not do this, they are culpable on grounds of negligence or malice.

This theory of the ancient revelation of knowledge of God is found in Holcot's commentary on the *Sentences* also.[127] Here the gentiles' failure is described not as a failure of intelligence or a lack of information but as a failure of nerve. The great philosophers had learned about God from the patriarchs, yet some of them, although believing in Him, did not worship Him through fear of tyrants or out of a desire to appease popular opinion. What, then, of St Paul's statement that 'the invisible things of him, from the creation of the world, are clearly seen, being understood by the things that are made' (Romans 1.20)? It would seem to follow from this that knowledge of God could have been obtained through rationalization based on knowledge of creatures. Yet Holcot maintains that we know of the existence of God only through revelation: but of course, once we know that He exists our powers of reason can find plenty of supporting evidence in creation. However, to those who employ well their natural ingenuity, God will reveal Himself in some way, thereby ensuring that such people possess knowledge of God in the sense of faith in God. If this were not true, astronomy would never have been invented, for in the *Historia Scholastica* it is said that Noah had a son called Ionith, who received from God a gift of wisdom which enabled him to found the science of astronomy.[128] If, with all this divine assistance, certain gentiles were still incapable of finding God, it was because they were looking in the wrong place: God is not to be found in vanity or carnality. And therefore they are inexcusable. The positive implication of this argument is obvious: those good pagans who looked in the right place, who developed their natural capacities and 'did what was in them', found God and their salvation.

We have come a long way from John of Salisbury and Jacob of Voragine, who emphasized that the salvation of the soul of Trajan was a unique event, not to be repeated in the case of any other good pagan. Jacob added that, because Gregory had dared to pray for one of the damned, he had to choose between being in purgatory for two days or being ill throughout his life.[129] Not unnaturally, he decided on the latter punishment. In the early fourteenth century the exception became the rule, when Holcot and his fellow nominalists, as it were, declared the gates of heaven open to all just men who had lived before the time of Christ, whether good Jews or good gentiles.

Holcot's views on the salvation of the heathen have been considered at some length because they represent the uttermost limits of fourteenth century investigation of the issue, or at least the most avant-garde excursus thereon which, to the best of our knowledge, was known to Chaucer.[130] Had he read Bradwardine's *De Causa Dei* as well, he would have found many nominalist positions being described in order to be refuted. This work, as we have seen, reaffirms with late-medieval emphases the conclusions which Augustine and Boethius had reached on those theological and philosophical problems raised by pagan theories of destiny. Despite the vast ideological differences between Holcot and Bradwardine, they shared at least a firm belief in the existence of many good pagans, and often grouped them with those resolute Old Testament Jews who had been the prophets and forerunners of Christianity. Similar attitudes were held by such major late-medieval compilers as Vincent of Beauvais, John of Wales, and Ralph Higden. Of course, it was held that the pagans had been very limited in their thinking, notably in their theology of gods and idols, and that some of them were much better than others, the Platonists and the Stoics having attained a high degree of metaphysical and moral enlightenment. The perfection of the pagans remained shadowy (to adopt John of Wales's idiom): it lacked real substance and it foreshadowed the total perfection embodied in the teaching and example of Christ. But perfection it certainly was, of an impressive kind.

In general, therefore, one may speak of the currency, in the age of Chaucer, of a more liberal attitude to the pagan past than had existed hitherto. The following chapters contain discussion of the extent to which this is reflected in

Chaucer's major poems about pagan antiquity, with special attention being paid to the intriguing manner in which he exploited the alleged limitations and achievements of ancient cultures.

CHAPTER III

Pagan Emotion and Enlightenment
in Troilus and Criseyde

The theologians, compilers and historians paraphrased above provide us with a perspective within which we can discuss Chaucer's treatment of and attitudes to the 'matter of antiquity' presented in *Troilus and Criseyde* and *The Knight's Tale*. In these works the philosophies of life ascribed to the characters (quoted out of context from Boethius, for the most part) are of a type believed to have been well within a pagan's powers; the religious practices (such as the worship of a plurality of gods, and Arcite's funeral by cremation) are, by fourteenth-century standards, historically accurate. It is generally recognized that in *Troilus and Criseyde* Chaucer considerably increased the pagan 'colouring' of *Il Filostrato*.[1] However, it has been argued also that 'instead of increasing the ancient colour of the *Teseida*, Chaucer has greatly reduced it' in *The Knight's Tale*.[2] I suggest that we are dealing with a difference of kind rather than of degree: what is in question is not the quantity of the 'paganism' found in Chaucer's poems, but its quality. Boccaccio's vision of antiquity possesses what may be regarded as a distinctive 'Renaissance' quality, and it is precisely this quality which Chaucer eliminated, substituting a classicism of the kind which has been described in our previous chapter. *Troilus and Criseyde* and *The Knight's Tale* present a comprehensive and consistent picture of the heathen past which is consonant with notions about pagans current in fourteenth-century England.

The present chapter describes some of the major features of this picture as presented in *Troilus and Criseyde*, in accordance with the following mode of procedure. First, we shall investigate the authorial stance adopted by Chaucer in *Troilus*, indicating the extent to which it is modelled on the literary role traditionally claimed by those late-medieval compilers who collected pagan materials and reported pagan matters. Then, four of the characters portrayed by this narrator shall be examined in ascending order of complexity and importance to the plot and central themes of the poem: Cassandra, Calkas, Criseyde and Troilus. Pandarus, the most pragmatic of all Chaucer's pagans and the main instigator of the action of the poem, will be considered in respect of his dealings with Criseyde and Troilus. This being done, we shall be in a good position to examine in more detail the tone and tenor of the so-called epilogue of *Troilus*, where Chaucer makes quite explicit the historical approach to pagan antiquity which characterises and controls the entire poem.

Enough has been said about the attitudes to good pagans held by Holcot, Bradwardine and others to indicate just how controversial and potentially dangerous much pagan lore was supposed to be. Any writer who wished to handle this material had to do so with considerable delicacy and diplomacy. Therefore, those medieval compilers who collected and co-ordinated pagan lore (including historians, encyclopaedists, and specialists in various disciplines) were obliged to develop firm principles of editorial practice and justification.

Some of the most comprehensive expressions of such principles were provided by John of Wales. In John's *Compendiloquium de vitis illustrium philosophorum* the lives of the pagan philosophers are placed within what, in the later Middle Ages, was regarded as a proper historical perspective. History was regarded not only as a collection of mere facts but also as a repository of *exempla* of virtues and vices which taught useful moral lessons: the reader or hearer was shown both what to imitate and what to avoid. One could not trust the pagans on tricky metaphysical matters, but in the area of ethics they were acknowledged experts. This supposed expertize is the basis of John's self-justification in the *Compendiloquium*.[3] Many gentiles, he claims, lived a life so good that they put Christians, who ought to know better and do better, to shame. This is attested by Isaiah 23.4, 'Be thou ashamed, O Zidon, for the sea has spoken'. As St Gregory says in his *Moralia in Job*, 'Zidon' signifies the stable New Law in which Christians live, while the 'sea' signifies the life of the gentiles. Well may Zidon be ashamed, for the life of virtuous pagans reproves life under the New Law, and the deeds of secular men confound the deeds of the religious. Christians preach but fail to practice what they receive as precepts, while the gentiles in their lives kept those things to which they were by no means bound by legal obligation. 'When gentiles, which have no law, do the things of the law, they are a law unto themselves' (Romans 2.14). For these reasons, John explains, he has thought fit to collect the notable sayings of the philosophers and imitable examples of virtuous men, in order to stimulate the young, to induce among those who wish to imitate the philosophers a salutary shame, to repress the elation of an arrogant heart, and to encourage humility in perfect men. They cannot be puffed up with pride when they hear how the gentiles did perfect things (in so far as these can be perfect without faith working through love) and endured much for honour and human glory.

This is why, John continues, the sayings and examples of the abovementioned philosophers are collected in the *Compendiloquium*: not because of rash presumption or vain curiosity or ambitious ostentation, but because of spiritual edification. After all, in their authentic books the saints placed the excellent sayings and exceptional examples of philosophers among their holy *sententiae*. Augustine does this in *De Civitate Dei* and elsewhere, as does Jerome in his *Contra Jovinianum* and in various epistles. But did not Jerome reject the works of infidels? John's answer is that the truths contained in gentile books were revealed by God out of his superlative goodness, as St Paul testifies—he falls back on the theory of ancient revelation. Therefore, such truths can fittingly be employed for the illumination of souls and in the expression of those Scriptural truths which pertain to ethics. In the epilogue to the *Compendiloquium* God is praised once again for having revealed certain truths to the gentiles: they received at least *gratia gratis data*, i.e. 'created grace', a specific gift of grace as opposed to habitual and sanctifying grace.[4] John of Wales, it would seem, was no nominalist. The upshot of his arguments is that certain pagans can assist Christians on the road to salvation. But what about their own salvation? John is silent on the issue, being content to stress the ethical achievements of the good pagans. Consequently, he is able to defend his pagan material on the grounds of its moral usefulness (*utilitas*).

Clearly, John of Wales favoured what may be called the principle of the ethical expertize of the pagans. Many other compilers, when justifying their handling of pagan material, preferred what I shall designate the principle of historical relativity. By emphasizing the paganism of the pagans on the one hand, and their own Christianity on the other, they distanced themselves from the actions and ideas which they were reporting—a spectacular case of eating one's cake and having it. Having taken great care to disassociate themselves from what the pagans had said, these compilers were prepared to let the pagans speak for themselves. This principle of historical relativity will now be illustrated in two ways: with reference to how one *historia* was 'placed' by different medieval compilers, and then by description of the 'disavowal of responsibility' techniques employed in the prologues to several major compilations.

The way in which certain pagans were allowed to speak for themselves (at least, according to late-medieval notions of what pagans were like) may be illustrated from the life of Alexander the Great as chronicled by Vincent of Beauvais in the *Speculum Historiale*, and by Ralph Higden who in the *Polychronicon* closely followed Vincent's account. Of special interest is their version of the tale of Alexander and the astrologer Nectanabus (a popular medieval story, which is alluded to in *The Miller's Tale* and paraphrased in Gower's *Confessio Amantis*).[5]

Vincent and Higden portray these pagans as fatalists who cannot escape their fate.[6] Nectanabus, having appeared in the likeness of the god Jupiter, corrupts and has his pleasure of Olympia, Queen of Macedonia. Alexander is begotten as a result of this incredible encounter, which the compilers seem to regard as faintly ridiculous. We are then provided with a prophecy of Alexander's death. A hen lays an egg in King Philip's lap which, when broken, reveals a serpent that crawls about but dies when it tries to re-enter its shell. This is interpreted as meaning that Philip now has a son who will be lord of all the world, but he will die if he returns to his birthplace. (This, we are told later, does happen: Alexander, flushed with success, disregards all warnings and enters Babylon, where he is poisoned.[7]) A similar sense of the inevitability of fate pervades the episode of the death of Nectanabus.[8] When Nectanabus is teaching the young Alexander astrology, this cynical pupil pushes him into a deep pit. Alexander proceeds to marvel at the ignorance of his tutor, who ought to have been forewarned of this event by the stars. Nectanabus replies that no man can flee from his fate: he knew by his science that his own son would cause his death.

Adhaec Magus, 'nulla mortalium contra fatum fuga est, olim per hanc scientiam cognoui me a filio interfectum iri'. Tunc Alexander, 'Num ego filius tuus?' tunc ille omnia confessus est, et Aegypti fugam, et qua arte Olimpiade potitus sit, et his dictis animam exaestuat.

[The magician replied, 'no mortal can escape from fate; by this science I knew in advance that I would be killed by my own son'. When Alexander replied, 'But I am not your son?', then he confessed everything, how he had fled from Egypt, and by what art he possessed Olympia, and having said these things he sent forth his spirit.]

Alexander's very attempt to shrug off fatalism has confirmed Nectanabus's prophecy and sealed his fate.

Fatalism would therefore seem to be a viable philosophy for a pagan—but not for a Christian. In his translation of the relevant passage from Higden's *Polychronicon* John Trevisa goes out of his way to disassociate himself from Nectanabus's statement that no mortal can escape his destiny. This man was a pagan witch, he protests, and it would be shameful for a Christian to believe his false statement, because if God so desires He can save a person from any destined misfortune.

Nectanabus seide þis sawe, and was a wicche, and þerfore it is nevere þe bettre to trowynge: but it were a vile schame for a Cristen man to trowe þis false sawe of þis wicche; for from every myshap þat man is i-schape in þis worlde to falle ynne, God may hym save if it is his wille.[9]

Similarly, in the prologues to their compilations Vincent of Beauvais and Ralph Higden disavow personal responsibility for the pagan beliefs which have merely been reported from *auctores*. Higden's justification of his literary role must be examined at some length, since it illustrates perfectly the principle of historical relativity.

Higden assures us that the gentile figments and pagan sayings contained in the *Polychronicon* actually serve the Christian religion and faith.[10] It was lawful for Virgil to seek the gold of wisdom in the clay of the poet Ennius, and for the children of Israel to despoil the Egyptians. Higden then claims that it is not possible to be equally certain about all things. Many incredible things are in fact true, as Jerome says, although one's doubts are often justified. One must respect the antiquity of diverse accounts, and accept the religion of ancient men, providing there is nothing dissonant with virtue or contrary to known truth. At this point in the argument the fifteenth-century translator of the *Polychronicon* adds the comment that 'If eny thynge be founde dissonaunte to feithe auþer diuerse or straunge to vertues in this werke, hit schalle be ascribede raþer to the tyme then to man'. This is a natural development of the principle of historical relativity which Higden is following. Full allowance, it is implied, must be made for the temporal context of each and every statement in his history book; care must be taken to identify precisely who is making the statement. St Paul, Higden points out, did not say that all that is written is true: he said that all that is written is written for our doctrine (Romans 15.4). Higden has excerpted his materials from diverse *auctores*, and so he cannot be blamed if some of these materials fall short of the truth. He will provide the names of the *auctores* who are his sources because they constitute a 'shield and defence' against detractors. Personal responsibility is admitted only for those statements which Higden has been careful to indicate with his initial.

John Trevisa was even more on the defensive than Higden had been; he had a firmer grip on the protective 'schelde' of the compiler:

þe auctores þat in the firste bygynnynge of þis book I take for schelde and defens, me for to saue and schilde aȝenst enemyes þat me wolde despise strongly and blame; first for my self and for myn owne name I write þis letter [R].[11]

This desire to avoid 'blame' is manifest throughout Trevisa's translation, though there is usually little basis for it in Higden's Latin. It is reflected by his eagerness to identify Nectanabus as a fatalistic witch whose opinion concerning destiny cannot be believed by a Christian, and by his criticism of Higden's use of a story about the philosopher Diogenes. Diogenes was told that a friend had slandered him.[12] His reaction was to doubt whether his friend had actually said such things, but it was quite clear to him that his informant had said them. Trevisa objects strongly to this 'lewd sophistry': the philosopher has failed to distinguish between the liar and the person who merely reports lies. Cases from the Bible are cited to prove the point:

Seint Iohn, in his gospel, seiþ nouȝt þat þe devel was in Crist; but Seint Iohn seiþ þat þe Iewes seide þat þe devel was in Crist; and Crist hymself despisede not God; but he reherseþ hou me bere hym on honde þat he despisede God: þat it followeþ in þe storie.

Here Trevisa is appealing to the common scholastic distinction between *recitatio* ('repetition', 'reporting', 'rehearsing') and *assertio* ('assertion').[13] Since the time of Vincent of Beauvais this distinction was a common feature of the literary theory disseminated with compilations. Vincent stated that he had added 'little and almost nothing' of his own to the authorial statements he had excerpted.[14] The authority involved belonged to the *auctores* themselves, while the credit for the organization and structuring of the diverse extracts was due to the compiler. While all *auctores* have authority, some have more authority than others. The pagans may not agree with each other or with revealed truth, but the compiler is not responsible for the truth or falsity of what they say. Vincent has merely 'reported' the views of different philosophers, leaving the reader to judge for himself.[15] In the prologue to his *Communiloquium sive summa collationum*, John of Wales displays a similar attitude to controversial authorities: he has simply narrated such things, and is not offering them as personal assertion.[16]

Sometimes the highly controversial nature of the 'reported' materials led the compiler to exploit the conventional idioms for disavowing responsibility. A major case in point is the one in which the materials involved the 'judicial art' of making particular predictions, that is, predictions about a particular human personality or about the fate of an individual.[17] At the end of his extensive account of the powers of the planets and their influence on human personality, Vincent of Beauvais makes a personal statement clearly labelled as such with the term *actor* (which means simply 'writer', in contradistinction to *auctor* which means 'authority').[18] We should, he warns, beware of inanely and obstinately attributing astral necessitation to those things which rest on the freedom of the human will.[19] Although the disposition of the stars at a boy's birth may dispose him, to some extent, to perform the corresponding actions, we believe by 'sane faith' that he has the power to act badly of his own volition or to live well through freedom of action assisted by divine grace. By the same token, although the Oxford astrologer John Ashenden was not a determinist, he felt obliged to guard against misinterpretation of his work.[20]. In a short treatise found in Oxford, Bodleian Library, MS Digby 176, a formal protestation is made concerning the contingency of his predictions. The predicted effects, Ashenden explains, will not inevitably or necessarily occur in consequence of the predicted conclusions. He has merely described the *signs* of future events, 'in accordance with astronomy and the opinion of those astronomers whom I have cited in this treatise'.[21]

Ashenden attributed to himself a similar dependent role in his *Summa Iudicialis de Accidentibus Mundi*, which became a standard reference book on astrology. In the prologue he complains that his science has often been misunderstood. Besides, he himself is not an authority: 'My intention is to compile the wise sayings of astrologers concerning the prognostication of occurrences which happen in this world by dint of the volubility of superior bodies . . .'.[22] Ashenden will add nothing out of his own head to the compiled rules and *sententiae*, apart from what seems to follow from the authoritative statements: his expressed wish is to 'by no means be reputed to be an author but only a compiler in this work'.[23] Here the compiler's typical disavowal of responsibility is functioning as a defence against those who distrust certain facets of astrology. As a compiler dependent on his author's statements, Ashenden cannot be blamed for the truth or falsity of the contents of his book.

This same kind of defence is found in the *Liber Judiciorum* preserved in Oxford, Bodleian Library, MS Bodley 581.[24] In its prologue, we learn that the compiler prepared this book of divinations for the consolation of King Richard II, but he does not want to be regarded as its *auctor*.[25] A good example of the corresponding idiom in Middle English is provided by the prologue of Chaucer's *Treatise on the Astrolabe*. Higden and Trevisa had regarded the compiler's typical disavowal as a shield against detractors: for Chaucer it was a sword to slay envy.

> But considre wel that I ne usurpe not to have founden this werk of my labour or of myn engyn. I n'am but a lewd compilator of the labour of olde astrologiens, and have it translatid in myn Englissh oonly for thy doctrine. And with this swerd shal I sleen envie.[26]

These words are ostensibly addressed to 'Lyte Lowys', but Chaucer is concerned with the response of a larger audience, as is made clear by his echo of Romans 15.4, 'All that is written is written for our doctrine'.

The detachment which Chaucer professes in the prologue is reinforced by an important statement in the treatise itself. When Chaucer comes to discuss the practice of making 'particular predictions' concerning the fate of an individual, he identifies this as a pagan belief which he, as a Christian, cannot accept:

> Natheles these ben observaunces of judicial matere and rytes of payens, in whiche my spirit hath no feith, ne knowing of her *horoscopum*.[27]

This may be compared with Chaucer's rejection of 'payens corsed olde rites' at the end of *Troilus and Criseyde*:

Lo here, of payens corsed olde rites,
Lo here, what alle hire goddes may availle;
Lo here, thise wrecched worldes appetites;
Lo here, the fyn and guerdoun for travaille
Of Jove, Appollo, of Mars, of swich rascaille!
Lo here, the forme of olde clerkis speche
In poetrie, if ye hire bokes seche.

(V, 1849–55)[28]

Precisely what is the significance of the verbal similarity? I suggest that, in the compilers' casuistry, Chaucer found an *apologia* for a portrait of pagan society which, in fourteenth-century England, would have been regarded as an historically plausible one, and a method of expressing his detachment from the beliefs of a noble but limited people.

The literary stance of the compiling historian seems to lie behind the role of the narrator in *Troilus and Criseyde*. Chaucer's narrator professes to be dependent on *auctores*, and so he cannot be praised or blamed for what (it is implied) he is merely repeating. This standard defence is amplified with the claim that he is translating as well:

> to every lovere I me excuse,
> That of no sentement I this endite,
> But out of Latyn in my tonge it write.
>
> Wherfore I nyl have neither thank ne blame
> Of al this werk, but prey yow mekely,
> Disblameth me, if any word be lame,
> For as myn auctour seyde, so sey I.

(II, 12–18)

Chaucer cannot be held responsible for the pagan beliefs (for example, belief in fatalism and in 'judicial matere') which are reported in the poem: he is not the assertor of such beliefs. An historian must allow the pagans to think and act as pagans—a perfectly acceptable procedure providing one's own Christian standards are asserted. This is what happens in the epilogue of *Troilus*, where both pagan love (that is, merely human love) and pagan lore (notably the 'corsed olde rites') are placed in a Christian perspective. Here Chaucer, in the manner of the compiling historian, ascribes the limitations of pagan society 'raþer to the tyme then to man' and shows how his gentile figments and pagan sayings can serve the Christian religion and faith. The tale of the unhappy love of Troilus and Criseyde may encourage 'yonge fresshe folkes' to turn aside from worldly vanity,

> And loveth hym, the which that right for love
> Upon a crois, oure soules for to beye,
> First starf, and roos, and sit in hevene above;
> For he nyl falsen no wight, dar I seye,
> That wol his herte al holly on hym leye.
> And syn he best to love is, and most meke,
> What nedeth feynede loves for to seke?

(V, 1842–8)

67

Christian knowledge is far superior to pagan knowledge: as Holcot says in the prologue to his *Wisdom* commentary, compared with Christ the philosopher's wisdom is stupidity.[29] Had the pagans been alive in the time of Christ, they would have been confronted with a kind of love which is beyond reason and beyond the contingency which pervades all earthly things, including human love.[30]

But since Troilus and Criseyde were born at the wrong time and in the wrong place, the option of Christian love was simply not available to them. Their human love, therefore, is part of Chaucer's *historia*, and he claims to be relying on his 'auctour' for information about the way in which people spoke of love and conducted their love affairs in the past. Forms of speech have altered over the centuries, and different lands have different customs; love also is subject to change and variation.

> Ye knowe ek that in forme of speche is chaunge
> Withinne a thousand yeer, and wordes tho
> That hadden pris, now wonder nyce and straunge
> Us thinketh hem, and yet thei spake hem so,
> And spedde as wel in love as men now do;
> Ek for to wynnen love in sondry ages,
> In sondry londes, sondry ben usages.
>
> (II, 22–8)

If any member of Chaucer's audience thinks that he would 'nat love purchace' in the manner described in the poem, he should remember that 'eech contree hath his lawes'. Indeed, it would be difficult to find among Chaucer's audience three people who have gone about the business of love in exactly the same way. Therefore, Chaucer is obliged to follow his 'auctour' (29–49). Faced with the changeable nature of human love, an historian must follow closely what his sources have to say about great loves of the past. (That, at least, is the role which Chaucer professes to have adopted; anyone who has read the actual sources of Chaucer's 'ancient' tale of the love of Troilus knows full well that he can be very cavalier in his treatment of them.) What I wish to emphasize is that the prohemium to book II and the ending of Troilus, considered as a single and consistent statement of the principle of historical relativity, tell us little or nothing about the quality of Chaucer's religious belief at the time of writing the poem. What we are offered is his version of a literary stance which medieval historians, encyclopaedists and other writers had evolved to defend their interest in pagan material. In it Chaucer found a sword to slay envy.

On the other hand, in *Troilus* he makes little appeal to the principle of the ethical expertize of the pagans, a principle which is of the first importance in other poems with an antique setting, namely *The Knight's Tale* and *The Franklin's Tale*. Of course, the moral virtue of Troilus is impressive, particularly when he is proving his worth to Criseyde, and we are invited to regard his planned suicide (IV, 1184–1211) as a manifestation of his courage and fidelity—Chaucer had available to him many pagan stories (including the tale of Seneca) in which suicide was the culmination of a life of exemplary virtue. But Troilus is by no means presented to the reader as a model of ethical behaviour.

The most direct allusion in *Troilus* to the notion of exemplary history is very brief. It occurs at the end of the poem, when Chaucer begs 'every gentil womman' not to be angry with him because Criseyde was untrue, and expresses his willingness to write about 'Penelopees trouthe and good Alceste' (V, 1772–8). Here he is thinking of Criseyde as an *exemplum* of faithless love which contrasts with Penelope and Alceste as *exempla* of virtuous and good love, as is made clear by an intriguing passage in *The Legend of Good Women*, a work which Chaucer seems to have conceived of as a sequel and complement to *Troilus*.[31] In both versions of the prologue to *The Legend*, the God of Love accuses the narrator of having defamed womankind by writing of the faithless Criseyde and by translating Jean de Meun's *Roman de la Rose* (F, 329–35; G, 255–72). The narrator protests, claiming that a true lover ought to praise him rather than blame him:

> 'Ne a trewe lover oght me not to blame,
> Thogh that I speke a fals lovere som shame.
> They oghte rather with me for to holde,
> For that I of Creseyde wroot or tolde,
> Or of the Rose; what so myn auctour mente,
> Algate, God woot, yt was myn entente
> To forthren trouthe in love and yt cheryce,
> And to ben war fro falsnesse and fro vice
> By swich ensample: this was my menynge'.
> (F, 466–74)

In respect of *Troilus*, this seems to mean that Criseyde was upheld as an *exemplum* of the faithless lover: the doctrine of virtuous love was taught obliquely by revealing the shame of a false lover, and thereby readers were warned away from falseness and vice. Such a description sums up very well Henryson's Cresseid, a self-proclaimed *exemplum* of infidelity, but it certainly does not define substantively the heroine of *Troilus* (a fact which shall be demonstrated fully below).[32] What we are dealing with in *The Legend* is a subsequent rationalization of Chaucer's portrayal of Criseyde, carried out by an I-persona whose attitudes and reactions are not necessarily to be identified with the poet's own. What we are dealing with in the *Troilus* epilogue is a standard comment by a Christian narrator who in general is concerned to emphasize the historical facts and temporal situation of Criseyde's infidelity rather than the moral implications thereof.

In the *Troilus* epilogue Chaucer is making fully explicit the detached historical approach to pagan antiquity which operates throughout the whole poem. He is amazingly deft at simultaneously allowing his pagan characters freedom of speech and signalling his personal detachment from their beliefs and sentiments. This view will now be substantiated with a detailed analysis of the text, with special reference to two episodes which constitute test-cases for the validity of our interpretation.

The pagans in *Troilus and Criseyde* avidly observe the 'rytes' of their heathen religion and 'honoure hir goddes ful devoute',

> But aldirmost in honour, out of doute,
> Thei hadde a relik, heet Palladion,
> That was hire trist aboven everichon.
> (I, 152–4)

The Palladium, as we are told by Benoît and Guido, was an image of Pallas Athene which fell from heaven in answer to the prayer of Ilus, the founder of Troy; Troy was safe from capture as long as it remained within the city.[33] Troilus first sees Criseyde in a temple during the 'servyse' of this relic (I, 169–322). On his first night of love with Criseyde, he accounts for his whereabouts with the excuse that 'he was gon to don his sacrifise' to Apollo and to receive the god's answer (III, 533–46). The success of this excuse, one may suppose, depended on the fact that Troilus often went alone to the temple

> Answered of Apollo for to be;
> And first to sen the holy laurer quake,
> Er that Apollo spake out of the tree,
> To telle hym next whan Grekes sholde flee
> (III, 541–4)

Much later, when Criseyde has been forced to leave Troy, the grief-stricken Troilus comes to believe that his impending death has been revealed to him by dreams and augury of birds (V, 316–27, 379–83). Troilus's sister Cassandre, who correctly interprets his most important dream-vision, is a creditable pagan prophetess of the kind praised by late-medieval writers, while Criseyde's father Calkas is a heathen 'astrologien' who by 'science' and by answer of his god 'Daun Phebus or Appollo Delphicus' has predicted the fall of Troy (I, 67–70). Criseyde may lack her father's learning, but she shares something of his fatalism. Hence, she is inclined to attribute her misfortunes to her horoscope:

> 'Allas!' quod she, 'out of this regioun
> I, woful wrecche and infortuned wight,
> And born in corsed constellacioun,
> Moot goon, and thus departen from my knyght'.
> (IV, 743–6)

However, the fatalism endemic to the pagan world of *Troilus and Criseyde* finds its most consummate expression in the fourth book of the poem, when Troilus concludes that human lives are governed by absolute necessity: 'al that comth, comth by necessitee' (958). In short, Chaucer's pagans fall into errors condemned by Bishop Tempier in 1270 and 1277, including the propositions that the human will is subject to the powers of heavenly bodies and that one's life is determined by the position of constellations and the aspect of fortune (cf. pp. 3, 42 above).

But there is a considerable difference between what Chaucer's pagans think and what his narrator thinks. A narrator who believes in 'necessitee condicioneel' is rehearsing the views of pagans who believe in 'symple necessitee'. A simply necessary fact is that all men are mortal, whereas a conditional fact is, *if* you know that someone is walking *then* it is necessary that he is walking (cf. Boethius, *De Consolatione Philosophiae* V pr. 6, and pp. 41–2 above). Applying this to *Troilus*, one can say that, whereas Chaucer's pagans believe they are fated, his narrator believes in their free will. The pagans regard their supposed destinies as necessary facts; the Christian historian regards them as conditional facts. By being so utterly convinced that their actions are fated, the pagans determine their actions. Two test-cases from the poem will elucidate this suggestion.[34]

The first concerns the processes by which Troilus and Criseyde fall in love with each other. These are described in such detail that, however much the characters may think their actions are fated, we the readers can see their free-will operating.[35] The narrator makes Troilus's behaviour in the temple serve as an *exemplum* of how the mighty and proud are suddenly made 'subgit unto love'. Yet, despite the reference to Troilus having been struck by the God of Love's arrow (209), there is no suggestion that Troilus's love is a necessary fact in the sense described above. Careful attention is paid to the psychological process of falling in love, which involves the free choice of the will. Criseyde makes a strong initial impression on Troilus, and this serves as a stimulus for his imagination (I, 365–78). Alone in his chamber, Troilus reasons long and hard about the matter (379–90). Eventually his will gives its full assent to the proposed course of action:

> with good hope he gan fully assente
> Criseyde for to love, and nought repente.
>
> (I, 391–2)

Here Troilus, although believing that he must love through his 'destine' (520), is presented by the narrator as freely choosing to follow his inclination to love Criseyde.

Even more obvious is Criseyde's free decision to love Troilus. After she watches the Mars-like Troilus return from battle, we are told that

> blisful Venus, wel arrayed,
> Sat in hire seventhe hous of hevene tho.
> Disposed wel, and with aspectes payed,
> To helpe sely Troilus of his woo.
> And, soth to seyne, she nas not al a foo
> To Troilus in his nativitee;
> God woot that wel the sonner spedde he.
>
> (II, 680–6)

The seventh heavenly house is the house of marriage, and Venus's presence there bodes well for Troilus; moreover, the favourable disposition of the planet at his birth had disposed him to love and to some extent determined his chances of success in love.[36] This is one of numerous occasions on which Chaucer makes precise and often subtle use of planetary configurations to provide the discerning reader with information about the personalities of his characters.[37] Indeed, so technically accurate is Chaucer's astrological lore that J. D. North has been able to date certain writings by working out the dates on which the stellar dispositions described by Chaucer occurred.[38] But this does not mean, of course, that Chaucer's spirit had any faith in the 'observaunces of judicial matere and rytes of payens' or any 'knowing of her *horoscopum*'. The pagans in *Troilus* may believe that they are determined by the stars, but the narrator clearly believes (with Bradwardine, Holcot, etc.) that men can freely accept or reject astral influences and temptations. He emphasizes, therefore, the process through which Troilus obtained the love of Criseyde:

For I sey nought that she so sodeynly
Yaf hym hire love, but that *she gan enclyne*
To like hym first, and I have told yow whi;
And after that, his manhod and his pyne
Made love withinne hire herte for to myne,
For which, *by proces and by good servyse,*
He gat hire love, and in no sodeyn wyse.

                                                          (II, 673–9. Italics mine)

Here we see, as it were, Criseyde's 'fre chois' in action. In coming to love Troilus she took her time and exercised her free-will; the stars did not force her into anything. It is significant that the passage describing the disposition of Venus (II, 680–6, quoted above) is introduced by an 'And also . . .' clause which implies that Venus, though a definite influence, was not the main factor in Criseyde's decision:

And also blisful Venus, wel arrayed,
Sat in hire seventhe hous of hevene tho . . .

As Chaucer says a little later (750), Criseyde is her own woman.

Our second test-case is provided by the occasion on which the weather prevents Criseyde from leaving Pandarus's house. It might seem that the stars have brought Troilus and Criseyde together for their first night of love:

The bente moone with hire hornes pale,
Saturne, and Jove, in Cancro joyned were,
That swych a rayn from heven gan avale,
That every maner womman that was there
Hadde of that smoky reyn a verray feere . . .

                                                          (III, 624–8)

But this follows a stanza which emphasizes that fortune and the stars are mere secondary causes subject to the controlling first cause, God:[39]

But O Fortune, executrice of wyrdes,
O influences of thise hevenes hye!
Soth is, that under God ye ben our hierdes,
Though to us bestes ben the causes wrie.

                                                          (III, 617–20)

Things do not happen by mere chance; neither are events predetermined by the stars. Saturn and Jove may be in conjunction within the zodiacal sign of Cancer, but it is up to Pandarus and Troilus to exploit the situation.

This involves much encouragement and stage-management by Pandarus. Troilus, terrified at the thought of meeting his beloved, invokes the assistance of every planet-god he can think of (but deliberately omitting the malevolent Saturn): Venus, Jove, Mars, Phebus, Mercurie and Diane (705–7, 712–32). For good measure, he appeals to the 'fatal sustren, which . . . my destine me sponne' (733–5). Pandarus, the most practical of all Chaucer's pagans, cuts short his friend's harangue in a way which highlights the humour of the situation:

> Quod Pandarus, 'Thow wrecched mouses herte,
> Artow agast so that she wol the bite?'
>
> (III, 736–7)

Invocation is no substitute for action. Moreover, despite the aid (real or imagined) of Venus *et al.*, Criseyde goes to bed with Troilus because she wants to:

> This Troilus in armes gan hire streyne,
> And seyde, 'O swete, as evere mot I gon,
> Now be ye kaught, now is ther but we tweyne!
> Now yeldeth yow, for other bote is non!'
> To that Criseyde answerde thus anon,
> 'Ne hadde I er now, my swete herte deere,
> Ben yold, ywis, I were now nought heere!'
>
> (III, 1205–11)

The fact that human beings are responsible for their behaviour is perfectly clear in Chaucer's mind. He is, therefore, able to depict the historically 'placed' paganism of his characters with considerable objectivity, though his sympathy with their predicament is apparent throughout the poem.

Having described the role of the narrator in Troilus, we shall proceed to describe the roles which he allocated to four of his characters, Cassandre, Calkas, Criseyde, and Troilus. The key to the character-types on which Cassandre and Calkas are based has been provided by the classicism described in our previous chapter. Cassandre is an enlightened and commendable sibyl while Calkas is a pagan 'astrologien' and fatalist of the kind so roundly condemned by John Trevisa. These two relatively minor characters help us to cope with the far more complex personalities of the two major characters, Criseyde and Troilus.

Calkas and Criseyde, father and daughter, are in their different ways motivated by the same emotion, the emotion of fear which (as has been demonstrated above) was supposed to have permeated pagan society. Earlier writers had established Briseida–Criseida as a type of the promiscuous and faithless woman. Chaucer, rejecting the traditional character-traits which identified her thus, transformed her into a figure who is simultaneously 'modern' and 'ancient', a courtly love heroine and an ancient pagan with fear as her ruling passion.

Cassandre and Troilus, sister and brother, are the two most enlightened pagans in the poem. What makes Troilus so interesting is the fact that he is a philosopher-lover; indeed, his emotions have a considerable effect on his philosophical position. To put it in terms of medieval psychology, the intellect (*intellectus*) of Troilus is now hindered, now liberated, by the alternating emotions of sorrow (*dolor*) and hope (*spes*) which he experiences in loving Criseyde.[40] On the other hand, the disposition (*affectus*) of Criseyde is influenced by fear (*timor*) to such an extent that all her good intentions come to nothing. This interaction of pagan emotion and enlightenment will now be considered in detail.

II   CASSANDRE THE SIBYL

In book 5 of *Troilus and Criseyde*, Troilus becomes convinced of the inevitability of his death, not only because of the lovesickness caused by the absence of Criseyde but also on account of his dreams of death which are apparently confirmed by the 'augurye of foules' (316–20). Later, he dreams of Criseyde kissing a boar (1244–41) and eventually asks his sister, the prophetess Cassandre, to expound this vision (1450–1540). There are two important elements in the character of Cassandre, her science and her paganism. Chaucer accepts the former, and places the latter in its historical context. Dreams can reveal something of the future, and wise men can expound dreams: in Chaucer's day this was scientific fact. There had been reliable pagan prophets and prophetesses: in Chaucer's day this was historical fact. The way in which these two types of fact are deployed in the poem will now be considered.

Fourteenth-century opinion concerning the scientific basis of significative dreams (*sompnia significativa*) may well be illustrated from lectiones 103 and 202 in Holcot's commentary on Wisdom, passages which (it has recently been argued) are the sources of the debate on divination through dreams included in *The Nun's Priest's Tale*.[41] In lectio 103 Holcot confirms that divine wisdom conveys herself into holy souls, making God's friends and prophets (Wisdom 7.27).[42] Three possible causes of significative dreams are then offered: they can originate in the body, from some dominant humour; from the mind; or from the influence of heavenly bodies. Fools, idiots and melancholics dream a lot, whence it is obvious that not all significative dreams are from God and hence genuinely prophetic.

These ideas are explained at greater length in lectio 202, where Holcot lists five causes of *somnia*: the human body, the soul, heavenly bodies, good spirits, and evil spirits.[43] A surfeit of phlegm can cause someone to dream that he is in water or drinking water; a surfeit of choler can cause dreams about fires and a burning house. An example of a mental cause of a dream is the way in which, out of solicitude for a friend, one dreams about him. On the other hand, the stars can cause men to dream of war, and of the fertility or sterility of the earth. It is obvious that Holcot is thinking here of general predictions only (cf. p. 46 above). Yet God, through the medium of good spirits or angels, can warn men of particular events in the future: hence Joseph was warned to take the Christ-child into Egypt to avoid the massacre of the innocents. In other cases, such a boon can be a reward for personal piety. However, dreams inspired by evil spirits can concern particular events also, such as the dream of Pilate's wife concerning Christ, which could have interfered with God's plan to redeem mankind (Matthew 27.19), or the dream of Cassius concerning the death of Caesar. From all this it would seem that various kinds of dream frequently occur, which are the signs of future events. From this follows Holcot's first conclusion, that divination through dreams is permissible.

His second conclusion, however, is that such divination should not be expected in respect of all dreams. Some dreams merely signify bodily conditions, not future events, and in any case significative dreams do not cause future events. This leads to Holcot's third conclusion, which is that to indulge in divination through dreams is hazardous, for several reasons: the possibility of diabolic suggestion, the ambiguous nature of much dream-imagery, which can refer equally well to several things, and the fact that different interpreters give different interpretations of the same dream. Moreover, since dream-images are merely the signs, and not the necessary causes, of future events, the foretold events need not come to pass. For example, clouds are the cause of rain, but when they mass together and thereby signify the future event of rain, they can be dispersed by some superior cause and consequently rain cannot fall. Similarly, a man may freely decide to perform some action in the future, but some stronger counsel may intervene to change his intention. Therefore, the interpreter of dreams cannot say determinately that a certain event will occur indeed just as the signs indicate, but conditionally that the event will occur provided no more powerful cause intervenes. Here Holcot is, in effect, arguing in favour of 'necessitee condicioneel'. The obvious inference is that it is hazardous to divine by dreams unless in very general terms (*communiter*). As the poet says, 'Do not trouble yourself about dreams, for dreams deceive many' (*Somnia ne cures, nam fallunt somnia plures*). Ecclesiasticus 34.1–7 clinches the matter: divinations, soothsayings and dreams are vain unless sent by God.

Troilus's dreams are, as subsequent events prove, accurate significations of the future. He will be killed (by Achilles: see V, 1806) and Criseyde has yielded, or will yield, to Diomede. But what caused these dreams? Pandarus argues that his dreams of death were merely caused by bodily disorder: Troilus was in a state of intense melancholy (V, 360–1). Besides, he continues, who can say for certain what dreams signify?

> 'For prestes of the temple tellen this,
> That dremes ben the revelaciouns
> Of goddes, and as wel they telle, ywis
> That they ben infernals illusiouns;
> And leches seyn, that of complexiouns
> Proceden they, or fast, or glotonye.
> Who woot in soth thus what thei signifie?'
> (V, 365–71)

Three of the causes of significative dreams as defined by Holcot's Christian and pagan clerks—God (operating through the medium of good spirits), diabolic suggestion, and bodily humour or condition—are here attributed to pagan priests of the temple. An antique veneer has been applied to contemporary scientific doctrine to obtain the correct period finish.

According to Troilus, his dream about Criseyde was a revelation of 'the blysful goddes, thorugh here grete myght' (1250–1). Chaucer has 'paganized' the Christian belief that God can cause dream-visions by ascribing this power to Jupiter, the supreme heathen deity:

75

This drem, of which I told have ek byforn,
May nevere come out of his remembraunce.
He thought ay wel he hadde his lady lorn,
And that Joves, of his purveyaunce,
Hym shewed hadde in slep the signifiaunce
Of hire untrouthe and his disaventure,
And that the boor was shewed hym in figure.

(V, 1443–9)

If the Christian reader interprets the pagans' faith in Jupiter as a stumbling attempt to know the one true God, he can accept Troilus's dream as a genuine divine revelation of particular future events. Because Troilus is, quite clearly, a noble and virtuous pagan, it seems quite possible that he should receive such a gift of grace. A more censorious reader might recall that dreams signifying particular events can be caused by demons also, and deduce that, since the pagan gods really were demons who purposed no good to mankind, some demon wanted to make Troilus suffer. Moreover, Pandarus's skepticism about Troilus's forebodings is a reminder of the attitude one was supposed to have concerning dream-visions, namely one of extreme caution. Holcot warns that much dream-imagery can refer equally well to different things, and that different interpreters can give different interpretations of the same dream. As if to illustrate this, Pandarus's interpretation of the 'figure' of the boar is very different from Troilus's (V, 1282–8; cf. 1245–51).

However, Cassandre vindicates Troilus's interpretation, and provides a fuller version of it. Chaucer's sympathetic portrayal of her is a radical departure from *Il Filostrato*. Boccaccio's Cassandra offers unsolicited advice.[44] Her brother, she exclaims, has been affected by 'that cursed passion which brings us to destruction, as we can see if we will'—a clear reference to the love of Paris and Helen which will result, as she has predicted, in the destruction of Troy. If this had to be, why did Troiolo not give his love to some noble lady instead of to 'the daughter of a depraved and vicious priest of low rank'. Troiolo is incensed, and attacks her as a malicious meddler.

'Or via andate con mala ventura,
poi non sapete ragionar; filate,
e correggete la vostra bruttura,
e le virtù d'altrui stare lasciate.
Ecco dolore, ecco nuova sciagura,
che una pazza per sua vanitate
quello ch'è da lodar riprender vuole,
e s'ascoltata non è, ne le duole'.

Cassandra tacque, e volentieri stata
esser vorrebbe altrove quella volta . . .

['Now go, and ill luck go with you since you are unable to talk sense. Be off and attend to your own defects, but leave the virtues of others as they are. What a sad thing and what a strange calamity it is when a madwoman foolishly tries to find fault where she ought to give praise, and complains about it if she is not listened to'. Cassandra fell silent and would willingly have been somewhere else at that time.]

By contrast, Troilus consults his sister as an expert. Cassandre is described as a 'Sibille' who knows many 'prophecyes by herte' (1450, 1494). John Gower, for his part, emphasized her wisdom:

> This, which Cassandre thanne hihte,
> In al the world as it berth sihte,
> In bokes as men finde write,
> Is that Sibille of whom ye wite,
> That alle men yit clepen sage.
> (*Confessio Amantis*, V, 7451–5)[45]

In our previous chapter we noted the high esteem in which certain sibylline prophecies were held by late-medieval scholars. Cassandre may not have managed to rise to a prophecy of Christ, as did some of the other sibyls, but of her science and wisdom there is no doubt; she may even be one of God's friends. This, I suggest, is the key to her character as envisaged by Chaucer.[46] Cassandre and Troilus, brother and sister, are the two most enlightened pagans in *Troilus and Criseyde*; they provide the norms of virtue and knowledge against which we may measure the other characters. Troilus has a significative dream which Cassandre interprets correctly: this seems to reinforce their family bond and link them together as beneficiaries of divine favour.

Cassandre smiles as she proceeds to tell Troilus the 'fewe of olde stories' that he must know in order to understand his dream fully (1457–8). She certainly is aware of her elevated status as prophetess: in medieval literature, superior female teachers (such as Dame Philosophy in the *De Consolatione Philosophiae* and the Pearl-maiden in *Pearl*) do not wear their authority lightly. Condescending that smile may be, to some extent, but their is nothing callous about it. It expresses affectionate recognition of her brother's habitual impatience with ancient lore (cf. I, 759–60), especially at a time as tense as this. She tells of how Diane, incensed because the Greeks would not sacrifice to her, caused a monstrous boar to destroy their corn and vines (1464–70). This boar was killed by Meleagre, the ancestor of Diomede, and so the boar in Troilus's dream signifies Diomede (1471–1515). As well as exemplifying the impressive scope of her learning, this long account firmly places Cassandre in her historical context. Her concluding statement is abrupt and perhaps tactless—possession of knowledge of the future would, doubtless, make one impatient with the vanity of human wishes.

> 'And thy lady, wherso she be, ywis,
> This Diomede hire herte hath, and she his.
> Wep if thow wolt, or lef! For, out of doute,
> This Diomede is inne, and thow art oute'.
> (V, 1516–9)

Yet her concern for and sympathy with her 'brother deere' are obvious.

Troilus's angry rejection of Cassandre's interpretation ironically echoes Pandarus's disbelief in the interpretation which he, Troilus, had offered of his dream:

'Thow seyst nat sooth,' quod he, 'thow sorceresse,
With al thy false goost of prophecye!
Thow wenest ben a gret devyneresse!
Now sestow nat this fool of fantasie
Peyneth hire on ladys for to lye?
Awey!' quod he, 'ther Joves yeve the sorwe!
Thow shalt be fals, peraunter, yet tomorwe!'

(V, 1520–6)

These words perform several functions. They serve to remind the Christian
reader of the kind of suspicious reaction he should have to pagan prophecy and
divination—an effect unparalleled in Boccaccio. Yet Cassandre is patently
right, and as a sibyl she commands our respect; Troilus's emotional outburst
constitutes a refusal to face facts. She seems fated to foretell the future for
Trojans who refuse to believe her.[47] Guido delle Colonne's Cassandra prophecies the fall of Troy no less than three times, with 'loud wailing, as if she were
mad', and eventually Priam puts her out of the way, 'under guard and in close
restraint'.[48] 'If her laments and complaints had penetrated the Trojan hearts
more effectively', Guido speculates, 'Troy perhaps would not in the least have
bewailed its eternal misfortunes'.[49] The refusal by Chaucer's Troilus to accept
his sister's pronouncement is, as it were, a domestic version of this universal
and tragic failure to listen to the expert.

In the *Historia Destructionis Troiae* Cassandra is praised for her excellence in
womanly virtue and in the liberal arts, especially astrology.[50] From Guido
Chaucer could have derived several pointers for his characterisation of Cassandre; the general esteem in which sibyls were held in his day would have done
the rest. The result is a sympathetic character whose science and good
character in general are not undermined by the limitations dictated by her
historical position. The contrast with Calkas, an untrustworthy devotee of an
untrustworthy god, could hardly be greater.

III   THE 'COWARD HERTE' OF CALKAS

Chaucer's Calkas is a perfect little portrait of a 'wicche' like Trevisa's Nectanabus, of a dubious pagan 'astrologien' who acts in a way which no Christian
historian could condone.[51] What Chaucer made of him can fully be appreciated
only in the light of the vicissitudes through which his character passed in the
works of earlier writers.

In Dictys, Dares and Joseph of Exeter, Calchas is a Greek priest.[52] In Benoît
and in Guido he is a Trojan traitor who has gone over to the enemy, yet despite
this Guido presents him as a pious man and the caring father of Briseida.[53] At
one point in the *Historia Destructionis Troiae* Calchas is referred to as 'the
traitorous Trojan priest' but usually the emphasis falls on his 'great knowledge
and experience'.[54] Indeed, it is apparent that his efforts to further the Greek
cause are attributable to pagan piety and devotion. Having travelled to the

island of Delos to consult Apollo, Calchas receives this answer: 'Calchas, Calchas, beware of returning to your country, but go at once in safety to the Greek fleet . . . For, by the will of the gods, it is to be that the Greeks will obtain the victory against the Trojans. You and your counsel and learning will be very necessary to these Greeks until they obtain the aforesaid victory'.[55] Learning that Achilles is in the same temple, Calchas hurries to him at once, and they receive 'each other in the bond of friendship'. The Greeks, delighted to learn that Calchas's oracle confirms the reply which Apollo has already made to Achilles, accept him as one of themselves: 'They welcomed this priest Calchas into their confidence and received him with sincere affection, promising to fulfill his wishes willingly in all things'. In this account, Calchas's defection is an act of obedience to the will of the gods.

Boccaccio, on the other hand, revealed Calchas in an unfavourable light: instead of meeting Achilles on Delos he flees from Troy to join the besieging army.[56]

> Fu 'l romor grande quando fu sentito,
> per tutta la città generalmente,
> che Calcàs era di quella fuggito,
> e parlato ne fu diversamente,
> ma mal da tutti, e ch'elli avea fallito,
> e come traditor fatto reamente;
> né quasi per la più gente rimase
> di non andargli con fuoco alle case.
>
> Avea Calcàs lasciato in tanto male,
> sanza niente farlene sapere,
> una sua figlia vedova . . .

[The outcry was great when it became generally known throughout the city that Calchas had fled. This was variously spoken of but condemned on all sides, and he was thought to have done wrong and committed an act of vile treachery. Indeed many people were almost inclined to go and set fire to his house. Calchas had left a widowed daughter of his in the midst of such dangers, without giving her any warning about them.]

Here the Trojan anger against Calchas as a deserter is evoked, rather than the Greek praise of a valuable ally. Moreover, there is a strong implication that Calchas has deserted his daughter, selfishly leaving her to whatever fate the angry Trojans choose to deal out: such an impression cannot arise from Guido's narrative, since Calchas changes sides on Delos and hence cannot involve his daughter, who is back in Troy. Certainly, Boccaccio's Criseida has a very low opinion of her father's character. When endeavouring to reassure Troiolo of her wish to return to him from the Greek camp, she suggests that the old age and avarice of Calchas can be turned to their advantage:[57]

> 'Egli è, come tu sai, vecchio ed avaro,
> e qui ha ciò che el può fare o dire:
> il che io gli dirò, se el l' ha caro,
> per lo miglior mi ci facci reddire,

mostrandogli com'io possa riparo,
ad ogni caso che sopravvenire
potesse, porre, ed el per avarizia
della mia ritornata avrà letizia'.

['He is, as you know, old and miserly, and has affairs that need to be dealt with or discussed here. And for that reason I shall tell him that if they matter to him, he had better let me come back here—showing him that I can protect his interests against all dangers that may arise. And his greed will make him glad to let me return'.]

We have come a long way from the reverent and revered sage presented by Guido.

Chaucer goes even further than Boccaccio in stressing the moral turpitude of Calkas. As in the case of the prophetess Cassandre, Chaucer brings out two main elements in his character, his paganism and his science, but the total effect is quite different. What we are left with is a thorough assassination of the character of this priest of Apollo.

Calkas has two sources of knowledge. In the first instance, he consults the pagan gods. In the first book of *Troilus* we learn that he

> Knew wel that Troie sholde destroied be,
> By answere of his god, that highte thus,
> Daun Phebus or Appollo Delphicus.
>
> (68–70)

In the fourth book Calkas says of the fall of Troy, 'Appollo hath me told it feithfully' (114). Phoebus and Neptune are angry with Troy, he assures the Greeks, and eventually will destroy the town. But Calkas is described as being expert in 'science' also: he learns 'by calkulynge' as well as 'by answer of this Appollo' (I, 67, 71–2). Apollo's revelation to him is substantially supported by rational inquiry:

> 'I have ek founde it be astronomye,
> By sort, and by augurye ek, trewely,
> And dar wel say, the tyme is faste by
> That fire and flaumbe on al the town shal sprede,
> And thus shal Troie torne to asshen dede'.
>
> (IV, 115–19)

Chaucer was prepared to accept Calkas's science but not, it would seem, his brand of paganism. In order to make this point clearly, it is necessary to consider in more detail the distinction between general and particular predictions which has briefly been touched on above.

This distinction is featured at the beginning of the second book of Ashenden's *Summa Iudicialis*, where it forms part of an introduction to a comprehensive treatment of general predictions.[58] Ashenden's version derives from the first proposition of the *Centiloquium*, in which Pseudo–Ptolemy had stated that it is not possible that particular forms of events should be declared by any person, however learned in the science of astrology, 'since the understanding conceives only a general idea of some sensible event, and not its particular form. It is, therefore, necessary for him who practises herein to adopt inference. They only who are inspired by the deity can predict particulars'.[59] This proposition may be elucidated by a genuine work of Ptolemy's, the *Tetrabiblos*, in which the validity of general predictions is defended with arguments which became part of the medieval heritage. Ptolemy stresses the basic principle that prediction is good, because with its help human beings can brace themselves for what is to come and thus mitigate hardship, just as men, forewarned of the coming of winter, are forearmed against it.[60] His most comprehensive classification of the two types of astrological prediction places foretellings of war, pestilence, floods, weather-conditions and fertility under the heading of general predictions, while such things as an individual's health, parents, and marriage are matters for particular prediction.[61] Ashenden classed storms, rains and floods, earthquakes, corruption of the air, pestilences and epidemics, and wars as general and hence predictable future events, and claimed that the astrologer can serve mankind by prognostication of this kind.[62] Similar sentiments are expressed by, for example, Thomas Aquinas, Roger Bacon, and Robert Holcot.[63] Astrology, Holcot declares, is not superstition if it confines itself to general predictions.

Chaucer did not call the 'science' of Calkas in question because his prophecy of the defeat of the Trojans and the fall of Troy was a general prediction of the kind condoned by fourteenth-century learning. Indeed, the allusions to the scientific basis of his knowledge are all Chaucer's own, without precedent in the sources. Calkas is 'a lord of gret auctorite' (I, 65), whose expertise in prediction must be accepted. Any astrologer who is sufficiently learned can make general predictions successfully: it does not matter whether one is a pagan or a Christian; neither need personal morality enter into it.

Instead, Chaucer destroyed his character's credibility in another way, by emphasizing his paganism and implying that there is a link between his supposed piety and his selfish behaviour. Every statement about Calkas's 'calkulynge' is juxtaposed with a statement about his other source of knowledge, the 'answere' of Appollo Delphicus. Apollo has intervened in human affairs to confirm Calkas's prediction of the fall of Troy, and this immediately raises the issue of Apollo's motives and the personal morality of Calkas. According to late-medieval discussions of heathen worship, demons forewarned the idolaters of old about certain unfortunate events simply in order to ingratiate themselves, that they might lead their dupes into sin and even greater trouble (cf. pp. 33–6 above). To this end, Holcot claims, demons gulled men into believing that secure knowledge could be acquired by the inspection of figures and the use of invocations.[64] But it is not possible, he continues, for the stars to imprint any active power on figures and characters: if there is some relationship between a figure and a star, this is the result of some pact made quite arbitrarily with demons which is therefore undependable. So heavily is Calkas involved in the 'payens corsed olde rites' that a Christian reader might wonder if the gods had fed him with correct information about the future simply in order to entrap his soul, to lead him into the mortal sins of covetousness and pride.

Certainly, Calkas the pagan prophet is presented quite differently from Cassandre the pagan prophetess. Cassandre's only fault was her paganism, and this is excusable to the extent that, historically speaking, she could not be expected to have as much knowledge of God as a Christian. By contrast, Calkas exploits his powers in a selfish and sordid way, and so obvious is the implication that we, as (nominally) superior Christian readers, should condemn him that in this instance Chaucer comes perilously close to a violation of the principle of historical relativity to which he has adhered so scrupulously elsewhere.

All this becomes clear in book IV, 1366–1414, where Chaucer amplifies the Boccaccio passage (quoted above) in which Criseida disparages her father's character. Chaucer goes far beyond Boccaccio in having his Criseyde deliver a bitter and full-scale attack on Calkas. Not only is he old and hence 'ful of coveytise', his greed is stronger than his religion and his science:

> 'So, what for o thyng and for other, swete,
> I shal hym so enchaunten with my sawes,
> That right in hevene his sowle is, shal he meete.
> For al Appollo, or his clerkes lawes,
> Or calkulyng, avayleth nought thre hawes;
> Desir of gold shal so his soule blende,
> That, as me lyst, I shal wel make an ende'.
>
> (IV, 1394–1400)

If Calkas is still unconvinced, Criseyde continues, she will tell him that he misunderstood the answer of the gods out of fear,

> 'For goddes speken in amphibologies,
> And, for a sooth, they tellen twenty lyes.
>
> Eke drede fond first goddes, I suppose—
> Thus shal I seyn,—and that his coward herte
> Made hym amys the goddes text to glose,
> Whan he for fered out of Delphos sterte'.
>
> (IV, 1406–11)

The statement that fear first caused the gods to exist in the world—probably based on Petronius's *Primus in orbe deos fecit inesse timor*—echoes the belief of Holcot, Ridevall and others that human fear was a major cause of the origin and survival of idolatory (cf. pp. 32, 39 above). A pagan has uttered what is virtually a condemnation of paganism; for a moment Criseyde speaks out of character, with a degree of insight which exceeds her usual abilities.

Equally significant is the fact that the accuracy of Calkas's predictions have seriously been called in question. If oracles are ambiguous, how can one be sure which interpretation is correct? Criseyde is not the only person to have such misgivings. Diomede mentions the possibility that Calkas may be manipulating the Greeks with ambiguities:

> 'And but if Calkas lede us with ambages,
> That is to seyn, with double wordes slye,
> Swiche as men clepen a word with two visages,
> Ye shal wel knowen that I naught ne lye . . .'
>
> (V, 897–900)

The implication is that Calkas may be telling lies—perhaps unwittingly, but more likely with intent to deceive. Like god, like worshipper: neither Apollo nor Calkas can be trusted. It would seem, then, that the priest of Apollo is not universally respected in the Greek camp. The contrast with Guido's Calchas, whom the Greeks welcomed into their confidence and regarded with sincere affection, is most striking. In sum, Chaucer's Calkas is an unscrupulous traitor with a 'coward herte', and Troilus's description of him cannot be bettered:[65]

> 'O oold, unholsom, and myslyved man,
> Calkas I mene, allas! What eileth the,
> To ben a Grek, syn thow are born Troian?'
>
> (IV, 330-2)

Judged with reference to Cassandre, who provides a sort of norm for commendable pagan prophets and prophecy in the poem, Calkas is found to be miserably wanting. His vices throw into sharp relief the goodness of the good pagans in *Troilus and Criseyde*.

IV   CRISEYDE, 'THE FERFULLESTE WIGHT THAT MYGHTE BE'

The scene in which Criseyde criticizes Calkas (IV, 1366-1414) may be considered from another point of view. Is it possible that these lines tell us as much about the character of Criseyde as they do about the character of Calkas? In some respects at least, Criseyde seems to be her father's daughter. Both are guilty of 'tresoun': he is unfaithful to Troy, she to Troilus (I, 85-91; cf. V, 1738). Moreover, she may share something of his pride. Criseyde is naive and perhaps arrogant in believing that she can exploit Calkas's character to suit herself. More importantly, she seems to share her father's fear; indeed, Chaucer describes her as 'the ferfulleste wight that myghte be' (II, 450). Criseyde's description of the 'coward herte' of Calkas, therefore, could be a case of one fearful wight recognizing another. The significance of this apparent family trait or failing will now be considered.

Indications of Criseyde's fearfulness abound in *Troilus and Criseyde*. 'I am of Grekes so fered that I deye', she tells Pandarus, and when he begins to declare Troilus's love she turns pale with fear (II, 124, 302-3). Her initial fears of falling in love having been overcome, Troilus becomes

> to hire a wal
> Of stiel, and sheld from every displesaunce;
> That to ben in his goode governaunce,
> So wis he was, she was namore afered . . .
>
> (III, 479-82)

Criseyde always needs a protector. When her father defected to the Greeks, 'of hire lif she was ful sore in drede', and sought the protection of Hector (I, 92–126). It is significant, therefore, that Pandarus should introduce Troilus to her as 'Ector the secounde': ostensibly he is comparing the brothers' prowess in battle, but for Criseyde the connection would have a special significance. When her 'wal of stiel' is removed, and when she has to pass beyond the walls of Troy to enter the camp of the dreaded Greeks, she is desperately in need of a new protector, and soon accepts Diomede for this role. This, of course, is the interpretation of C. S. Lewis, who argues that fear was the fatal flaw which led to the personal tragedy of Criseyde: 'If fate had so willed, men would have known this flaw only as a pardonable, perhaps an endearing, weakness; but fate threw her upon difficulties which convert it into a tragic fault, and Criseyde is ruined'.[66] As a piece of psychological character-analysis in the best modern manner which fits the facts of the text extremely well, this critique cannot be bettered. It is possible, however, to see Criseyde's exemplification of and interest in the fear motive (which is unparalleled in earlier versions of the story) as but one facet of Chaucer's historical approach to pagan antiquity. In his characterization of Criseyde, as in his characterization of Calkas, Chaucer makes specific and personal the emotion of fear which, according to late-medieval scholars, permeated pagan society and was at the very root of pagan religion.

The crucial phrase is 'drede fond first goddes' (IV, 1408), Criseyde's claim that the pagan gods originated in the emotion of fear. Robert Holcot attributed this *sententia* to Petronius, and identified the first person to tell the tale as Diophanes of Lacedæmon.[67] A much fuller discussion is provided in the first chapter of Ridevall's *Fulgentius Metaforalis*.[68] Citing the story of King Cirophanes (sic) of Egypt who caused an image of his dead son to be made and worshipped, Ridevall explains that Fulgentius thought the source of idolatry was unrestrained and excessive love, while its continuation was due to adulation and fear. Inordinate love was, as it were, the follower and executor of an illicit and perverse cult which sprang from inordinate affection, and so Fulgentius adduces the verse of Petronius, *Primus in orbe deos fecit inesse timor*. The same statement, Ridevall points out, is found in the *Thebaid* of Statius and in the commentary of Cassiodorus on psalm 21. What great iniquity such inordinate fear caused, he continues, is touched on by the saints. For example, St Augustine, commenting on psalm 79, says that all criminal misdeeds were committed either through ardent desire (*cupiditas*) or through humiliating fear. 'Examine therefore your consciences, inquire into your hearts, lest there may be therein sin due to fear or cupidity. All sins in men are caused by two things, namely cupidity and fear'. Ridevall then applies this doctrine to the story of Cirophanes. Because malefactors feared to undergo the punishments justly meeted out to them because of their sins, in order to evade them they practised idolatry, whereas adulators did this out of cupidity, because of their desire to please Cirophanes.

This excursus throws considerable light on Calkas, since it helps to explain the manner in which, in Chaucer's depiction, his cowardice and sin are inextricably linked with his pagan religion. It cannot be said that Criseyde is biased in her view of his character, out of a wish to mollify Troilus or whatever, since her assessment is confirmed by the comments of both Diomede and Troilus (as quoted above) and by the rather jaundiced way in which the narrator recounts Calkas's grovelling request in the Greek assembly that Antenor should be exchanged for Criseyde (IV, 64–133). It would be facile, however, to conclude that we are meant to regard Criseyde in the same contemptible light. The emphasis which late-medieval scholars placed on fear as the motivating emotion of much pagan behaviour may well have influenced Chaucer's attitude to the actions of both Calkas and Criseyde: fear lies behind his infidelity to Troy and her infidelity to Troilus. Yet this emotion is treated very differently in each case. Calkas's historical position in the pagan past highlights his selfishness and avarice. It seems appropriate that a man so deeply involved in the 'corsed olde rites' of a fear-based religion should be a moral coward. By contrast, the historical fact that Criseyde suffers in large measure the fear which permeates pagan society helps us to understand her eventual falseness. Chaucer was not interested in *moralizatio*; neither was he writing moral history of the didactic and exemplary type. His aim was to report or 'rehearse' rather than to condemn, leaving the declaration of his Christian values and criteria of judgment until the very end of the poem. This almost breaks down when he comes close to condemning Calkas (as has been suggested above), but it is at its most obvious in his treatment of Criseyde.

This interpretation may best be recommended through a process of comparison and contrast: it will be considered in relation to a different interpretation which, although very tempting, in the final analysis seems untenable. The next few paragraphs will present the argument that the heightened emotion which Troilus feels for Criseyde is supposed to be, metaphorically speaking, a kind of idolatry which Chaucer intended to condemn.[69] I shall argue this case as strongly as I can (expanding and attempting to substantiate readings by Robertson and Frankis), and then offer my own, very different, views.

Inordinate affection (in the sense meant by Holcot and Ridevall) caused idolatry to come into existence; perhaps inordinate affection is the raison d'etre of the love-affair described in *Troilus and Criseyde*. After all, Wisdom 14.12 tells us that 'The beginning of fornication is the devising of idols'. At the outset it will be useful to hear what Holcot had to say about that passage of Scripture.[70] His explanation begins with a reminder that demons were wont to reside in the idols of the gentiles. By diabolic suggestion these images were made, to the displeasure of God. Pagan idols, therefore, cannot be respected, because 'the beginning of fornication' of the soul as it recedes from God 'is the devising of idols, and the invention of them is the corruption of life'; the life, that is, of the rational creature which naturally is disposed towards the cult of the true God. Fornication, according to Papias, is derived from *fornix*, which means an arch or curve in a wall or building, because in such places harlots display themselves in public. For fornication is love freed from and unrestrained by lawful marriage, the freedom of satisfying and following lust. Taking the term in its widest sense, the Scriptures understand by fornication the corruption of all that is legal, as is idolatry and avarice. It is, therefore, a transgression of the divine law, as is attested by psalm 72.27, 'You throw away from you all those who fornicate'.

So much for the literal exegesis of Wisdom 14.12. Holcot proceeds to expound the text *moraliter*. According to the moral understanding there are four kinds of idol in the church. The fourth, 'the idol of incontinence and enticing disposition', is of most interest to us. This, Holcot says, is like a woman meretriciously prepared with adornments, disposed and ornamented all over like a temple, with the intention of captivating souls. Ezechiel described it well as 'the idol of jealousy' which was set 'to provoke to jealousy' (Ezechiel 8.3). Harlots are idols in which, as it were, demons give responses which are fallacious and excite lust. They shine with gold and silver, and gems and precious clothes, yet notwithstanding they are made of cheap clay inside. As the verse says, the pot may be clothed in gold colouring to give it a noble air, but it is still made of clay. St Jerome rightly attacks ornate refinements which entice a man or woman to illicit love. Clearly, no man who is just and good can respect such an idol.

Holcot then quotes from the ninth chapter of Ecclesiasticus: 'Look not upon a woman that hath a mind for many, lest you fall into her snares'; 'Turn away thy face from a woman dressed up, and gaze not about upon another's beauty' (verses 3 and 8). These creatures are those of whom it is said in Wisdom 14.11, 'the creatures of God are turned to an abomination, a temptation to the souls of men, and a snare to the feet of the unwise'. In this snare, the snare of incontinent desire, King David was caught. Indeed, the idol of incontinence and enticing disposition led the wise Solomon into idolatry in the literal sense of the term: 'when he was now old, his heart was turned away by women to follow strange gods' (III Kings 11.4).

These female idols are to be avoided, Holcot insists, and not curiously sought out, because, as the text says, 'the beginning of fornication is the devising of idols'. It is not possible for a curious and lascivious man to associate with them and be uncorrupted. By diligently searching them out, and imaginatively thinking of the nature of women, he will make to himself an idol, thereby preparing his own downfall. In the *Vitae Patrum* the story is told of a certain saint who would not speak to any woman, not even his own mother, unless he had his eyes closed. And it is said that the old men of that time would not look at women lest they should think about them, because such thoughts or imaginings are, as it were, disquieting pictures arising out of the memory of things seen. In conclusion, the best precaution against this idol is to flee, for it is very difficult to fight against. St Paul assures us that God 'will not suffer you to be tempted above that which you are able, but will make also with temptation issue, that you may be able to bear it. Wherefore, my dearly beloved, fly from the service of idols' (I Corinthians 10.13–14). This means that, although you are liable to be tempted, you will not be tempted beyond that which you can bear. On the other hand, it would be presumptuous to look for trouble: therefore, fly from the service of female idols!

On the face of it, Holcot's exegesis contains many ideas which seem very relevant to Chaucer's poem. Considered according to the strict criteria of scholastic theory of love and marriage, Troilus and Criseyde commit the sin of fornication, love freed from and unrestrained by lawful marriage. Fornication, understood in its widest sense, is the corruption of all that is legal, as is idolatry, and by this token their illicit love and their illicit religion are essentially linked. Applying Holcot's moralization, Criseyde might be considered as an idol of incontinence and enticing disposition—at least, this is what she becomes to Troilus. 'Simple of atir' in her widow's habit, she can hardly be identified as a woman meretriciously prepared with adornments, but it is obvious that her 'blake wede' becomes Criseyde well (I, 169–82). Under this 'cloude blak' is obviously a bright star, as Troilus recognizes all too clearly for his comfort:

She, this in blak, likynge to Troilus
Over alle thing, he stood for to biholde . . .
                                        (I, 309–10)

Having beheld her as intently as good manners will allow, Troilus returns to his palace and proceeds to picture her in his mind. Clearly, his imaginings arise out of the memory of what he saw in the temple:

his spirit mette
That he hire saugh a-temple, and al the wise
Right of hire look, and gan it newe avise.

Thus gan he make a mirour of his mynde,
In which he saugh al holly hire figure . . .
                                        (I, 362–6)

Here Troilus may be making to himself an idol (in the imaginative manner which Holcot warned against), and in the process preparing his own downfall.[71] Having gazed upon another's beauty, he has fallen into the snares of a woman who, as it transpires, has a mind for many. What a pity that Ecclesiasticus was written long after the time of Troilus . . .[72]

Certain details in the text of *Troilus* lend some credibility to this approach. It is interesting that Troilus should first catch sight of Criseyde in a pagan temple during the service of an idol and relic, the Palladium, and that on his first night of love with her he is (the excuse goes) supposed to be performing his sacrifice to Apollo. Throughout the affair he tends, like Palamon in *The Knight's Tale*, to regard his beloved as a goddess rather than as a flesh-and-blood woman, and Pandarus has constantly to remind him that she is a living creature. Troilus's persistent appeals to the pagan deities to further his suit serve to reinforce the apparent connection between the two kinds of idolatry. But perhaps most interesting of all is the scene in which the lovelorn Troilus, faced with the empty house of Criseyde, has the urge to kiss it as one might kiss a relic:

'fayn wolde I kisse
Thy colde dores, dorste I for this route;
And farwel shryne, of which the seynt is oute!'
                                        (V, 551–3)

Perhaps it is not over-fanciful to suggest that this application of the idea of a saint living in his shrine was suggested to Chaucer by the common late-medieval conception of pagan idols as the dwellings of demons.[73] When the animating spirit leaves its home, all that remains is cold and lifeless matter.

'The beginning of fornication is the devising of idols'. At the beginning of his affair, Troilus made an idol to himself in his imagination; at its end, all he is left with are memories, a heap of images divorced from empirical reality. He even manages to mistake a 'fare-carte' for his returning beloved (V, 1158–62). This at once indicates the gulf, at this point in the narrative, between Troilus's fantasies and the facts, and also serves as a reminder of the great yet dubious power of the image-making faculty of the mind.[74]

It is precisely because I find this alternative interpretation so (superficially) attractive that I have been able to play devil's advocate at such length. But reject it I must, because in my opinion it does not fit all the facts of the text. It would be perverse to read into Chaucer's poem a moral framework which he systematically sought to avoid.

A recent study of attitudes towards marriage in English and French medieval literature concludes that Criseyde is a highly sensual creature— witness her lustful thoughts which make her 'wex al reed' as she watches manly Troilus returning from the battlefield (II, 652)—who undertakes the love-affair with full knowledge that it is illicit and will remain that way.[75] Since she acts of her own free will, it is argued, she is morally culpable; Troilus, for his part, succumbs to unbridled lust for her. The standards of behaviour on which these judgments are based are, not surprisingly, taken from scholastic discussions of love and marriage, with a preponderance of antifeminist and antimatrimonial texts. Of course, judged by these standards, which to some extent are reflected by Holcot's exegesis of Wisdom 14.12, Troilus and Criseyde are reprehensible. The question is, are these standards appropriate, that is, did Chaucer mean his audience to have such criteria in mind when listening to or reading his poem? I think not, and I am convinced that this can be proved through a consideration of his presentation of pagan love in the light of other presentations, beginning with the treatment generally favoured by the Latin clerical group of writers on the Trojan war, which included Simon Capra Aurea, Joseph of Exeter, Albert of Stade, and Guido delle Colonne.[76]

These works are permeated with the notion of a conditional necessity or fate which may be changed by one's retreat from a course of morally irresponsible action.[77] The fall of Troy is often seen as an ultimate consequence of human pride and lust. When Joseph of Exeter and Guido describe how Helen and Paris, and later Polyxena and Achilles, fall in love at first sight, they obviously are influenced by the stock scholastic view of the sequence according to which lust develops.[78] Joseph's Helen (the one with the ticklish liver) is so impressed by the beauty of Paris that 'she would have liked to display her entire face and her naked breast' to him, 'but her modesty reproved her and held in check the full-blown excess'.[79] 'So great was the lust battering his violent heart' that Paris can hardly wait to abduct her; Helen, for her part, welcomes his piracy and heedlessly abandons her marriage bed. For Guido the story of Briseida is an *exemplum* of faithless womankind in general. Throughout the *Historia Destructionis Troiae* he takes every opportunity to call his reader's attention to women's moral frailty and treacherous inconstancy. This antifeminism comes out, for example, in a direct admonition of Troilus (which has no precedent in Benoît) for having been taken in by Briseida:

Sed, O Troile, que te tam iuuenilis coegit errare credulitas ut Briseyde lacrimis crederes et eius blanditiis deceptiuis? Sane omnibus mulieribus est insitum a natura ut in eis non sit aliqua firma constancia, quarum si vnus oculus lacrimatur, ridet alius ex transuerso, quarum mutabilitas et uarietas eas ad illudendos uiros semper adducit, et cum magis amoris signa uiris ostendunt, statim sollicitate per alium amoris sui demonstranciam instabilem repente uariant et commutant. Et si forte nullus solicitator earum appareat, ipsum ipse, dum incedunt, uel dum uagantur sepius in fenestris, uel dum resident in plateis, furtiuis aspectibus clandestine sibi querunt. Nulla spes ergo est reuera tam fallax quam ea que in mulieribus residet et procedit ab eis. Vnde fatuus ille iuuenis merito censeri potest et multo fortius etate prouectus qui in mulierum blanditiis fidem gerit et earum demonstracionibus sic fallacibus se committit.[80]

[But oh, Troilus, what youthful credulity forced you to be so mistaken that you trusted Briseida's tears and her deceiving caresses? It is clearly implanted in all women by nature not to have any steady constancy; and if one of their eyes weeps, the other smiles out of the corner, and their fickleness and changeableness always lead them to deceive men. When they show signs of greater love to men, they at once at the solicitation of another suddenly change and vary their inconstant declaration of love. If perchance no seducer appears to them, they seek him themselves, secretly with furtive glances while they are walking or more frequently, while they wander through shops or while they linger in the public squares. There is truly no hope so false as that which resides in women and proceeds from them. Hence a young man can deservedly be judged foolish, and one advanced in years even more so, if he puts his trust in the flattery of women and entrusts himself to their false declarations.]

This passage occurs at the end of the scene in which Troilus and Briseida enjoy their last night of love prior to her departure. Benoît had treated Briseida sympathetically at this point in the narrative, but for Guido her emotional behaviour is proof positive of woman's inconstancy: if a woman can scratch her face, tear out her hair, swoon incessantly, etc., yet still be false, of what treachery is she incapable?[81] Similarly, when Briseida's love for Troilus begins to wane shortly after her arrival in the Greek camp, Guido asks what can one say about the inconstancy of women who, by the very nature of their sex, are weak-willed and subject to changes of mind in the briefest time?[82] Men are incapable of describing their inconstancy and guile!

It may be added that, although Boccaccio was not interested in Guido's moral framework, on several occasions he emphasized the lascivious nature of Criseida, who seems determined to gather rosebuds as long and as often as she may. In particular, one of the arguments she uses to convince Troiolo that elopement is not the answer to their problems reveals her as a self-determining and forceful wanton. It runs as follows. There is nothing so worthless that, if guarded well, does not come to be desired with ardent longing, and the more one burns to possess it, the sooner does one's heart turn away from it if it is openly seen and possessed.[83] 'The reason why our love is such a delight to you is that you are able to attain this paradise only rarely and by means of stealth. But if you were able to possess me without difficulty, the torch of passion which now makes you burn would quickly be put out, and the same would happen with me. Thus if we want our love to last, we must always enjoy it secretly as we are doing now'. Significantly, Chaucer did not place this argument in the mouth of his Criseyde. It squares with a statement made some time previously by Boccaccio's Criseida, when she was considering what response should be made to Troiolo's suit: 'Water gained by stealth is a much sweeter thing than wine that can be taken freely—so in love the pleasure that remains secret far excels that of constantly embracing a husband'.[84] Although Boccaccio's interests and prejudices were not the same as Guido's, he seems to have learned from the Latin writer. Indeed, Guido's admonition of the young Troilus (which has been quoted above) may lie behind the conclusion of *Il Filostrato* which admonishes young men not to trust any woman too easily, and declares that 'a young woman is both inconstant and eager for many lovers'.[85]

Guido was writing didactic and exemplary history; Benoît de Sainte-Maure was not. *Le Roman de Troie*, which is dedicated to Eleanor of Aquitaine, is 'a courtly romance with an emphasis on *fin amor*, on rich descriptions of armour, banners, splendid furniture, magnificent sepulchers, and on long drawn-out dialogues designed to demonstrate the gallantry, sentimentalism, and courtly amorousness of his characters'.[86] Women like Briseida are, for Benoît, a debilitating and demoralising influence on the knight and lover; they betray or obstruct the ideal of courtly behaviour.[87] Thus Briseida's teasing treatment of Diomedes reduces him to a snivelling wreck, and her infidelity causes Troilus to condemn all women as fickle. But for Benoît she is the exception rather than the rule.[88] The good women of Troy, he assures us, 'feel great hatred towards her and wish her the worst of ill luck. They no longer love her as they did, for she has brought shame upon all of them and will always be notorious for doing so'.[89] Benoît, writing in a genre different from Guido's and under the influence of different literary conventions, produced a different view of women in general and of Briseida in particular.

To some extent, Chaucer did to *Il Filostrato* what Guido did to *Le Roman de Troie*: he placed the action firmly in the past and narrated the events as an historian (although, as we have seen, Chaucer's conception of his role as historian and attitude to the pagan past were at variance with Guido's). But it is equally true that Chaucer was even more interested in *fin' amors* than was Benoît. Troilus and Criseyde conduct their affair in accordance with the code of fashionable behaviour in vogue in Chaucer's day; the influence of the *Roman de la Rose* of Guillaume de Lorris and Jean de Meun is writ large throughout the first three books in particular. Indeed, *Troilus* is to some extent a mirror for lovers, a work designed to demonstrate to its immediate audience the rules of the game of love. In the end Criseyde may be untrue, but *in medias res* she is portrayed sympathetically as (among other things) a romance heroine and a fit object of romantic veneration.

When Troilus falls in love at the first sight of Criseyde, the psychology Chaucer employs in describing his mental condition can be paralleled in *Le Roman de la Rose* and in innumerable courtly romances in Old French and in Middle English. To be sure, a similar psychological pattern was regarded by scholastic writers as the sequence whereby lust develops, but that was within a different genre. The function of the imagination, the image-making faculty of the mind, is commonly emphasized in medieval love-poetry, without possessing the moral significance which Holcot gave to it in his account of the idol of incontinence and enticing disposition.[90] Religious imagery of veneration and worship is a stock feature of the language in which literary lovers describe their feelings towards their ladies; its use in *Troilus and Criseyde* need not carry the implication that Troilus is doubly reprehensible as an idolater in love and in religion. Criseyde's blush at the erotic impact which the sight of Troilus makes on her is, in context, indicative not of all-consuming lust but of the normal sexual urges which she shares with the healthy heroines of, for example, *Sir Degrevant William of Palerne, Sir Isumbras* and *Floriant and Florete*. Chaucer, I suspect, was primarily concerned to convey her self-consciousness and modesty—which she shares with Troilus, who also blushes in this episode, embarrassed by the praise of the Trojan people (II, 643–8). To make the point in terms of medieval literary theory, different 'senses' can be imposed on the same 'matter'. Or, to put it in the language of contemporary structuralist criticism, meaning is determined by the structure within which that meaning exists.

It is relatively easy to say what Criseyde is not; it is very difficult, perhaps impossible, to say what she is. She is not Benoît's exception to the courtly rule, or Guido's example of faithless womankind, or Boccaccio's self-determining and forceful wanton, or Holcot's idol of incontinence and enticing disposition. In search of what she is, let us turn yet again to that crucial scene in book IV in which Criseyde explains to Troilus the arguments she intends to use with Calkas.

This scene is crucial because it is pure rehearsal: we never see it enacted. In book V, 694–5 Criseyde briefly mentions that her father was unimpressed with her arguments, but here in book IV there is nothing to call them in question. By contrast, in Guido's *Historia* Briseida confronts her father directly, and comes off very badly.[91] How, she asks, were his senses deceived, when he, who used to be esteemed and richly rewarded for great wisdom among the Trojans, became a traitor to his country? 'You have been deceived', she cries, 'by the trifling replies of Apollo, who, you say, ordered you to desert your ancestral home and your gods in bitter hatred and to attach yourself thus closely to your enemies. Obviously it was not the god Apollo, but rather, I think, a band of infernal furies from whom you received such a reply'. On this note Briseida, 'overwhelmed by many sobs and tears', ends her distraught speech. Her father's reply is brief and direct. Does she think that it is safe to 'spurn the orders of the gods'?[92] He knows 'for certain through the promises of the infallible gods that the present war cannot be extended for a long time and that the city of Troy will be destroyed and ruined within a short time'. Therefore, Calchas concludes, 'it is much better for us to be here than to perish by a hostile sword'. Briseida's accusation comes across as an unconsidered and highly emotional outburst, part and parcel of a reaction against being parted from Troilus and Troy which soon is revealed as excessive and even hypocritical. Guido notes that before the day is done she has changed her allegiances and prefers to be with the Greeks in general and with Diomedes in particular. Briseida's outburst is long and verbose; Calchas's is short and to the point; his superior knowledge, piety and prudential grasp of the realities of their situation command respect, and throw into sharp relief Briseida's flightiness, both sexual and mental.[93] 'In such a short time', Guido laments chauvinistically, 'so suddenly, and so unexpectedly, she became inconstant and began to change in every thing'.[94] No man, he claims, can possibly describe the fickleness and wiles of women.

Here the emphasis is on the male superiority of Calchas—and, of course, of the moralistic historian Guido. During her rehersal of arguments in book IV of *Troilus* Criseyde is very definitely the superior party, describing her father's vices accurately and ably reassuring her lover with practical plans, unhindered by any hints from the narrator of her future infidelity. Chaucer places the emphasis on Criseyde's wise insight that the pagan gods originated in fear. The emotion of fear is the intrinsic flaw of pagan religion, of her father's character, and—although she does not admit it—of her own character. The 'ancient' and 'modern' elements in Criseyde's character meet and merge superbly well: a heroine who illustrates the 'modern' system of love and courtship has, as the basis of her personality, the characteristically pagan failing of fear. Chaucer seems to regard this failing primarily as an historical fact to be recorded objectively rather than as a moral fault to be condemned. As we have seen, the late-medieval compiling historians commonly claimed the right to report past events and to repeat or 'rehearse' ancient beliefs without making value-judgments on their materials; their disavowals of personal responsibility and protestations of objectivity placed the onus of judgment on the reader. One must respect the antiquity of diverse accounts, and accept the religion of ancient men, Ralph Higden declared, providing there is nothing dissonant with virtue or contrary to known truth (cf. p. 64 above). In the final book of his poem, Chaucer makes it clear that pagan religion falls considerably short of the revealed truth of Christianity (V, 1835–48) and that Criseyde's infidelity was dissonant with virtue (1772–85), but in general his attitude to the past is very similar to that held by Higden's anonymous translator: 'If eny thynge be founde dissonaunte to feithe auþer diuerse or straunge to vertues in this werke, hit schalle be ascribede raþer to the tyme then to man'.[95] To the extent that Criseyde's fear, and the infidelity which it occasions, can be regarded as *res facte* they become the more comprehensible and acceptable—fear was, after all, supposed to be one of the dominating emotions in pagan society. The narrator of *Troilus* ostentatiously suspends his moral judgments in the face of the historical facts.

This comes to the fore in book V, where Criseyde, 'the ferfulleste wight that myghte be', is forced to leave her lover and 'wal of stiel' and live 'among the Grekis stronge' (V, 688). Diomede soon goes on the offensive, exploiting her fears by assuring her that the fall of Troy is inevitable (V, 841–952). Benoît and Guido depicted Briseida as the selfish manipulator of Diomedes; in Chaucer's poem it is Diomede who is the manipulator and Criseyde who is the victim. 'Let me then be true to this man', says Benoît's Briseida of Diomedes, 'who is a most valiant and worthy knight'[96]. She has substituted one ideal lover for another. Criseyde, by contrast, loses by the exchange. Diomede is certainly a good warrior, but he is not as worthy as Troilus: Chaucer describes him as impetuous ('sodeyn') and as verbally adept ('of tonge large'), with the implication that his deeds do not always match his words. In this context Criseyde's 'To Diomede algate I wol be trewe' (1071) is resigned and pathetic, having nothing of the guilty defiance of Briseida's similar statement. But in general we have little contact with Criseyde in book V. Chaucer deliberately distances her from us; she seems to recede far into the pagan past.

In large measure this effect is achieved by allusion to background details of the history of Troy and by ostentatious deference to the *auctores* who are Chaucer's alleged sources:

> And after this the storie telleth us
> That she hym yaf the faire baye stede,
> The which he ones wan of Troilus . . .
>
> (V, 1037–9)
>
> I fynde ek in the stories elleswhere,
> Whan thorugh the body hurt was Diomede
> Of Troilus, tho wepte she many a teere. . . .
>
> (1044–6)

92

But trewely, how longe it was bytwene
That she forsok hym for this Diomede,
Ther is non auctour telleth it, I wene,
Take every man now to his bokes heede;
He shal no terme fynden, out of drede.

(1086–90)

Actually, the *auctores* named elsewhere in the poem ('Omer', 'Dares' and 'Dite') were not interested in Briseida-Criseyde. Chaucer is, as usual, alleging their *auctoritas* to impress on the audience that they are reading *historia*, an account of occurrences removed in time from the recollection of the recent age. Two of the real sources of book V, Benoît and Guido (but not Boccaccio), had found plenty to say about Briseida's prompt infidelity; Chaucer is chiding Criseyde far less than their version of the story would allow. When the narrator wishes to avoid explicit condemnation of the heroine of the type which Guido and to a lesser extent Benoît had provided, he professes to be limited by what his *auctores* have said. Ralph Higden described the *auctores* whom he listed at the beginning of his *Polychronicon* as a shield and defence against detractors.[97] It might be suggested that Chaucer used the same shield to protect Criseyde, a woman whom, he admits, he 'wolde excuse . . . yet for routhe' (1119) even if no other excuse were possible.

Despite the appeal to the relative superiority of Christ as ever-faithful lover (1845–6), and the hints that Criseyde's promiscuity might be considered as an *exemplum* of the kind of love which ought to be avoided at all costs (1772–8; cf. 1527), the prevailing impression given by the last book of the poem is that Chaucer's narrator, like the narrator of Robert Browning's *A Toccata of Galuppi's*, lacked

the heart to scold.
Dear dead women, with such hair, too—what's become of all the gold
Used to hang and brush their bosoms?[98]

In book V of *Troilus and Criseyde*, Criseyde the fearful pagan found two protectors, Diomede and the narrator—one for the time, the other for posterity.[99]

V   THE ACHIEVEMENT AND LIMITATIONS OF TROILUS

The transformation of Troiolo the prostrated lover into a gentile philosopher capable of wise speculation about the nature of the universe was a personal stroke of genius by Chaucer, quite unprecedented in previous versions of the story though perfectly comprehensible in view of late-medieval interest in the extent to which virtuous heathen had anticipated some of the truths of Christianity.[100] Guido's Troilus was a young fool to have fallen in love with Briseida. The youth and inexperience of Chaucer's Troilus are obvious, yet it would seem that his love for Criseyde makes him better morally and intellec-tually. Inspired by the consummation of this love, he rises above the general level of fatalism and polytheism to formulate the most enlightened pagan philosophy offered in the poem, a monotheistic vision of divine harmony (III, 1744–71). But that, of course, is not the end of the story. When he learns that Criseyde must leave Troy, he reverts to his previous fatalism and provides a full philosophical rationale for it (IV, 958–1078). Troilus, in the final analysis, is swayed by his emotions; his world-view alters as he moves from sorrow to joy and back to sorrow again.[101] This vacillation between different forms of paganism will now be considered, beginning with Troilus's fatalism.

When Pandarus offers to help Troilus in book I, Troilus replies that he cannot be helped because fortune is his foe:

> 'Ful hard were it to helpen in this cas,
> For wel fynde I that Fortune is my fo;
> Ne al the men that riden konne or go
> May of hire cruel whiel the harm withstonde;
> For, as hire list, she pleyeth with free and bonde'.
>
> (836–40)

He believes that he must love through his destiny (520) and, like Nectanabus as reported by Vincent of Beauvais and Ralph Higden, is convinced that no man can escape his destiny. Because he cannot trust in the efficacy of his own actions, Troilus renders himself incapable of any action. He cannot cease loving Criseyde; neither can he declare his love to her. The presence of Pandarus, therefore, is absolutely necessary for the furtherance of the plot. Troilus's inaction is in marked contrast with the practice recommended in the *Roman de la Rose*, where the lover is encouraged to display ostentatiously his love-symptoms before his lady, in the hope that she may notice and take pity on him. Although he is to some extent a 'modern' romance hero, Troilus is primarily an 'ancient' pagan, and we are never allowed to forget this. With the intensity of youth, Troilus takes to extremes the fatalism current in the society in which he lives.

Troilus's ignorance of the nature of fate and fortune at this early point in the poem is similar to that professed by Boethius's narrator in book I of *De Consolatione Philosophiae*, and Pandarus's teaching on these subjects, as is generally recognized, is derived from the speeches of Dame Philosophy in book II, prosa 1—metrum 3. Pandarus is essentially a pragmatist, and his wisdom is of the most basic kind, consisting of the notions that 'Fortune is comune / To everi manere wight in som degree' and that change is part of fortune's very nature (I, 843–4; 848–54). Troilus, his friend advises, should act in the hope that fortune will bring him a more pleasant lot. Dame Philosophy had regarded these arguments as 'gentle and pleasant physic' of only medium strength which would prepare the way for 'stronger medicines'. Nicholas Trevet identified these gentle remedies for removing sorrow (*dolor*) as 'reasons taken from the general conditions of fortune'.[102] He argues that in morals universal statements are of limited efficacy because, as Aristotle says in the *Ethics*, when we are discussing actions particular statements come nearer the heart of the matter, while general statements are of less worth. The 'stronger medicines' of Boethius have as their essential ingredient the belief that God is the author of fortune, but Pandarus never moves to apply such remedies: he consistently regards fate 'as effect' and never 'as the effecting of the divine will' (to apply Bradwardine's useful distinction). His advice to Troilus does serve its purpose in the context of the first two books of the poem, but in book III the pupil moves beyond his master to a higher level of wisdom, to a vision of an ordered universe governed by Jove, the author of nature and of fortune.

But the judgments of Troilus, it would seem, are a parcel of his fortunes.[103] In book IV he returns to his fatalistic view of the world, and pushes it to what he regards as its logical conclusion, namely, that 'symple' or absolute necessity rules. The consistency of Troilus's character as portrayed by Chaucer is impressive: the fatalistic lover of books I and II is indubitably the same person as the fatalistic philosopher of book IV. 'Al that comth, comth by necessitee'; from eternity God has predetermined all future events, including the departure of Criseyde. Therefore, one's destiny must be accepted as irrevocable. No human action apparently can alter the necessary course of events; there is no freedom of the will:

> '. . . men may wel yse
> That thilke thynges that in erthe falle,
> That by necessite they comen alle. . . .
>
> And this suffiseth right ynough, certeyn,
> For to destruye oure fre chois every del'.
> (IV, 1048–59)

These ideas are, as is well known, taken from *De Consolatione Philosophiae* V, pr. 3. Dame Philosophy had proceeded to refute them, by proving that fate and divine providence are one and that free will is utterly compatible with divine omniscience. Troilus's statement resembles one of the propositions condemned in 1277 by Bishop Tempier of Paris, who in this case upheld Boethius's conclusion as the norm of orthodoxy:

Quod nihil fit a casu, sed omnia de necessitate eveniunt, et, quod omnia futura, que erunt, de necessitate erunt, et que non erunt, impossibile est esse, et quod nichil fit contingenter, considerando omnes causas—Error, quia concursus causarum est de diffinitione casualis, ut dicit Boetius libro de Consolatione.[104]

[That nothing occurs by chance, but everything proceeds from necessity, and that all future things which will be will be from necessity, and those things which will not be, cannot possibly exist, and that nothing at all occurs contingently, all the causes having been considered—an error, because the order of causes is by definition fortuitous, as Boethius says in his book *The Consolation*.]

However, Troilus never reaches this Boethian conclusion: he gives credence to a philosophy which is a charter for quietism.

Once again, Pandarus must accuse Troilus of being a foe to himself, and stir him to action (IV, 1086–1127). But he does not attempt to refute Troilus's arguments: his notion of 'common fortune' does not stretch so far. Pandarus is no speculative philosopher and, besides, is as fatalistic and polytheistic as the next pagan. To the Christian narrator and audience the views expressed by Troilus are, of course, unacceptable. Putting it in terms of the literary theory channelled by late-medieval compilations, Chaucer is repeating or 'rehearsing' views in which he has no personal belief and for which he wishes to accept no personal responsibility. Troilus is the assertor or author of the fatalistic beliefs found in book IV of *Troilus and Criseyde*; Chaucer is merely their reporter or compiler (though on occasion he empathizes with his characters' points of view). A philosophical statement which admirably suits the fatalistic pagan as envisaged in the fourteenth century has been quoted out of context from the fifth book of *De Consolatione Philosophiae*.[105]

Trevet's commentary on the relevant part of Boethius's fifth book is translated on our Appendix, in order to bring out the manner in which Trevet's *divisio textus*—the way in which he divided up the text in order to explain it—seems to have influenced Chaucer's understanding of Boethius. Suffice it to say here that if we follow in Chaucer's footsteps by reading the relevant Trevet glosses the extent to which our author was deliberately quoting out of context becomes much more apparent.

In the third prosa of the fifth book, Trevet explains, Boethius raises an objection (the verb used is *obicio*) concerning those things which have been said previously, by showing that it is not possible for providence to co-exist with the freedom of the will. Concerning this the *auctor* does two things: first he says there is an uncertainty or doubt (*dubitacio*) relating to those aforesaid things, and secondly he considers the reason for this doubt. Further subdivision of the text follows, as Trevet expounds Boethius's fatalistic argument in prosa 3 and the supporting exclamation made in metrum 3 to the effect that providence and free-will are incompatible. At the beginning of his commentary on prosa 4 Trevet announces that Dame Philosophy will now solve the *dubitacio*. It is crucial to realize precisely what these technical philosophical terms mean. *Quaestio est dubitabilis propositio*, Boethius had said in his commentary on Cicero's *Topics*: 'a question is a proposition carrying doubt'.[106] This tenet became a cornerstone of the scholastic system of debate, of the procedure of adducing arguments for and against a proposition in order that its true nature should be seen and the question (*quaestio*) subsequently resolved. The arguments for and against were brought into play, as M.-D. Chenu says,

> not with the intention of finding an immediate answer, but in order that, under the action of *dubitatio*, research be pushed to its limit. A satisfactory explanation will be given only on the condition that one continue the search to the discovery of what caused the doubt. . . . It should be well understood that in stating the pro and con the arguments are not . . . simply lined up and juxtaposed one after another. On the contrary, they are interlocked with the purpose of leading the mind on to the knottiest part of the problem.[107]

To object (*obicere* or *objicere*) meant to set forth or offer arguments within this procedural framework, not to object in the modern sense of arguing against a previously established thesis. Applying this to Boethius's *dubitacio* as identified by Trevet, research on the topics of providence and free-will is being pushed to its limits in Boethius's fatalistic argument. This is a means to an end, not an end in itself. The search for truth may continue once the reason for the doubt is discovered; through the interaction of alternative arguments the mind is led to the very heart of the matter and ultimately (to employ Boethius's own idiom) to 'the unloosing of the knot of the question' (III pr. 5, 18).

To be more specific, Trevet 'frames' Boethius's *dubitacio* as follows. The author, he explains, introduces his argument by saying that there is 'an uncertainty even more difficult', for sometimes greater uncertainty is encountered in the explanation of truth than in the explanation of falsity. Many people, in trying to avoid a difficulty, forsake truth and relate falsehood, as is clear from the case of Zeno who, wishing to avoid the difficulty concerning the crossing of infinities, went so far as to deny the existence of motion. It would appear from this that Trevet regarded Boethius's *dubitacio* as an attempt to meet a difficulty directly, thereby furthering the explanation of truth. The other end of Trevet's 'frame' is found at the beginning of his exposition of V, prosa 4. Here Dame Philosophy had identified Boethius's argument as arising from 'the old complaint about providence, one powerfully dealt with by Cicero when he was classifying kinds of divination' (1–3).[108] Trevet identifies this as an allusion to *De Divinatione*, wherein Cicero, not being able to solve the difficulty, completely denied divine providence and prescience of future events in order to save the freedom of the will. Troilus, it would seem, has gone to the other extreme by denying free will in order to save divine providence and prescience. To some extent, therefore, he resembles Cicero's traditional opponents, the Stoics, who (according to Augustine and Bradwardine) believed that the order of causes is fated, or is fate itself. This order of causes was supposed to dispense the power of that great and all-disposing god whom they called Jove. Similarly, for Troilus the 'ordre of causes' is governed by strict necessity, and the ultimate cause of all is 'Almyghty Jove' (IV, 1017; 1079). Whether or not Chaucer was modelling his Troilus on the standard picture of the Stoic philosopher, in Trevet's commentary he would have found Boethius's fatalistic argument carefully 'framed' by statements which indicated its limitations.

What for Boethius (according to Trevet) was a *dubitacio*, an interim stage in a dialectical process, was for Troilus a conclusion, the end of the process. But the narrator of *Troilus and Criseyde* is quite aware that the last word on the subject of 'necessitee' had not been said, as is manifest by the way in which he 'framed' Troilus's *disputatio* with himself.[109] At the outset we are warned that on that particular day Troilus had fallen into despair to such an extent that he wanted to die. He was utterly wretched when he formulated his argument in favour of absolute necessity:

> And shortly, al the sothe for to seye,
> He was so fallen in despeir that day,
> That outrely he shop hym for to deye.
> For right thus was his argument alway:
> He seyde, he nas but lorn, so weylaway!
> 'For al that comth, comth by necessitee:
> Thus to ben lorn, it is my destinee'.
>
> (IV, 953–9)

Chaucer has planted in his reader's mind the idea that the following soliloquy may tell us more about Troilus's state of mind than it does about the nature of the universe. After all, for a Christian despair is a mortal sin. The entire 'argument' is convincing psychologically as the product of extreme emotion: one can expect a forlorn man to believe that his condition is fixed and insuperable. This impression is confirmed by the other end of Chaucer's 'frame':

> Thanne seyde he thus: 'Almyghty Jove in trone,
> That woost of al this thyng the sothfastnesse,
> Rewe on my sorwe, and do me deyen sone,
> Or bryng Criseyde and me fro this destresse!'
>
> (IV, 1079–82)

In other words, Troilus is not convinced that he has reached the heart of the matter; only God (that is, Jove) knows what that is. This frank admission hardly inspires confidence in the reader—an effect which is quite deliberate.

Moreover, Troilus's prayer for Jove to intervene in the affairs of men, to bring about some change for good or ill on behalf of Criseyde and himself, is quite illogical. He has just proved that fate is inexorable, and therefore neither God nor man can do anything which will change the predetermined course of events. Indeed, so rigid is the 'ordre of causes' that advance knowledge of the future is of no avail since it cannot be altered:

> 'and thus the bifallyng
> Of thynges that ben wist bifore the tyde,
> They mowe nat ben eschued on no syde'.
>
> (IV, 1076–8)

Such a view was unacceptable not only to medieval Christians but also to those pagans who, according to medieval Christians, were the most enlightened of their kind. This may be illustrated from the *Secreta Secretorum*, generally believed to have been written by Aristotle, the greatest pagan philosopher, for Alexander, the greatest pagan king. We have already noted Bradwardine's high regard for this work as a repository of pagan wisdom. Pseudo–Aristotle attacked those who think that, because God has predetermined all things and so the future is unalterable, it does not profit a man to be warned of future events. One of the Middle English versions translates the relevant passage as follows:

> þere ben oþer, no lesse þan fols, sayn, þat god
> haues purueyd and ordeyned alle þynges at þe
> ferste bygynynge, wherfore þay say it profites noght
> to knowe þynges to come, sithen þay nedys moste come.

These 'fols' are in 'gret errour', because men can brace themselves when they know that trouble is ahead and in various ways mitigate its force. Moreover, they can pray to God for an alternative fate:

> Wherfore men oghte wyth byse prayers bysek þe heghe
> destynour, þat he by his mercy torne þe euyls þat er
> to come, and þat he wille oþerwyse ordeyne, and for

þat men awe to praye to goddys pitee in orysouns,
deuociouns, prayers, fastynge, seruices, and almesse,
and oþer goode dedys, bysekand forgyfnesse of hir trespas,
and be rependant of hir synnes. And so þay shal mowe sothly
trowe, þat god almyghty shal turne fro hem þat þat þey drede.

But Troilus has rejected such 'necessitee condicioneel' in favour of a mechanistic universe where human effort is useless and divine intervention impossible. Judged by the high standards of 'Aristotle', his fatalism is foolishness and great error.

In book IV of *Troilus and Criseyde* we are made very aware of Troilus's limitations as a philosopher. In book III, by contrast, there is no undercutting of the beautiful vision of 'Love, that of erthe and se hath governaunce', which is allowed to emerge as the apex of Troilus's philosophical achievement. It has long been recognized that III, 1751–71 is based on *De Consolatione Philosophiae* II met. 8, but only recently has Trevet's gloss on this passage of Boethius been brought to bear on Troilus's song in praise of love. Because a translation of Trevet's entire exposition is provided in our Appendix, only the more important facets and implications need be touched on here.

Trevet explains that, because at the end of the previous prosa Boethius had said that friends are the most precious kind of riches, in this metrum he commends love. Divine love is commended in the first twenty-one lines, where he shows the way in which earthly concord is obtained by it. Boethius, therefore, states in the first instance that the love which governs 'earth and sea and sky' (14–15), that is, the divine love which produces and governs creatures, 'binds the series of things' (13), that is, the concord of things. In regular concord the world moves through its changes (1–2), in accordance with the four seasons of the year and the alternation of day and night. Similarly, the greedy sea is restrained from extending its limits, so that it does not overwhelm totally the earth. All things are 'now held by mutual love' (17) in the sense that concord brings them together: here love is taken to be concord, because love in the true meaning of the term is not to be found in irrational things. In his commentary on *De Consolatione Philosophiae* IV met. 6 Trevet had explained 'the love common to all things' (44) as the general appetite of all creation which tends towards, as to its end, the *summum bonum*, the Creator who 'sits on high, and ruling the universe guides its reins' (34–5). Irrational creatures incline towards Him in as much as they represent Him and partake of His being, and therefore the same natural appetite by which something wishes to exist inclines it towards its own ultimate end. Rational creatures, on the other hand, pursue Him through the conscious activity of intellect and will. In the light of this explanation, it is clear that Trevet supposed the term *amor* to have been used in a broad sense in II met. 8, to cover both the natural appetite of irrational creatures and the self-conscious emotion of humans.

From line 22 until the end of the metrum, Trevet continues, Boethius commends the love of men, showing the way in which human friendship (*amicicia*) is obtained by it. 'Love joins people too by a sacred bond' (22–3), the bond of friendship, and 'ties the holy knot of chaste married lovers' (24–5). Trevet interprets the 'holy knot' as a reference to the sacrament of matrimony, and the 'chaste married lovers' as being a man and his wife. Love also imposes laws of *amicicia* on 'all faithful friends' (26–7). Because all this proceeds from divine love as from its origin, Boethius adds that the race of men is happy 'if the love that rules the stars', that is, the divine love which causes concord in celestial things, 'may also rule your hearts' by causing in them the concord of friendship (28–30).

The fact that Trevet instantly identified lines 14–15 (referring to the love which governs earth and sea and sky) as the thematic centre of this metrum may explain why Troilus begins his hymn to love thus: 'Love, that of erthe and se hath governaunce' (III, 1744). Trevet had noted that Boethius used the term *amor* in a broad sense to cover both the love of rational creatures and the natural appetites of irrational creatures. Chaucer happily exploited this ambiguity to create a splendid celebration (true to the spirit of the original as interpreted by Trevet) of that divine concord which unites the entire universe within itself and with its Creator. The doctrine of Troilus's hymn is not essentially Neoplatonic; there is no need to interpret it as an illustration of the process whereby the philosopher may move from the love of an individual (in this case, Criseyde) up the ladder of being to the true object of love, absolute and heavenly beauty. Trevet's appeal to the Aristotelian doctrine that everything tends towards the good as its end, is quite sufficient to justify the attribution of the hymn to Troilus as an estimable pagan philosopher.

Even more interesting are the ways in which Chaucer altered the Boethian metrum to suit the character of Troilus. According to Trevet, the last lines of the metrum are to be interpreted impersonally as a reference to the divine love which causes concord in celestial things and which can cause the concord of friendship in men's hearts. Chaucer personalises this in terms of the divine will: God, the author of nature, wished to encircle every heart with his great bond of love, so that not a single creature might escape:

> 'So wolde God, that auctour is of kynde,
> That with his bond Love of his vertu liste
> To cerclen hertes alle, and faste bynde,
> That from his bond no wight the wey out wiste;
> And hertes colde, hem wolde I that he twiste
> To make hem love, and that hem liste ay rewe
> On hertes sore, and kepe hem that ben trewe!'
>   (III, 1765–71)

Thus, Troilus believes that this all-powerful God—obviously Jove in this context—has the power to intervene in human affairs: He can twist cold hearts to make them love and feel pity for the 'hertes sore' of others, and He can help true lovers (1769–71). We are far away from the mechanistic universe envisaged in book IV, wherein human effort is useless and divine intervention is impossible. Here in book III Troilus has attained the high degree of enlightenment described by 'Aristotle' in the *Secreta Secretorum* (as quoted above). The monotheistic import of the hymn places Troilus in the good company of Socrates and the Platonists, who thought that the plurality of gentile gods should be reduced to one alone, while its implicit theory of causality links him with the Stoics, who believed that the power of omnipotent Jupiter was disseminated through the series of secondary causes. By rationalizing from his own experience and 'doing what was in him', Troilus has transcended the polytheism and fatalism which he espouses elsewhere in the poem.[111]

In Trevet's interpretation of *De Consolatione Philosophiae* II met. 8 the love between men (*amicicia*) and the chaste married love of man and wife are brought together as two instances of the benevolent operation of divine love in human affairs. *Amicicia* plays a major role in the action of *Troilus and Criseyde*.[112] Pandarus is prepared to move mountains for Troilus out of friendship; his tireless and selfless service cannot be explained merely by reference to the traditional role of the *ami*, the trusted confidant of the courtly lover, which is described so well in *Le Roman de la Rose*. What Pandarus feels for Troilus, and Troilus for Pandarus, is far deeper and more comprehensive than that; certainly it goes far beyond the comradeship of Boccaccio's two young men of the world. Extending the concept of *amicicia* beyond its normal limit of friendship between men, the caring and easy friendship of Pandarus and Criseyde, which is one of the most appealing features of Chaucer's poem, could be regarded as another instance of the way in which love imposes laws of companionship on all faithful friends.

But whereas in his interpretation of II met. 8 Trevet had emphasized the love between men, in his adaptation of this metrum Chaucer emphasizes the love between a man and a woman. Hence, the statement that God can twist cold hearts to love and pity comes across, at least in part, as a declaration of the power of heterosexual love to strike where it will, as it did when the cold heart of Troilus was warmed with love for Criseyde. For the precise reference to the 'holy knot of chaste married lovers', glossed by Trevet as the sacrament of matrimony which unites man and wife, Chaucer substituted a vague allusion to love's power to cause 'couples . . . in vertu for to dwelle' (III, 1749). Those who believe that Chaucer regarded the liason of Troilus and Criseyde as sinful and wicked will doubtless seize on this contrast as further evidence of Chaucer's implicit condemnation of the affair, but in my opinion it is rather an indication of the careful way in which he assimilated his diverse source-materials to each other.

The failure of the lovers to get married, or even to discuss the possibility of marriage, is an historical fact which must be accepted as such.[113] As Chaucer reminds us in the prohemium to book II,

> to wynnen love in sondry ages,
> In sondry londes, sondry ben usages.
> (27–8)

In view of this historical and cultural relativity, a 'modern' reporter of past events is obliged to follow his 'ancient' *auctores*. No *auctor* and/or source had said that Troilus and Criseyde became man and wife, and, while on occasion Chaucer could be cavalier with what his authors had said, he could not dismiss them altogether, especially in a matter so crucial for the rationale of the story. Had a marriage taken place, the Trojans could hardly have exchanged the wife of a royal prince for a warrior, however noble, and the plot requires that Criseyde should be forced to live in the Greek camp. Chaucer the compiling historian would not have wished to alter the *res facte* beyond all recognition, especially when to have done so would have created enormous problems for him as a writer.[114]

The question of marriage did not arise in Benoît's *Roman* or Guido's *Historia* because Briseida, as the promiscuous woman par excellence, was simply not the marrying kind. Boccaccio's Criseida considered marriage but preferred the greater thrill of the occasional encounter. Chaucer ennobled the character by refusing to portray her as casually promiscuous (*pace* Benoît and Guido) and by removing her taste for 'water gained by stealth' (*pace* Boccaccio). On the positive side, he emphasized Criseyde's isolation in the Greek camp and the pressure brought to bear on her by circumstances—and by the 'sodeyn Diomede'—which her fearful nature could not withstand. It seems altogether perverse to read Chaucer's poem in a way which, as it were, reverses the direction in which all the changes he made to his sources tend. Chaucer the poet of human love was writing a love story full of human interest, not a moral tract on the vice of cupidity.

Troilus's hymn to love is anticipated by and is wholly consonant with a celebration of 'Benigne Love' as the 'holy bond of thynges' (III, 1254–74); indeed, it amplifies and clarifies ideas canvassed in this earlier passage. The identification therein of the astrologized deity Citherea-Venus as the mother of 'Love' and 'Charite' (these terms being used synonymously) has been taken as an indication of Troilus's failure to distinguish between cupidinous and charitable love.[115] This reminds the audience of the existence of a higher love, the argument goes, namely *caritas* or divine love, and it reveals the absurdity of elevating sexual passion onto a metaphysical and mystical plane. In fact, in the lines under discussion Chaucer is thinking of the divine love which, as he makes clear in Troilus's hymn to love, is the source of concord in the fabric of the universe and in human relationships. The term *charite* is anachronistically yet appropriately applied to this high kind of love.[116] In *De Consolatione Philosophiae* II met. 8 Chaucer found the fullest vision of love which could be attained through philosophical wisdom, without bringing to bear theological knowledge concerning the God of Love who died for love of mankind. In III, 1254–74, as in III, 1751–71, he is adapting this vision to suit the needs of his narrative, by generally 'paganizing' it and specifically stressing the element of heterosexual love. This accounts for the absence of the distinctions which a Christian moralist would apply.

But such distinctions are, of course, invoked at the end of *Troilus*, and the manner in which the epilogue firmly places Troilus's philosophical achievement in its historical perspective demands fuller investigation. In order to establish the appropriate ideological structure within which valid interpretation may take place, we shall once again turn to two of the sources of Chaucer's classicism, Trevet's commentary on Boethius and Holcot's commentary on Wisdom.

In Book III of *De Consolatione Philosophiae* Dame Philosophy had identified true happiness (*beatitudo*) as the highest of all goods, which contains all goods within itself. All men strive to obtain happiness by various paths, but they are led astray after false goods (III pr.2, 10–15). Five false goods are then described in turn: material wealth, honour, power, fame, and bodily pleasure. When expounding this discussion Nicholas Trevet took his cue from Aristotle's statement at the beginning of the *Ethics* that 'the good' is 'that at which all things aim' by dint of natural inclination or appetite. According to Aristotle, there is an elaborate hierarchy of superior and inferior goods or ends with the *summum bonum* at the very top, and this is the ultimate end towards which all things tend. The lesser goods or ends are not to be condemned or despised, but their limitations must be recognized: singly or collectively, they are no substitute for the *summum bonum*, which Christian scholars identified with God. Chaucer could have read these views also in Jean de Meun's prologue to his Old French *Boece*, which is a translation of the Latin prologue to the first 'Aristotelian' commentary on Boethius, written by William of Aragon.[117]

The false felicity of bodily pleasure, including the pleasure of love, is therefore to be seen as limited and restricted rather than as essentially contemptible. True happiness cannot consist in sensual delight (*voluptas*), Trevet explains, because it is common to man and beast and because of the many troubles which attend on it.[118] As Dame Philosophy says, the longing for bodily pleasure is full of anxiety and its satisfaction is full of repentance (III pr. 7, 1–3). Moreover, the human body is subject to rapid change and decay. 'How brief is the brightness of beauty, how swiftly passing, more quickly fleeting than the changing loveliness of spring flowers' (III pr. 7, 21–2). If, as Aristotle says, men had the sight of the lynx, which has the power to penetrate obstances, the superficially very beautiful body of Alcibiades would seem most vile when its innards could be seen. Medieval scholars generally supposed that this was a reference to a beautiful woman:[119] in fact, Alcibiades was a Greek general and the intimate friend of Socrates. Trevet repeats the gloss of William of Conches to the effect that 'she' was a lovely prostitute. When Aristotle's pupils took their master to look at her, he exclaimed that if men had lynx's eyes so that they could see through the exterior to the inside, what appeared most beautiful would seem most vile.

This female Alcibiades, the type of superficial beauty, reappears in Holcot's exegesis of Wisdom 13.2–3.[120] Here, Holcot argues, the holy Spirit reprehends those gentiles who exalted and worshipped created things, such as fire (named Vulcan), the swift air (named Jupiter), and so forth, thereby falling into the errors of polytheism and idolatry. Certain gentiles were deceived in this way because they took too much delight in the beauty of created things, thereby mistaking them for gods, instead of trying to know 'the Lord of them' who 'is more beautiful than they, for the first author of beauty made all things' (verse 3). Holcot warms to the theme that certain men take excessive delight in earthly beauty. There are some who revel in their own comeliness, not realizing that they are vain and superficial, brief and temporal. As Boethius says in *De Consolatione Philosophiae* III pr.7, the sleek looks of beauty are more ephemeral than the blossoms of spring. If we could see right through things with lynx's eyes, even the body of Alcibiades, so fair on the surface, would look thoroughly ugly. Holcot then moralizes Ovid's story of Narcissus, who is said to represent those who vainly glory in insubstantial bodily appearance, and become useless flowers instead of men. As Isaiah 40.6 puts it, 'All flesh is grass, and all beauty is like the flower of the field'. Other men take excessive delight in the beauty of others. To them one must repeat the words of Daniel to the lecherous elders, 'Spawn of carrion, not of Judah, beauty has seduced you, lust has led your heart astray' (Daniel 13.56). Susanna, a woman of great beauty, led the elders to their deaths. Likewise, Judith made Holofernes weak with the beauty of her countenance, then killed him (Judith 16). David was captivated by the appearance of Bathsheba (II Kings 11). Therefore, one should heed the warning of Ecclesiasticus 9.8, 'gaze not on another's beauty'. Many perish on account of the beauty of women; because of this beauty concupiscence blazes up like a fire. Nothing, Holcot insists, is more capable of subverting the human heart than concupiscence and love of appearances.

Of course, Chaucer never suggests that Criseyde has led Troilus morally astray: indeed, the opposite seems to be true, because of the ennobling power of *fin' amors*. Neither does Criseyde cause Troilus's death, although she may be regarded as the cause of his 'double sorwe'. Yet Holcot's linking of polytheistic paganism with excessive delight in created beauty does throw some light on Chaucer's depiction of Troilus: it indicates Troilus's basic weakness, namely that he remains too attached to earthly beauty, and it identifies this as a failing characteristic of certain pagans. In this manner of speaking, Criseyde can be said to have impeded his spiritual development.

Perhaps here is the key to the pagan hymn to love at the end of the third book of *Troilus and Criseyde*. Troilus's vision is limited for two reasons: it does not go far enough, and it is of short duration. In the first instance, he does not build on the philosophical wisdom of the hymn, by proceeding to acquire fuller knowledge of the divine source of love, of the first author of beauty who created all beautiful things. To put it in Aristotelian terms (following Trevet), Troilus cannot relinquish the inferior good of bodily pleasure and move towards the supreme good of true happiness. In the second instance, the vision is too dependent on created beauty to survive; Troilus is unable to sustain it when the stimulus of requited and joyful love is threatened and eventually removed.

Troilus does not become aware of these limitations until he looks down from the 'eighthe sphere' on 'this litel spot of erthe',

> and fully gan despise
> This wrecched world, and held al vanite
> To respect of the pleyn felicite
> That is in hevene above . . .
>
> (V, 1816–9)

At last he realizes that one cannot trust earthly things because of their ephemeral nature, and that the human emotions connected with them are vain:

> And in hymself he lough right at the wo
> Of hem that wepten for his deth so faste;
> And dampned al oure werk that foloweth so
> The blynde lust, the which that may nat laste . . .
>
> (V, 1821–4)

If Criseyde was faithless, so are all earthly things,[121] and so her faithfulness, if not excusable, is at least understandable and perhaps forgivable, all passion having been spent. The brightness of human beauty is indeed more ephemeral than the changing loveliness of spring flowers, or, as the Christian narrator puts it,

> al nys but a faire
> This world, that passeth soone as floures faire.
>
> (V, 1840–1)

This is the height of philosophical wisdom. Sadly, Troilus attains this degree of enlightenment only in death, when his intelligence is unhindered by his emotions.

Heterosexual love, whether within or outside marriage, is not being condemned at the end of *Troilus*, merely being recognized as an inferior good or end, subordinate to true happiness: we should, following Trevet, read Boethius on false felicity, and hence the *Troilus* epilogue, with an Aristotelian gloss. There is, moreover, no need to postulate that the pagans were congenitally incapable of having successful love-affairs or contracting happy marriages.[122] Criseyde's infidelity becomes a symbol of that earthly mutability of which it is part and parcel. The fall of Troy occurred long ago in the past; the pagans' old rites must now be regarded as 'corsed' by the Christian. That is not to say, however, that Christian standards can directly be applied to the pagan past. The principle of historical relativity, which operated throughout the entire poem, has attained full definition: hitherto the compiler-narrator had reported 'ancient' beliefs and practices in which his spirit has no faith; now his 'modern' credentials are being displayed openly. Chaucer's attitude to the 'lust' and 'lore' of *Troilus* is similar to Higden's attitude to the pagan 'doctrine' in his *Polychronicon*. St Paul did not say that all that is written is true, he reminds us; he said that all that is written is written for our doctrine.[123] Much of what Chaucer had written certainly was not true in terms of Christian belief and morality, but it had been written for the doctrine of readers who enjoyed stories about pagans. Chaucer cited this Pauline dictum when, in the 'retracciouns' appended to *The Parson's Tale*, he sought to excuse in some measure *Troilus* and other works which, he then feared, might lead the reader into sin.[124] This concern would seem to indicate a new conviction that the compiler's standard defence of reporting or 'rehearsing' ancient and authoritative materials did not absolve the writer of responsibility for what he had written. In *Troilus* he professes to think the opposite.

Chaucer is silent on the issue of whether the good pagan, by 'doing what is in him', can merit salvation. All we are told is that Troilus's soul went where Mercury, the pagan psychopomp, 'sorted hym to dwelle' (V, 1827). The amount of scholarly debate on precisely where the 'eighthe sphere' was and what this implies concerning the ultimate destination of Troilus's soul has made clear at least just how vague Chaucer's lines really are.[125] That this vagueness was deliberate is suggested by the fact that it is present also in book IV, in the episode in which Troilus, believing Criseyde to be dead, contemplates honourable suicide. On that occasion we are told how

> His swerd anon out of his shethe he twighte,
> Hymself to slen, how sore that hym smerte,
> So that his soule hire soule folwen myghte
> Ther as the doom of Mynos wolde it dighte . . .
>   (1185–8)

There is no hint of what the decree of Minos, the pagan judge of the dead as described by Virgil, Statius and Claudian, might be.

However, *Troilus* contains one intriguing reference to a pagan entering hell. When Pandarus calls on Criseyde and her ladies he interrupts their reading of a 'romaunce . . . of Thebes' (presumably Chaucer had in mind the Old French *Roman de Thebes*)[126] at a significant point in the narrative:

'And here we stynten at thise lettres rede,
How the bisshop, as the book kan telle,
Amphiorax, fil thorugh the ground to helle'.

(II, 103–5)

Much later in the poem, Cassandre refers to the same incident in the same language, but without mentioning hell (V, 1500). In *Le Roman de Thebes* Amphiorax is portrayed as a somewhat cowardly and occasionally ridiculous astrologer-priest, rather reminiscent in some respects of Chaucer's Calkas.[127] Having predicted that most of the Greek kings will die fighting the Thebans, and that he himself will be devoured by the earth, he goes into hiding to avoid being taken on the expedition. Foolishly, he entrusts the secret of his whereabouts to his wife, who betrays him to the Greeks, and so he is forced to accompany them to Thebes and to his doom. On a certain morning Amphiorax comes out on the battlefield in his chariot, whereupon the earth opens up and swallows him and his companions. John Lydgate, amplifying the crucial passage in a manner clearly indebted to the *Troilus* epilogue, regards this awful fate as a punishment for the bishop's idolatry, old rites, incantations, necromancy and astronomy:

And thus the devel / for his old outrages,
lich his decert, paiëd hym his wages.
For he ful lowe / is descendid doun
Into the dirk and blake Regyoun
wher that Pluto / is crownyd and ystallyd
with his quene / proserpina I-callyd.
with whom this bisshop / haþ made his mansioun
Perpetuelly / as for his guerdoun.
  lo here the mede / of ydolatrie,
Of Rytys old / and of fals mawmetrye.
lo: what auayllen Incantaciouns
Of exorsismës / and coniurisouns;
what stood hym stede his Nigromancye,
Calculacioun / or astronomye;
what vayllëd hym / the heuenly manciouns,
Diuerse aspectis / or constellaciouns?
The ende / is nat bot sorowe and meschaunce,
Of hem þat setten / her outre affiaunce
In swiche werkes supersticious,
Or trist on hem /: he is vngracious.[128]

(III, 4039–58)

The Greeks, shocked at the sudden demise of their sage, all fear that they may go to hell too.

Is Troilus, then, on his way to hell or some pagan equivalent? It is highly unlikely that Chaucer meant us to think thus, in view of the general tenor of his classicism and the specific import of the closest analogue of the 'ascent' scene in the *Troilus* epilogue, the passage of the soul of Arcita to the 'concavity of the eighth sphere' (perhaps the lunar concave) as described in Boccaccio's *Teseida*.[130] On his deathbed, Arcita had prayed that Mercury should take him 'into the midst of the pious souls who dwell in Elysium'.[130] 'I do not believe', he exclaims, 'that I ought to dwell among blackened souls [that is, among the damned in hell], and I am not worthy of heaven and do not ask for it. It is precious enough for me to stay in Elysium'. Elysium, as Boccaccio tells us in his own gloss on this passage, is 'a delightful place in which, according to the opinion of the ancients, were the souls of those who had been valiant and good men, who had not, however, deserved to become gods'.[131] Since Elysium was often located in the lunar concave, it would seem that the psychopomp answers Arcita's prayer, that this is 'the place that Mercury had chosen for him'.[133] Clearly, Arcita was a more worthy pagan than Amphiorax.

Chaucer may have conceived of Elysium as the ultimate destination of Troilus's soul also. Indeed, at one point in the poem Criseyde had expressed the hope that she and her lover might be united there, though she appears to have thought in terms of descending rather than ascending to it:

'For though in erthe ytwynned be we tweyne,
Yet in the feld of pite, out of peyne,
That highte Elisos, shal we ben yfeere,
As Orpheus with Erudice, his fere.
(IV, 788–91)

In view of her infidelity, it seems highly unlikely that Criseyde ever did enter that happy region,[133] but Troilus may well have done. The only limitation for which he was personally culpable (it being impossible to blame him for the limitations attendant on his unfavourable historical position) was that he had pursued the false beauty of this world. So had Arcita—but that, it would seem, had not barred him from Elysium.[134]

Chaucer, however, is non-committal about what happened to Troilus after death, being more interested in his virtuous behaviour and philosophical vision in life. It is the achievement of Troilus that remains uppermost in our minds rather than his failure to push his speculations to their ultimate conclusion. Chaucer was prepared to give him credit wherever he could. Troilus's perfection may be shadowy, but certainly it is impressive.

In *Troilus and Criseyde*, late-medieval notions about the pagan past are employed to depict an ancient society and to characterize a group of pagans living under natural law without the benefit of revealed truth. Judged by the standards of the day, the extent of Chaucer's antiquarianism is remarkable,[135] as is the consistency with which he deploys it in the poem. It is, however, to his further credit that the characters are not mere mouthpieces for this antiquarianism: they actually come alive as individuals who live, love and philosophize in a way which is touchingly human and wholly credible. All the relevant knowledge which Chaucer derived from a wide range of sources—including histories, mythographies, commentaries on *auctores*, and compilations of various kinds—was made personal and specific in terms of character and action. *Moralizatio* has receded before *narratio*, tropological sense before literal sense, and *fabula* before *historia*. The result is a tragical history of human love which turns on the complex relationship between pagan emotion and pagan enlightenment.

Making Virtue of Necessity:
The Noble Pagans of The Knight's Tale

In *Troilus and Criseyde*, we are given a firm impression of both the achievements and the limitations of the pagans. By contrast, in *The Knight's Tale* the
pagans' achievements in ethics, politics and metaphysics are very much to the
fore. This difference between the poems is related to a major difference of
narrative technique. Whereas in *Troilus* the narrator provided an explicit
Christian standard against which the pagan standard was measured and
ultimately found wanting, in *The Knight's Tale* the narrator empathizes with
his characters and allows them to define their pagan standard without direct
interference. There is no thoroughgoing condemnation of paganism, no
attempt to assert openly the superiority of Christian belief.

In the General Prologue to *The Canterbury Tales*, we are told that the Knight
fought 'for oure feith' against the 'hethen' (I, 47–66), which may be taken as an
explanation of his interest in pagan chivalry and belief[1] Only at one point in the
tale does the Knight feel the need to justify this interest. When he comes to
Emelye's pagan 'ryte' in honour of Diana, he coyly assures us that a man who
means well should be granted the freedom to describe such things at length:

> But hou she dide hir ryte I dar nat telle,
> But it be any thing in general;
> And yet it were a game to heeren al.
> To hym that meneth wel it were no charge;
> But it is good a man been at his large.
> (I, 2284–8)

An appeal is then made to the *auctoritas* of 'ancient' books, including the
Thebiad of Statius:

> Two fyres on the auter gan she beete,
> And dide hir thynges, as men may biholde
> In Stace of Thebes and thise bookes olde.
> (I, 2292–4)

Naturally, no mention is made of Boccaccio's *Teseida*, the 'modern' work
which was Chaucer's main source both for this episode and for *The Knight's
Tale* as a whole. Chaucer wished to establish the historical credentials of the
tale, so that his 'ancient' pagans could be allowed to speak for themselves (cf.
pp. 63–4 above). The Knight's most explicit criticism of paganism is so slight
that it could be missed, consisting as it does of a casual witty remark to the
effect that, when the trees are being felled for Arcite's funeral,

> the goddes ronnen up and doun,
> Disherited of hire habitacioun,
> In which they woneden in reste and pees,
> Nymphes, fawnes and amadrides . . .
>
> (I, 2925–8)

For the rest, the Knight's Christian standard is implicit; it emerges in the way he tells the story.`

This narrative technique will now be considered in some detail, beginning with an examination of the reciprocal relationship between gods and men which the Knight seems to postulate. The personality of each pagan is defined in relation to the personality of his special god; the strengths and weaknesses of each god are mirrored by his worshipper. Yet, in the final analysis, the pagan deities fare very badly from this comparison, and the characters of the men transcend the characters of the gods they serve. This being done, we shall examine the degree of enlightenment which the Knight allows to Theseus, Emelye, Arcite and Palamon respectively. All the pagans in *The Knight's Tale* appear to be virtuous and good, but clearly some are better than others. In particular, the mature Duke Theseus is far more enlightened than are the young people.[2] Any limitations which any human character may have, however, pale into insignificance when we are confronted with the caprice and cruelty of the pagan gods. The two major revelations of this divine malevolence will be described in turn: how an ambiguous oracle gives Arcite false hope, and how the planet-god Saturn indulges his ancient malice against Thebans by condemning this worthy man to death. In *The Knight's Tale* the 'payens corsed olde rites' are open to much criticism, but the good pagans can only be commended for the way in which they make virtue of necessity.

I   THE SOURCES OF CHARACTER-TYPES

From the *Teseida*, Chaucer took the characters of Teseo, Arcita, Palemone and Emilia, and created them afresh.[3] Whereas Boccaccio's main interest was in Arcita while Palemone was portrayed less fully, Chaucer provided the cousins with equally important though very different personalities. Emelye was made into a fatalistic and acquiescent person; Theseus became even more noble than he was in *Il Teseida*. I wish to suggest that these changes were carried out with a large measure of consistency, and that to some extent this was due to the operation of a single basic principle: the main sources of Chaucer's character-types were traditional descriptions of the *natura deorum gentilium*.

Most of the evidence marshalled in support of this interpretation comes from two acknowledged Chaucer sources, the *Ovidius Moralizatus* which constitutes book XV of Bersuire's *Reductorium Morale*, and Alain de Lille's *Anticlaudianus* (1182–3)[4]; popular repositories of astrological commonplaces have been consulted also. Indeed, one can find a precedent for the process of character-creation itself in one of these works, the *Reductorium Morale*. As has been show in Chapter I, Bersuire provided an historical explanation and a series of anthropocentric moralizations for each of the gentile gods (Saturn as a Cretan king, as a depraved old man, and so on), a method of exposition which probably has its *raison d'etre* in the medieval belief that the gods were mere humans who had superstitiously been deified. By interpreting the gods as historical individuals and moral types, Bersuire, as it were, reversed this process. So, in a different manner, did Chaucer, by modelling the characters of his pagans on the characters of the gods they worship.[5] Euhemerism has become a principle of characterization. Moreover, Chaucer's gods, like Bersuire's, are astrologized deities, and therefore another factor influencing characterization in *The Knight's Tale* would have been the notion that a man's character was affected (but not determined, of course) by the planet-god or planet-gods in the ascendant at his birth. Some knowledge of these sources of Chaucer's character-types will help us to understand what he really did to *Il Teseida*.

In Boccaccio, Arcita's character has primacy. He sees Emilia first and may therefore be said to have the prior claim on her, yet he acts reasonably and with superhuman patience towards the cousin who cannot control his passion for the same woman. A pugnacious Palemone continually insists on fighting a reluctant Arcita—it seems somewhat ironic that Arcita should pray to Mars while Palemone prays to Venus, for clearly Palemone is the aggressor.[6] Chaucer was more precise in relating human nature to the *natura deorum*. The cousins' prayers on the eve of the tournament (2209–70; 2367–437) confirm the general impression one gains of each character in the poem as a whole: their personalities are such that one cannot imagine Arcite praying to Venus or Palamon praying to Mars.[7] Equal in prowess, virtue and worth, in nature they are quite different.[8] Arcite may be described as a Mars-type, and Palamon a Venus-type.

This suggestion may be substantiated by reference to the stock 'pictures' of astrologized deities provided by medieval scholars. The source of Chaucer's description of armed Mars, standing 'upon a carte' with a rapacious wolf at his feet (2041–50) was probably Bersuire's *Ovidius Moralizatus*, as has already been mentioned above (p. 20).

> Erat ergo figura Martis ymago furibundi hominis in curru sedentis, galeam habentis in capite et flagellum in manu portantis. Ante eum vero lupis pingebatur quia scilicet illud animal sibi ab antiquis gentilibus specialiter consecrabatur. Iste enim Mavors id est mares vorans, et deus bellorum dicebatur a gentibus . . .[9]

> [The figure of Mars, therefore, was in the likeness of a man surrounded by fire and sitting in a chariot, having a helmet on his head and carrying a whip in his hand. In front of him, indeed, a wolf was painted because that animal was specially consecrated to him by the ancient gentiles. This certainly is from *mavors* 'devouring males', and he was said to be the god of battles by the gentiles . . .]

Allegorically, Bersuire explains, by this god and image can be understood worldly princes and tyrants and most of all bellicose men. They are said to be seated in a cart because of their lack of stability; the wolf which accompanies them signifies the cruel officials who always accompany tyrants to prey on their subjects. Earlier in the *Reductorium Morale*, in the fifth book, Bersuire had described Mars as a hot and dry planet, which gives men born under it a choleric complexion.[10] These astrological details were derived from the *De Proprietatibus Rerum* of Bartholomaeus Anglicus, here quotes in John Trevisa's translation:

> Mars god of bataile and of werre was iholde amongis naciouns. For he is an hoot planete and drye, male, and a ny3t planete, and so haþ maistrie ouer colera and fire and colerik complexioun, and disposith to boldnesse and hardinesse, and to desire of wreche. þerfore he is iclepid god of bataille and of werre. . . . he disposiþ þe soule to vnstedefast witte and li3tnes, to wraþþe, and to boldnesse, and to oþir colerik passiouns.[11]

Much of the same information is provided in Alain de Lille's *Anticlaudianus*. Alain recounts how Prudence is stunned by the heat of the palace of Mars: here the fiery planet-god holds sway, abundant in wrath, eager for disputes, the destroyer of peace and treaties.

> Imperat hic Mars igne calens, fecundus in ira,
> Bella serens siciensque lites nostrique sititor
> Sanguinis, excuciens pacem fedusque recidens . . .
> Tabe sua uiciat comitem, sociumque planetam
> Vel seuum seuire docet, uel forte benignum
> Nequicia docet esse truncem leditque ueneno.

[Mars, glowing with fire, here holds sway, prolific in wrath, sowing the seeds of war, thirsty for disputes, thirstier still for our blood, banishing peace, wiping out treaties. . . . By his corruptive influence he affects his companion and neighbouring planet and in his malice teaches the violent to show more violence or the mild to turn savage and he wounds with his venom.][12]

Fuller accounts of the actions and influence of the planet are provided in works of a rather different kind, the technical treatises on astrology such as Ashenden's *Summa Iudicialis* and the *Exafrenon* of Richard of Wallingford (died 1336).[13] We may assume that Chaucer, a proficient astrologer-astronomer, knew the standard description of Mars as an unfortunate planet which, when it governs alone, generally causes such mischiefs and destruction as are consonant with dryness. According to Ashenden, these include wars both foreign and civil, divisions, captivity, slaughter, untimely death, violations of treaties and all kinds of violence.[14]

This medieval lore throws considerable light on Arcite's character. Chaucer has Palamon see and love Emelye first, and to some extent Arcite's decision to pursue his suit appears as an act of aggression. It is Arcite who rejects the family tie and breaks the blood-brother code, as Palamon is quick to point out:

> 'It nere', quod he, 'to thee no greet honour
> For to be fals, ne for to be traitour
> To me, that am thy cosyn and thy brother

Ysworn ful depe, and ech of us til oother,
That nevere, for to dyen in the peyne,
Til that the deeth departe shal us tweyne,
Neither of us in love to hyndre oother,
Ne in noon oother cas, my leeve brother;
But that thou sholdest trewely forthren me
In every cas, as I shall forthren thee,—
This was thyn ooth, and myn also, certeyn;
I woot right wel, thou darst it nat withseyn'.

(I, 1129–40)

One is reminded of Mars's traditional role as the destroyer of peace and treaties, the bringer of strife. Arcite finds it impossible rationally to refute Palamon's prior claim (1152–1186). He labours under the disadvantage of, as it were, having come in second—in *Il Teseida* it was Palemone who laboured under this disadvantage. Mars's destructive capability is stressed heavily in Chaucer's description of the temple of Mars (1967–2035). Arcite's destructive capability is stressed also: it is he who exclaims,

'Wostow nat wel the olde clerkes sawe,
That "who shal yeve a lovere any lawe?"
Love is a gretter lawe, by my pan,
Than may be yeve to any erthely man;
And therfore positif lawe and swich decree
Is broken al day for love in ech degree'.

(I, 1163–8)

The logical conclusion of Arcite's proposition is anarchy and the destruction of positive law, those legal institutions established by generations of wise men. 'Positif lawe and swich decree' is constantly broken in war, Mars having no regard for such things.

Of course, Arcite and Palamon are equally brave as knights and equally ardent as lovers. Both feel 'wraþþe' because of the other's love of Emelye, and both are worthy to wed her, as Theseus says (1831–2). Yet the essential difference between them emerges quite clearly during Palamon's prayer to Venus. Palamon makes his plea through a series of negatives which, by implication, define Arcite's character:

'I kepe noght of armes for to yelpe,
Ne I ne axe nat tomorwe to have victorie,
Ne renoun in this cas, ne veyne glorie
Of pris of armes blowen up and doun;
But I wolde have fully possessioun
Of Emelye . . .
For though so be that Mars is god of armes,
Youre vertu is so greet in hevene above
That if yow list, I shal wel have my love'.

(I, 2238–50)

Arcite seems to see everything—including his love for Emelye—in black-and-white terms of 'victorie' or death; the 'renoun' or 'glorie' he gladly will give to Mars. Convinced that Emelye must be won by force of arms, Arcite asks Mars for his 'helpe or grace':

> 'For she that dooth me al this wo endure
> Ne reccheth nevere wher I synke or fleete.
> And wel I woot, er she me mercy heete,
> I moot with strengthe wynne hire in the place,
> And, wel I woot, withouten help or grace
> Of thee, ne may my strengthe noght availle.
> Thanne help me, lord, tomorwe in my bataille . . .
> And do that I tomorwe have victorie.
> Myn be the travaille, and thyn be the glorie! . . .
> Yif me victorie, I aske thee namoore'.
>
> (I, 2396–420)

There is something sadly bitter about his belief that Emelye does not care what happens to him and that she must be forced to respond. One gains the impression of a man who, faced with an inhospitable world and cruel gods, has come to place his trust in martial 'strengthe'.

It is, therefore, typical of Arcite that he should almost die of his 'loveris maladye' (1355–79) and that, unlike Palamon, he should first describe his love for Emelye in terms of killing, dominance and death:

> 'The fresshe beautee sleeth me sodeynly
> Of hire that rometh in the yonder place,
> And but I have hir mercy and hir grace,
> That I may seen hire atte leeste weye,
> I nam but deed; ther nis namoore to seye'.
>
> (I, 1118–22)

The abruptness of this protestation also befits a Mars-type: unlike the Venus-type, he cannot be loquacious about love. Arcite is a man of action rather than of words, and it seems perfectly appropriate that he should bluntly ask Mars for victory in battle: 'Yif me victorie, I aske thee namoore' (2420). When all due allowance is made for the influence of traditional complaint about the *femme fatale* (which, of course, influenced Palamon's professions of love also), Arcite's rather morbid preoccupation with love and death seems to go far beyond the stock idioms of *fin' amors*. And the reasons for this are rooted in his 'martian' character.

The basis of Palamon's character may be sought in late-medieval descriptions of the planet-god Venus. As Twycross has pointed out, Chaucer's description of naked Venus, 'fletynge in the large see', wearing a 'rose gerland' and holding a 'citole' (1955–65), is derived from mythographic tradition.[15] Close literal parallels are found in Bersuire:

Fingebatur igitur Venus puella pulcherrima nuda et in mari natans et in manu sua dextera concham marinam continens atque gestans, que rosis erat ornata, a columbis circumvolantibus comitata . . . Ante quam tres

astabant nude iuvencule que tres Gracie vocabantur . . . Cui scilicet
Cupido filius suus alatus et cecus assistebat . . .[16]

[Therefore, Venus was feigned as a most beautiful naked girl, swimming
in the sea and holding and bearing in her right hand a sea-shell; who was
adorned with roses, accompanied by doves flying all around . . . In front
of whom stood three naked young girls who were called the Three Graces
. . . Cupid, her son, winged and blind, stood beside her . . .]

The mythographers stressed the voluptuous and foolish nature of Venus, a
view which Chaucer fully recognized in his description of the temple of Venus
(1918–54).[17] Bersuire, following Fulgentius, interpreted Venus as the voluptuous life or a certain luxurious person, depicted as a woman because of
woman's inconstancy. She is said to be naked because of her inevitable
indecency, to float in the sea because she wants always to wallow in sensual
pleasures.[18] 'Mythographus tertius' says of the roses of Venus that, just as roses
blush and prick with their thorns, so sensual desire indices blushing because of
the disgrace of shame, and pricks with the goad of sin.[19] The Venus worshipped
by Boccaccio's Palemone is basically of this type; she functions as the patroness
of his violent and destructive passion.

However, Venus fared much better in the accounts of the astrologers, and
this is significant because Chaucer's Venus, unlike Boccaccio's, is an astrologized deity. Bartholomaeus Anglicus explains that

Uenus . . . is an goodliche planete, female, and a nyȝt planete, in his
qualities, in hete and moisture, temporat. . . . This planete . . . hatte
Venus for, as me seiþ, by his qualite, hoot and moist, a excitiþ to loue of
Venus, as Isidir seiþ. . . . He haþ colour whiȝt and schinynge as *electrum*,
þat is metalle þat is most whit and briȝt . . . For among alle sterres Venus
schiniþ most comfortabilly and whitly, and þerfore he is iclepid 'cleernes-
se' . . . In mannes body he disposiþ to fairnesse, volupte, and lykynge in
touche and gropinge, in smyl, in taast and in songe; and þerfore he makeþ
singers, louyers of musik . . . Vndir him is conteyned wey, loue, frend-
schipe, and pilgrimes, and tokeneþ wynnynge and ioye and blisse; and he
is trewe.[20]

Richard of Wallingford compares the planet's benevolent influence with that
exercised by Jupiter:

in wynter principaly, and in ver, she temperis the yere, in moysture, and
the drowght of somer and harveste she schiwes, fore she manote use hir
ladyshipe but in gudenesse namore than Jupiter.[21]

John Ashenden says that when Venus is alone in domination, honour and joy
will attend mankind.[22] Happy marriages will be contracted and the fortunate
couples will have many children. Every undertaking will prosper. Wealth will
increase, and the conduct of human life will altogether be pure, simple and
pious, due reverence being paid to all holy and sacred institutions, and
harmony existing between princes and their subjects. In such descriptions
Chaucer could have found valuable hints for the rather mystical personality of
Palamon.

It is perfectly appropriate that Palamon the Venus-type should see Emelye first and fall in love with her first, and that his love should be consummated in a happy marriage:

> now is Palamon in alle wele,
> Lyvynge in blisse, in richesse, and in heele;
> And Emelye hym loveth so tendrely,
> And he hire serveth al so gentilly,
> That nevere was ther no word hem bitwene
> Of jalousie or any oother teene.
>
> (3101–6)

At first, Palamon does not know whether Emelye is a woman or the goddess Venus herself:

> 'I noot wher she be womman or goddesse,
> But Venus is it soothly, as I gesse'.
> And therwithal on knees doun he fil,
> And seyde: 'Venus, if it be thy wil
> Yow in this gardyn thus to transfigure
> Bifore me, sorweful, wrecched creature,
> Out of this prisoun help that we may scapen'.
>
> (1101–7)

Arcite tells him that

> 'Thyn is affeccioun of hoolynesse,
> And myn is love, as to a creature'.
>
> (1158–9)

—which seems perfectly accurate. Palamon is the type who will see something of Venus in every beautiful woman. Viewed in the context of the pagan religion in the poem, Palamon seems to have the makings of a visionary: he can see the invisible in the visible, the uncreate in the created. If he were a Christian, one would expect him to go on pilgrimages and to have a strong 'affective' devotion to the Virgin Mary.[23]

In this regard, it is interesting to note that Bersuire managed to allegorize certain planetary properties of Venus as qualities of the Virgin Mary. Bartholomaeus had said that she is a benevolent, feminine, and nocturnal planet that always accompanies the sun. Such is the blessed Virgin, Bersuire exclaims, because she is feminine on account of her piety, benevolent on account of her generosity, and nocturnal and occult with regard to her humility, and she always accompanies the sun who is the incarnate Christ.[24] Bersuire also moralizes the planetary motions of Venus in terms of the mental activity of the perfect man, who elevates his intellect in meditation of heavenly things and extends his disposition (*affectus*) in loving the invisible. But such a high degree of perfection is not possible for a pagan who, because of his unfortunate historical position, lacks the revealed truth of Christianity. As things stand in the ancient world of *The Knight's Tale*, Palamon's total devotion

115

to Venus hints at his eventual 'wynnynge and ioye and blisse' in a matter of human love.

Such was Chaucer's concern for symmetry in *The Knight's Tale* that his parallelism of pagan gods and men extended to the minor characters Lygurge and Emetreus. Boccaccio allocated only four lines to Lygurge, in contrast with Chaucer's twenty-seven; Emetreus was Chaucer's invention. These alterations to the *Teseida* were dictated by Chaucer's wish to provide Arcite the Mars-type and Palamon the Venus-type with champions of appropriate personalities. Arcite's martian character is emphasized by Emetrius's choleric complexion, golden apparel and distinctive appendages (2155–78).[25] Lest we should miss the point, Emetrius is said to have come 'ridynge lyk the god of armes, Mars'. By contrast, Lygurge's black hair and beard, and yellow and red eye-circles, clearly mark him as a saturnian man (2128–52). It is fitting that the Saturn-type should champion the Venus-type, because in the pagan heaven Saturn champions his daughter Venus at least to the extent that he puts her claim on a par with that of Mars (who, after all, had granted his knight's request first in the narrative), and at best to the extent that his way out of the gods' dilemma, while perfectly satisfactory to Mars, leaves the Venus-type alive and in possession of Emelye at the end of the tale.[26]

Emelye's personality is modelled on the personality of the goddess she serves; she may be called a Diana-type. In her case Chaucer drew on the mythographic tradition which described Diana as the chaste huntress of the woods. Bartholomaeus Anglicus explains that

> in fablis he is clepid Prosperina, for naciouns clepiþ þe mone goddes of sedis þat ben iþrowe in þe erþe. Also he is iclepid Diana, goddesse of woodis and of groves, for he ȝeueþ liȝt to wilde bestis þat gadren her mete by nyȝe in woodis and grovis. And þerfore nacyouns clepiþ þe mone goddes of hunters, for huntinge is ofte in woodis and in groves. And þerfore þey peyntid a goddes wiþ a bowe in hire honde, for hunters vsen bowes.[27]

Similarly, Bersuire states that Diana is depicted 'in the form of a lady carrying an arrow and bow, hunting the horned deer', and stresses her virginity by allegorizing her as the Virgin Mary.[28] In his description of the temple of Diana—which has no equivalent in *Il Teseida*—Chaucer refers to Diana's chastity and love of hunting (2051–88). These are Emelye's defining characteristics also, which emerge on the one occasion on which Chaucer allows her to speak, namely when she prays to Diana:

> 'Chaste goddesse, wel wostow that I
> Desire to ben a mayden al my lif,
> Ne nevere wol I be no love ne wyf.
> I am, thow woost, yet of thy compaignye,
> A mayde, and love huntynge and venerye,
> And for to walken in the wodes wilde,
> And noght to ben a wyf and be with childe.
> Noght wol I knowe compaignye of man'.
>
> (I, 2304–11)

When Emelye prepared herself for this prayer, she engaged in another activity traditionally associated with her goddess, namely bathing:

> This Emelye, with herte debonaire,
> Hir body wessh with water of a welle.
> (I, 2282–3)

Perhaps Chaucer had in mind the story of Acteon, who was transformed into a deer and killed by his own dogs because he had seen Diana bathing 'al naked': significantly, this story is mentioned twice in *The Knight's Tale*, in Chaucer's description of the temple of Diana (2065–8) and during Emelye's prayer itself (2302–3). It would seem, then, that Emelye is a sort of earthly counterpart of Diana. Is Chaucer implying that she is equally deadly to men who unwittingly come into contact with her, as Palamon and Arcite did when they looked upon her in the garden?

Duke Theseus, the benevolent 'Firste Moevere' of the world of the poem, is the perfect human counterpart of his special god, Jupiter. In *De Proprietatibus Rerum* Jupiter is described as follows:

> Errour of naciouns and feynynges of poetis menen þat Iubiter was hiȝest fadir of goddis. . . . þis Iubiter coniunct with goode planetis makeþ goode and profitable impressiouns in þise neþir elementis, and þerfore astronomers tellen þat in mannes body he helpiþ to fairnesse and honeste. . . Vndir Iubiter is conteyned honour, richesse, best cloþynge. In iugement and dome of astronomers he tokeneþ witte and wisdome and resoun, and is tristy and trewe. And þerfore, as astronomers tellen, whanne he is iseye in his cercle þat hatte *assendens*, he tokeniþ reuerence and honeste and fey and lore; and he schal be ende to saluacioun.[29]

These details are repeated in the fifth book of Bersuire's *Reductorium*.[30] According to Ashenden, when Jupiter is alone in domination, he promotes honour, happiness, content and peace.[31] The planet induces favours, benefits, and gifts emanating from royalty, and adds greater lustre to kings themselves, increasing their dignity and magnanimity. For Chaucer it would have been a short step from a kingly planet to an ideal king whose character was an amalgam of the qualities invariably associated with that planet. After all, the good rule of the planet-god Jupiter was praised often, and contrasted with the bad rule of Saturn.

At one point in the poem, Chaucer actually compares Theseus to a god:

> Duc Theseus was at a wyndow set,
> Arrayed right as he were a god in trone.
> (I, 2528–9)

We need not wonder which god Chaucer had in mind. Jupiter was traditionally depicted as sitting majestically on a burnished throne, holding the symbols of his supreme power:

Iupiter Saturni filius cui celum et celi regimen in sorte cessit, pingebatur homo in throno eburneo in sua mayestate sedens sceptrumque regni manu tenens, fulmina eciam altera manu inferius mittens et Gigantes repressos fulmine tenens sub pedibus et conculcans.[32]

[Jupiter the son of Saturn who in turn succeeded to heaven and the government of heaven, was painted as a man sitting in his majesty on a burnished throne, holding the sceptre of royalty in one hand and with the other despatching thunderbolts downwards, and holding the giants, restrained by lightning, under his feet and treading them down.]

Bersuire provides an historical interpretation of this 'picture' in terms of the King of Crete who repressed his enemies (the Titans) and deposed his father Saturn.[33] This interpretative process, which is found in all the major medieval compilations of pagan history and myth, could have provided Chaucer with the precedent for his 'humanizing' of Jupiter (or at least Jupiter's more admirable traits) in the person of Theseus.

Theseus possesses the jovian qualities of 'witte and wisdome and resoun' in abundance; he wields absolute power and exercises considerable control over the pagan world of the poem. His excellence in rule and judgment is obvious; he wants to judge others as fairly as he would wish to be judged himself (1863–4). When, in the woods, Theseus judges Arcite and Palamon for their transgressions against him, his 'resoun' has supremacy over his 'ire'; he tempers justice with mercy (1762–86). In the monotheistic vision which serves as the climax to the poem, Theseus's 'lore' finds its consummate expression (2987–3040).

Certain mythographers spoke also of the supreme power of Jupiter,[34] and this attribute is reflected by his devotee in *The Knight's Tale*. Theseus proceeds from one war to another without respite (864–993); the city of Thebes is destroyed 'bothe wall and sparre and rafter' (an incident which has no parallel in Boccaccio).[35] Moreover, he sentences Arcite and Palamon to life-imprisonment without hope of ransom (1020–32), releases one cousin but not the other (1189–1208), initiates the tournament for the possession of Emelye (1845–69), and eventually decides that Emelye should marry the survivor (3067–98). None of these decisions is questioned, either by the other characters or by Chaucer's Knight. Theseus's *fiat* is supreme; his expressed 'wyl' rarely brooks any 'repplicacioun' (1845–69; cf. 2533–60). If some of the man's actions seem rather arbitrary and even harsh, they may be related to the dark side of the character of his god.

However, Theseus is 'jovial' in the modern sense of the term also. John Ridevall, following 'Mythographus tertius' (whom he identifies erroneously as Alexander Neckam), comments on the good humour of Jupiter as follows:

Sexta pars picture est de dei Iovis hilaritate. Pingitur enim Iupiter a poetis cum vultu hilari et ameno, sicud et de hoc tractat Virgilius, ut recitat Alexander Nequam in sua mithologia. Astrologi eciam dicunt Iovem preesse sanguini; unde sanguinei sunt Iovis filii.[36]

[The sixth part of the picture is of the hilarity of the god Jove. For Jove is painted by the poets with a cheerful and amenable expression, just like

Virgil also treats of this, as Alexander Nequam reports in his mythology. The astrologers say that Jove is the leader of the sanguine, whence sanguine men are sons of Jove.]

Theseus certainly shares his god's sense of humour. He soon sees the funny side of the situation in the woods: their love for the same woman has brought the cousins into a ridiculous situation.

> 'Now looketh, is nat that an heigh folye?
> Who may been a fool, but if he love?
> Bihoold, for Goddes sake that sit above,
> Se how they blede! be they noght wel arrayed?
> Thus hath hir lord, the god of love, ypayed
> Hir wages and hir fees for hir servyse!'
>
> (1798–803)

But the best joke of all is that Emelye knows nothing of their plight:

> 'But this is yet the beste game of alle,
> That she for whom they han this jolitee
> Kan hem therfore as muche thank as me.
> She woot namoore of al this hoote fare,
> By God, than woot a cokkow or an hare!'
>
> (1806–10)

There is nothing malicious nor even condescending about Theseus's humour here, because he proceeds to admit that during his own youth he suffered similar distress on account of love.

The planet Jupiter was regarded as the bringer of peace. In his *Anti-claudianus*, Alain de Lille recounts how Prudence makes her way into the undamaging fires of Jupiter, the joy of his calm peace and the smiling regions of the celestial pole. Here the star of Jupiter shines, bringing tidings of safety to the world, and tempering the fury of Mars. Jupiter will befriend any evil star that is joined with him, thus turning gloom to laughter, lament to applause, and tears to joy.

> Hic sydus Iouiale micat mundoque salutem
> Nunciat et Martis iram Martisque furorem
> Sistit et occurit tranquilla pace furenti.
> Cui si stella mali prenuncia, preuia casus
> Iungitur, ille tamen inimicum sidus amicat,
> Alternansque uices, in risus tristia, planctum
> In plausus, fletusque graues in gaudia mutat . . .

[Here the star of Jupiter glows, brings tidings of safety to the world, checks Mars' rage and fury and opposes his madness with serene peace. Even if a star that is a herald of evil and a precursor of misfortune is joined to him, Jupiter makes friends with the unfriendly star and brings about a change in him, turning gloom to laughter, lament to applause, bitter tears to joy.][37]

Bartholomaeus Anglicus explains how Jupiter can temper the malice of the other unfortunate planet, Saturn; similar statements are found in Vincent's *Speculum Naturale*, Ashenden's *Summa Iudicialis*, and Bersuire's *Reductorium Morale*.[38] Chaucer's Theseus is a peace-maker also, a quality not marked in Boccaccio's Teseo. When he discovers Arcite and Palamon fighting in the woods, Theseus's first reaction is that they lack a 'juge or oother officere' (1710–3). Later, Theseus organises a proper tournament and proclaims strict rules; his order that no blood should be shed is obeyed. Thus, the fury of Mars is tempered; violence is restrained and minimized. When death has removed Arcite from the contest, Theseus takes delight in bringing peace and joy by organising the marriage of Palamon and Emelye. This he interprets as the will of Jupiter:

> 'What may I conclude of this longe serye,
> But after wo I rede us to be merye,
> And thanken Juppiter of al his grace?
> And er that we departen from this place
> I rede that we make of sorwes two
> O parfit joye, lastynge everemo.
> And looketh now, wher moost sorwe is herinne,
> Ther wol we first amenden and bigynne'.
>
> (3067–74)

Gloom has been turned to laughter, lament to applause, and tears to joy. Moreover, this marriage has resolved the long conflict between Thebes and Athens. Theseus's final speech is made in the Athenian parliament; before Palamon and Emelye were summoned the lords had discussed the issue of an alliance with Thebes:

> ther was a parlement
> At Atthenes, upon certein pointz and caas;
> Among the whiche pointz yspoken was,
> To have with certein contrees alliaunce,
> And have fully of Thebans obeisaunce.
>
> (2970–4)

This passage, unparalleled in Boccaccio, has given rise to the charge that Theseus was a crass political opportunist, and that his speech in praise of 'the faire cheyne of love' had a very practical objective, namely a marriage of convenience.[39] But Chaucer would doubtless have seen Theseus's political acumen as an essential virtue in a prince. Surely the significance of the episode turns rather on the realization that one marriage can produce so much peace and harmony, both personal and political.

In would seem, then, that in *The Knight's Tale* very considerable comparisons can be drawn between the humans and their respective deities. Yet the contrasts one can make between men and gods are equally significant and ultimately more important. Arcite moves far beyond the limitations of Mars when, on his deathbed, he makes a supreme gesture of reconciliation by commending Palamon to Emelye (2792–6). Here he invokes 'Juppiter so wys', the bringer of peace. Moreover, the dishonourable and murderous activities described in the temple of Mars (1995–2038) are unparalleled in Arcite's life. Similarly, the unpleasant qualities of Venus listed in the description of her temple (1918–50) find no echo in Palamon's character. If Emelye is a *femme fatale* she is an innocent and unwilling one: she has no desire to emulate her goddess by causing the deaths of men. In his descriptions of the gods' temples, Chaucer provided both a focus for Christian suspicion of pagan religion, and an indication that his pagans deserve better gods than the ones they worship.

Most interesting of all is the contrast between Theseus and Jupiter. One of the man's most attractive qualities is the positive way in which he responds to the importunities of women. This cannot be criticized as vacillation because on each occasion feminine influence brings out some good quality in his character. The Theban widows move him to right their grievous wrong (893–1000); the company of courtly ladies move him to temper justice with mercy by pardoning Arcite and Palamon (1748–81). Theseus responds in a noble manner to male friends also. At the request of Perotheus he frees Arcite (1189–1218); he turns to his father Egeus for wise and consoling counsel (2837–52). By contrast, Jupiter is vacillating and indecisive. Feminine influence (the shrewish demands of Venus) hardly brings out the best in him, and when he turns to his father, Saturn, it is for an easy way out of a dilemma. Egeus and Saturn, the two fathers, are similar only in age and quantity of experience; in quality of experience and type of character they are quite different.

Consideration of the major role played by Saturn in *The Knight's Tale* will be reserved until the end of this chapter, since it can best be appreciated after the goodness of the good pagans in the poem has been described more fully. We shall, therefore, proceed to discuss the ways in which late-medieval notions about pagan achievements and limitations (as summarized in previous chapters) influenced Chaucer in his transformation of Boccaccio's poem. The varying degrees of perfection attained by Theseus, Emelye, Arcite and Palamon will be considered in turn.

II   THE SHADOWY PERFECTION OF DUKE THESEUS

Duke Theseus is the most perfect of all Chaucer's good pagans: indeed, he is the closest Chaucer ever got to portraying a hero.[40] His perfection may be said to have two facets, ethical-political and metaphysical.[41] The former is manifest throughout the tale; the latter receives full articulation in Theseus's fine monotheistic vision of the first and unmoved mover who made the fair chain of love which forms the bond of the universe (2987–3074).

Theseus is credited with the virtues of wisdom, true nobility, chivalry, pity, 'gentillesse', truth, worthiness and might; he is a paragon of ethical and political virtue. Chaucer avoided referring to his faithlessness to Ariadne, which he did describe in *The Legend of Ariadne*.[42] As portrayed by the Knight, Theseus is wholly honourable in his treatment of women, and susceptible to their entreaties (see 952–64, 1760–81).

Particular emphasis is placed on his role as a 'rightful lord and juge' (1719).

Those who would appear to have some cause to complain about his judgments fail to do so. Although Theseus has sentenced Arcite and Palamon to life-imprisonment, they tend to blame their plight on fortune and the stars and not on their captor. Besides, Theseus's subsequent generosity to the cousins dispels any doubts that the reader may have concerning his treatment of them. Particularly illuminating is the episode in which he interrupts their fight to the death in the woods. Among the reasons for his anger is the fact that they are fighting 'withouten juge or oother officere' (1712), improperly conducting a trial by combat. Palamon instantly sees the situation from Theseus's point of view (yet another indication that the Duke's standards are supreme in the poem) and accepts that, judged by the canons of absolute justice, he and Arcite should be condemned to death. But of course, Theseus's 'resoun' soon gains control over his 'ire', and he recognises that in this case justice should be tempered with mercy.

> And softe unto hymself he seyde, 'Fy
> Upon a lord that wol have no mercy,
> But been a leon, bothe in word and dede,
> To hem that been in repentaunce and drede' . . .
> (I, 1773–5)

The man who can rule himself is fit to rule others, as we are assured in many a late-medieval 'Regiment of Princes'.

The basic principle on which Theseus operates is that he will judge others as he would wish to be judged himself:

> 'God so wisly on my soule rewe,
> As I shal evene juge been and trewe'.
> (I, 1863–4)

This seems to be the pagan equivalent of Matthew 7.2: 'With what judgment you judge, you shall be judged: and with what measure you mete, it shall be measured to you again'. These sentiments, the emphasis on the Duke's abilities as a judge, and his anger at the improper conduct of a trial by combat, are all without precedent in *Il Teseida*.

Ample precedent may be found, however, in a different kind of writing, namely, in stories of virtuous pagan kings and/or judges. A wealth of such *exempla* is provided in the first part of the *Communiloquium*. There John of Wales, following John of Salisbury, claims that the prince is 'the public power, and as it were an image on earth of the divine majesty' (cf. our discussion on p. 117 above).[43] Moreover, according to Plutarch's *Instructio Traiani*, the prince, being the 'chief judge' and head of the body politic, has to instruct and inform those persons who are its members. His justice should be dispensed without prejudice or favour.[44] Mercy is essential in a prince, as the Emperor Trajan recognized when he said that a man is insane who, having inflamed eyes, prefers to dig them out rather than cure them.[45] Likewise, nails which are too sharp should be trimmed and not plucked out. Just as a cithar player can correct the fault of a string which is out of tune by tuning it and not breaking it, so should the prince moderate his acts—now with the rigour of justice, now with the leniency of mercy—so that he may make his subjects all of one mind.

Therefore, the ethical writer (Ovid) says, 'The true prince is slow to punish, swift to reward, and grieves whenever he is compelled to be severe'. Trajan was inclined by nature to be merciful towards all, though he was stern towards the few who deserved his wrath. All these noble qualities are present in Duke Theseus, the ideal ruler and chief judge of *The Knight's Tale*.

In *St Erkenwald*, the unnamed good pagan whose body is miraculously preserved in order that it might be baptised and his soul saved thereby, was a judge of 'the gentile law'.[46] Indeed, he was the 'king of keen judges' because of the superlative excellence of his decisions, and hence when he died his body was buried with the trappings of kingship.

> 'I was committid & made a mayster mon here,
> To sit upon sayd causes þis cite I ʒemyd
> Vnder a prince of parage of paynymes laghe
> (& vche segge þat him sewid þe same fayth trowid). . . .
> Quen I deghed for dul denyed all Troye,
> Alle menyd my dethe, þe more & the lasse,
> & þus to bounty my body þai buriet in golde,
> Cladden me for þe curtest þat courte couthe þen holde,
> In mantel for þe mekest & monlokest on benche,
> Gurden me for þe gouernour & graythist of Troie,
> ffurrid me for þe fynest of faith me wytinne;
> ffor þe honour of myn honeste of heghest enprise
> þai coronyd me þe kidde kynge of kene iustises,
> þer euer wos tronyd in Troye oþir, trowid euer shulde
> And for I rewardid euer riʒt þai raght me the septre'.
>
> (201–56)

The heathen people who lived in 'New Troy' (=London) were unruly, but he administered justice according to his conscience, without showing undue favour to anyone, no matter how rich or powerful. Even if his own father had been a murderer, he would not have been swayed from his duty, but if necessary would have seen him hanged. This is reminiscent of the action of the just Emperor Trajan, in refusing to show favour to his own son. When Trajan's son accidentally killed a widow's son, the Emperor gave the widow his son in place of hers (cf. p. 54 above). Of course, in *The Knight's Tale* Theseus is not called upon to make a personal sacrifice of that kind, but it is quite clear that he has the superlative virtue necessary for such a feat of justice.

In order to establish this superlative virtue at the outset, Chaucer drastically abbreviated the first two books of the *Teseida*, where Boccaccio dealt with Teseo's great wars against the Amazons and the Thebans respectively. As a result of this drastic abbreviation the episode of Theseus and the widows becomes all-important. Boccaccio had employed this as a link-passage between Teseo's two wars, but in Chaucer the episode is more important than the wars. Chaucer's selection of material might have been influenced by popular tales about that other pagan champion of widows, Trajan. Trajan's decision to give a widow his son in place of her dead son, has just been mentioned. Even more significant in this context is the occasion on which the Emperor was hindered from going to war by a widow who, seizing his stirrup and miserably lamenting, besought him that she should have justice (cf. pp. 53–4 above).

Trajan promised to give her satisfaction on his return. The widow then asked what would happen if he did not return. Higden takes up the story thus:

> Traian themperour seide, 'My successor schalle iugge and do to the satisfaccioun'. The wedowe seide, 'What schalle that profite the and if thy successour do satisfaccion for me or eny other; þow arte dettor to me to receyve after thy meryte, and hit is a frawde not to restore that is dewe; hit is sufficiaunte for þy successor if he do satisfaccion for hym selfe'. Traian themperour, hauenge compassion of that wedowe, lepede downe of his hors, and did satisfaccion to the wedowe, wherfore he hadde an ymage sette in the cite of Rome made to his similitude.[47]

By contrast, Theseus, returning from one war, sets off on another war on behalf of a group of wretched widows who were once married to high-ranking aristocrats. Yet in each case a widow appeals to a pagan lord renowned for his nobility and justice, and in each case the lord puts the widow's grievance before self-interest. Chaucer may have regarded his Theseus as a Greek Trajan.

Particularly impressive is the way in which Theseus manages to avoid mass slaughter at the tournament: by the standards of Chaucer's age, he was positively squeamish.[48] Boccaccio's Teseo merely imposed limits on the numbers of fighting men and on the arms they could carry, expressing the pious hope that unnecessary bloodshed should be avoided.[49] During the battle, some knights are captured but a great many are killed, so that Emilia fears the curses of the bereaved 'mothers, fathers, friends, brothers, sons and others'.[50] At the beginning of the tenth book of Il Teseida a series of cremations is described briefly: each king lights 'a fire for his dead on the pyres built in sorrow'.[51] The instructions of Chaucer's Theseus are precise and strict: there is to be no bloodshed at all.

> 'The lord hath of his heigh discrecioun
> Considered that it were destruccioun
> To gentil blood to fighten in the gyse
> Of mortal bataille now in this emprise.
> Wherfore, to shapen that they shal nat dye,
> He wol his firste purpos modifye'. . . .
> (2537ff.)

Knights who are overcome in battle are not to be killed, but 'brought unto the stake' where they must await the outcome of the contest without further participation. Consequently, 'of hem alle was ther noon yslayn' (2708), although they all can display honourable wounds. Only one cremation is described towards the end of The Knight's Tale—that of Arcite, who is the victim of Saturn and not of Palamon or any of his company of knights.

Theseus's decree against bloodshed is universally commended by the people:

> The voys of peple touchede the hevene,
> So loude cride they with murie stevene,
> 'God save swich a lord, that is so good,
> He wilneth no destruccion of blood!'
> (I, 2561–4)

Similarly, the company assembled in the woods praise Theseus's judgment of Arcite and Palamon (1870–80). The exceptional virtue of this good pagan, therefore, is acknowledged by all, and there is no reason to suspect any of the famous (or infamous) Chaucerian irony in his portrayal.[52] In his final speech, a shrewd political move—the marriage of Palamon and Emelye, which will ensure peace between Thebes and Athens—is shown to have not only ethical but also metaphysical sanction. The philosophy of Duke Theseus is internally consistent, comprehensive, and enlightened.

But precisely how enlightened is Theseus; what degree of perfection has he attained? The answer lies in his final speech, which will now be considered at some length. It shall be argued that the Boethian ideas found therein are quoted out of context from *De Consolatione Philosophiae* every bit as much as was the argument in favour of strict necessity which Chaucer put in the mouth of Troilus. Once again, Chaucer is using material drawn from Boethius not to investigate the nature of truth but to characterize a pagan philosopher of a type envisaged in the sources of his classicism.

Theseus's monotheistic vision provides the climax of *The Knight's Tale*, in marked contrast with the *Teseida* wherein Arcita's death and funeral serve this function. Chaucer transformed the episode in which Teseo, acting imperiously and somewhat overbearingly, decrees that Palemone and Emilia should marry. Every man must die, declares Teseo, and when it shall please the god 'who sets the limits of the world, we who are living now shall also die. Therefore, we ought to bear up cheerfully under the pleasure of the gods, since we cannot resist it'.[53] Here is the key to what Teseo means by making 'a virtue of necessity'. Since we all have to die, it is best to die well, 'when life is a joy'. The valiant man ought not to care how or whence death will come, because fame will preserve the honour he deserves. Consequently, if we thought deeply about this, we would emulate Arcita instead of grieving for him, turning 'our efforts towards a valiant life that would win us glorious fame'. This is the opening speech in a debate with Palemone, who has to be persuaded that to marry Emilia would not negate his love for Arcita. Emphasizing that he is following the pleasure of great Teseo rather than his own volition, Palemone seeks the approval of 'merciful Jove' who governs 'the earth and heavens with prudence and who gives each and all equally their ever-lasting place'.[54] He prays also to Diana, Venus, and any other goddess who has power in matrimony, and finally asks pardon, if pardon is necessary, of the 'piteous shade' of Arcita.

By contrast, in *The Knight's Tale* it is Theseus alone who speaks. His reasoning is altogether more substantial and comprehensive than Teseo's, and Palamon does not reply to him but accepts Emelye with joy and without even a token protest. Only one god is mentioned,

> 'Juppiter, the kyng,
> That is prince and cause of alle thyng'
> (I, 3035–6)

This monotheistic precision contrasts with the references to a plurality of gods made in the speeches of Boccaccio's Teseo and Palemone, although it should be noted that both these pagans make vague allusions to an omnipotent god. The main change, however, that Chaucer wrought was the introduction of ideas from *De Consolatione Philosophiae*. For example, from II met. 8 and IV met. 6 is derived the notion that the divine love which produces and governs creatures binds 'the series of things' so that the world moves through its changes in regular concord, all things being 'held by mutual love' (cf. pp. 99–100 above).

> 'The Firste Moevere of the cause above,
> Whan he first made the faire cheyne of love,
> Greet was th'effect, and heigh was his entente.
> Wel wiste he why, and what thereof he mente;
> For with that faire cheyne of love he bond
> The fyr, the eyr, the watèr, and the lond
> In certeyn boundes, that they may nat flee.
> That same Prince and that Moevere', quod he,
> 'Hath stablissed in this wrecched world adoun
> Certeyne dayes and duracioun
> To al that is engendred in this place,
> Over the whiche day they may nat pace,
> Al mowe they yet tho dayes wel abregge'.
>
> (I, 2987–999)

Here the Creator who 'sits on high, and ruling the universe guides its reins' (IV met. 6, 34–5) is identified with the Aristotelian first mover and primary cause, perhaps under the influence of the Aristotelian theory of causality which, as we have seen, permeates Trevet's commentary on Boethius (cf. pp. 102–3 above).[55] But the Boethian philosophy in lines 2987–3016 is much more than a mere preliminary to the free adaptation of Teseo's speech provided in the lines which follow—it is the main guiding principle behind that adaptation, and provides the perameters within which interpretation thereof should operate. Theseus's views on necessity and fame must be considered in Boethian terms, as I now hope to demonstrate.

The world, Theseus claims, is subject to those general fortunes which are dispensed by secondary causes. From on high the eternal and stable Mover has decreed that

> 'speces of thynges and progressiouns
> Shullen enduren by successiouns,
> And nat eterne, withouten any lye'.
>
> (I, 3013–5)

Natural things go through the phases of their existence and eventually cease to be; towns 'wane and wende'; human beings die. No living creature can resist these things:

> 'heer-agayns no creature on lyve,
> Of no degree, availleth for to stryve'.
>
> (3039–40)

This might appear to be similar to Troilus's postulation of strict necessity, which Chaucer derived from *De Consolatione Philosophiae* V pr. 3,

126

'al that comth, comth by necessitee:
.Thus to be lorn, it is my destinee'.
(IV, 958–9)

—but in fact it is quite different in origin and import. The relevant Boethian analogue is to be found in IV pr. 6, where Dame Philosophy explains the way in which 'the generation of all things, and the whole development of changeable natures, and whatever moves in any manner, are given their causes, order and forms from the stability of the divine mind' (22–25). Trevet explains that the necessity involved here is not absolute but conditional (cf. pp. 41–2 above). God ensures that certain things (such as the balance of elements, the seasonal cycle, and the normal successions of creatures) result necessarily only to the extent that these things have proximate causes which are contingently necessary. Causes which, in so far as they are contingent, are changeable, can yet be disposed in a fixed order by divine providence. This stability is not absolute but conditional, dependent on a higher authority. As Theseus puts it, the fixed pattern of the ever-changing series of events is made by

> 'Juppiter, the kyng,
> That is prince and cause of alle thyng,
> Convertynge al unto his propre welle
> From which it is dirryved, sooth to telle . . .'
> (I, 3035–8)

Conditional necessity means that neither God nor man is a mere cog in a mechanistic universe. Men are free to meet the common fortunes of life with dignity and courage.[56] We have the power to

> 'maken vertu of necessitee,
> And take it weel that we may nat eschue,
> And namely that to us alle is due.
> And whoso gruccheth ought, he dooth folye,
> And rebel is to hym that al may gye'.
> (I, 3042–6)

This may be compared with the attitude to future contingents recommended by 'Aristotle' in the *Secreta Secretorum* (cf. pp. 98–9 above). Some say that, since things must come 'of force', there is nothing we can do about it, even in those cases in which we are warned of future evils by astrological prediction. 'Aristotle' rejects this view and espouses a positive approach which has much in common with that of Theseus: things which we expect to happen may be 'moor lightly suffred, moor wysly passand, and so in manere eschewed; ffor yn als mekyl als þey ar forsey yn oure knowynge, we take hem mor discretly to passe withoutyn heuynesse and most harme'. This argument is substantiated by reference to the seasonal cycle:

Als by ensample, whanne men trowyn wynter þat it is cold, men ordeyns herbergage and cloþing, and warmstores of cole and woode, and of many oþer þynges; And þerfore whanne þe wynter comes, þay er noght harmyd of þe cold. And yn somer of þe same maner þurgh cold metys and dyuers spyses þay kepe hem fro þe hete of somer; and yn þe same maner, when men knowyn byfore ȝeres of nede and hunger, þurgh kepynge and holdynge of whete and of oþer þynges, men suffren þe tyme mor lightly.[57]

This entire discussion, and Theseus's final speech, presuppose a belief in the freedom of the will, a belief which Troilus, in his most fatalistic mood, could not accept (IV, 1058-9). The logical conclusion of Troilus's thought is quietism and gloomy acceptance of fate: by contrast, Theseus insists on the importance of action. Thanks to conditional necessity, real virtue is possible, and it may be rewarded, according to Theseus, with 'a worthy fame'.

To be fair to Troilus, at the end of book III of *Troilus and Criseyde* he attained a vision of love as the 'holy bond of thynges' similar to that ascribed to Theseus, which also entailed belief in conditional necessity (cf. p. 100 above). But Troilus was unable to maintain this enlightened position for long. When the stimulus of earthly beauty was removed he reverted to his previous fatalism and polytheism. Theseus's wisdom, however, is mature and secure: he does not vacillate between variant forms of paganism; his vision is not dependent on the stimulus of earthly beauty. In death, Troilus realized that one cannot trust earthly things because of their ephemeral nature, that human joy and grief are vain. By contrast, in *The Knight's Tale* this type of insight into the transitoriness of the sublunary world and the vanity of human wishes is presented as the height of pagan wisdom, which Theseus is able to attain in life. Coming as it does at the end of the poem, his wisdom is presented as the distillation of the experience and thought of a lifetime.

Yet Theseus's wisdom is limited. He fails to move from the notion of Jupiter, prince and primary cause, to the notion of a loving god who can intervene in the determined course of events and suspend the normal operation of secondary causes.[58] Similarly, he does not push his understanding of earthly mutability to what a Christian (like the narrator of *Troilus*) would regard as a logical conclusion, namely, the rejection of the earthly and mutable in favour of the divine and permanent. Instead Theseus opts for the spurious eternity of human fame:

> 'And certeinly a man hath moost honour
> To dyen in his excellence and flour,
> Whan he is siker of his goode name . . .
> Thanne is it best, as for a worthy fame,
> To dyen whan that he is best of name'.
> (I, 3047-56)

Chaucer's personal skepticism about human fame may be inferred from *The House of Fame*, in which Fame's dwelling is said to be made of glass and built on ice.[59]

> Thoughte I, 'By seynt Thomas of Kent!
> This were a feble fundament
> To bilden on a place hye.
> He ought him lytel glorifye
> That hereon bilt, God so me save!'
> (1131-5)

Some of the virtuous people who approach the 'gentil lady Fame' are granted 'good fame' but others are not; some will have neither 'good ne harm' spoken of them while others will actually be slandered (1549–1635). A company of people who have been idle all their lives are granted as much renown as those who 'han doon noble gestes, / And acheved alle her lestes' (1727–1770). It would seem, therefore, that the confidence which Theseus has in Arcite's 'goode name' is utterly misplaced: the fame of this worthy man may endure, but then again it may not. Only time will tell; it is all a matter of fortune and luck, and posterity may afford some 'ydel' fellow as much respect as he.

To be more precise, what is in question at the end of *The Knight's Tale* is the status of fame as a good, the extent to which it is a fitting object of human endeavour. Since this issue is not discussed in *The House of Fame* we must turn once again to the sources of Chaucer's classicism, paying special attention to the late-medieval understanding of Boethius's statements on *gloria* and *fama*.

Robert Holcot's views on the subject emerge in his treatment of the *dubitacio*, is it virtuous for a man to neglect his fame?[60] It would seem that fame should be neglected, since it is a matter of good fortune or luck and, as Boethius proves in the first two books of *De Consolatione Philosophiae*, such matters are to be abandoned by the virtuous man. This is what those saints did, who gave up everything for Christ. Indeed, it seems to be the case that fame is to be contemned, because this kind of positive contempt is conducive to true happiness. As Christ told his followers, 'Blessed are ye when they shall revile you, . . . and speak all that is evil against your name' (Matthew 5.11). Furthermore, II Corinthians 6.4 teaches us to exhibit ourselves to God in such a way that we shall not take pride in good estimation nor be concerned about bad estimation. However, against the proposition that fame should be neglected one can cite Ecclesiasticus 41.15, 'Take care of a good name: for this shall continue with thee, more than a thousand treasures precious and great', and also Proverbs 22.1, 'A good name is better than great riches'. Holcot then 'responds' with his own opinion, which turns out to be a reiteration of what Augustine says in *De Communi Vita Clericorum* about the distinction between conscience and fame. These are two distinct things: conscience is necessary to us in respect of ourselves; fame, in respect of our neighbours. To contemn proper fame would be a mortal sin, while to neglect it would be sin either venial or mortal, depending on the degree of negligence. The reason for this is, that to neglect fame would be directly contrary to charity, which involves the instruction of one's neighbour by good edification or conversation. Holcot proceeds to refute the arguments in favour of the proposition as follows. Matters of good fortune are to be abandoned only if they impede virtue, yet *bona fama* does not hinder virtue but greatly promotes it. However, the love or desire for good fame can be excessive, as can the love of food, drink or clothes, each of which is necessary for life. Against the second argument, it may be pointed out that what was being praised was the patience with which the saints in question endured infamy inflicted unjustly, not the neglect of good fame. All this seems to point to the conclusion that fame can be a good thing if sought in the right manner and to the right extent.

Attacking those who are wholly preoccupied with the glory of fame, Holcot paraphrases five arguments from *De Consolatione Philosophiae* II pr. 7.[61] First is the spatial argument: the whole earth is but a mere point in comparison with the heavens, as Ptolemy and Alphorabius prove. Only a quarter of the earth is habitable, which further indicates the narrowness of the limits within which fame can spread. Secondly, it is impossible to spread one's name widely because of defective communications and the difficulty of travel. Thirdly, there is a wide variety of customs in the world: what one race approves of and commends, another may deride and contemn. Fourthly, men die, and the memory of their name fades away. As Boethius asks in the following metrum, who now remembers the good Fabricius or Cato or Brutus? Names written in a few letters are all the fame that is left to them, and by reading these letters we cannot gain knowledge of the people themselves. Fifthly and finally, he who hopes to live in the memories of men suffers two deaths—one of his body, the other of his name.

Here Holcot appears to be adapting the *divisio textus* or breakdown of arguments offered in Trevet's commentary on *De Consolatione Philosophiae* II pr. 7. Of special interest to us is Trevet's gloss on Boethius's deliberations on the question, 'what has fame to offer men of the best sort, whose means to glory has been their virtue—what indeed, . . . after death has finally destroyed the body?' (77–80). He expands the author's statement that virtuous men either die totally or, if the soul lives after the death of the body (which we must believe) it travels to heaven.[62] If such men die totally, glory will be no concern of theirs; if their souls continue to live, being in heaven they will scorn all earthly things and consequently care nothing for human glory. One thinks of the souls of Boccaccio's Arcita and Chaucer's Troilus, rejecting mundane values as they travel towards their eternal home. Later in *De Consolatione Philosophiae*, in III pr. 6, glory or fame is firmly placed as one of the five inferior goods which are no substitute for the *summum bonum* of true happiness. As a type of false felicity, fame is not to be sought inordinately.

By placing Teseo's praise of fame in a Boethian context which encouraged the reader to identify it as one of Boethius's types of false felicity, Chaucer was bringing closer to the surface the principle of historical and cultural relativity which, I suspect, underlies Boccaccio's treatment of his pagan warlord in the final book of *Il Teseida*. Teseo's special interest in renown as a reward is absolutely typical of virtuous heathen as envisaged in the later Middle Ages.[63] Robert Holcot was expressing a commonplace of late-medieval classicism when he remarked that in 'ancient' writings we read that those men who did great and wonderful things, or things which were of great benefit to the state, were not only commemorated by their successors but also were placed in eternal memory to be worshipped as gods.[64] For example, Dionysius, the first to demonstrate the way in which grapes are cultivated, was called the father of wine by the Greeks, and deified. In a similar manner, Hercules and Ulysses, Ajax and Hector, perpetuated their fame by bellicose deeds. Another commonplace of late-medieval classicism was that the desire for fame had actually motivated many pagans to perform virtuous actions. According to Augustine in the fifth book of *De Civitate Dei*, 'love of country and thirst of praise' were 'the two things that set all the Romans upon admirable action'.[65] Boccaccio, aiming at historical accuracy in this matter, has Teseo recommend that all men should turn their efforts towards a valiant life that would win them glorious fame.[66]

In the extensive discussion of earthly glory provided in book V of *De Civitate Dei*, Augustine invoked the principle of the ethical expertise of the pagans. Christians should be shamed from boasting of their deeds for the eternal country by the superlative feats of virtue achieved by the Romans for their temporal city and for merely human glory.[67] For example, why is it so much to despise all this world's vanities for eternity, when Brutus could kill his own sons (supporters of the power-seeking Tarquin) for fear his country should lose bare liberty, a deed which the heavenly country compels no one to do?[68] Virgil erects Brutus 'a monument of unhappiness' for killing his sons, though otherwise he praises him. So then, if a pagan father could kill his sons for mortal freedom and thirst of praise, both transitory desires, what great matter is it, if we do not kill our sons, but count the poor of Christ our sons, and for eternal liberty free men, not from Tarquin but from the devils and their king? The obvious implication is that what Christians are obliged to do is altogether more reasonable and appropriate, and certainly more pleasing to God. The virtue that serves human glory, Augustine declares, 'is not comparable even with the imperfect beginnings of the saints' virtues, whose assured hope stands fixed in the grace and mercy of the true God'.[69] These views were reiterated frequently by late-medieval classicizing scholars, including the compiler of the *Speculum Morale*, John of Wales, and Pierre Bersuire.[70] Bersuire summed up the prevailing opinion succinctly: 'Fame, indeed, is the thing that the noble heart seeks most eagerly; and for that reason the ancients performed all their lofty deeds for the sake of acquiring fame, and they longed for glory and fame as the final reward of their deeds; and this they did because they were ignorant of the true glory of heaven and the true, everlasting reward'.[71]

This throws considerable light on the attitude of Boccaccio's Teseo and Chaucer's Theseus to 'worthy fame' and 'goode name'.[72] It was perfectly proper, and indeed commendable, for pagans to conceive of human fame as the final reward of their deeds, especially since, by dint of their unfavourable historical position, they were ignorant of the true glory of heaven and the true, everlasting reward. Therefore, in so far as the pagan desire for fame which Theseus articulates is conducive to virtue, it may be accepted and even approved of by the Christian reader of *The Knight's Tale*. However, such a reader cannot accept either Theseus's trust in fame or his inclination to establish it as the fit objective of human endeavour. The truth of the matter is that the virtuous man should not care greatly about the perpetuity of human fame and glory after death, although charity dictates that, in the interests of his neighbours, he should not neglect fame during his lifetime. 'Fame is the spur that the clear spirit doth raise' to superlative feats of virtue and valour, but it is also (as Augustine and Boethius recognized) the 'last infirmity of noble mind'.[73] Thus, the strengths and weaknesses of Theseus's philosophy of life are evident.

III   THE YOUNG FATALISTS: EMELYE, ARCITE AND PALAMON

Chaucer's Emelye is a puzzling character, and quite unlike her counterpart in Boccaccio. Boccaccio's Emilia has a positive and quite forceful personality.[74] For example, during the tournament she complains of the evil that love has wrought, and of the effect of her beauty, 'the price of which had to be a horrible, wicked, and ruthless conflict waged here only because of my face! How heartily I wish that it might have been kept veiled always, rather than that so much blood should be spilled for it, as I now see here in the place below'.[75] The sorrowful spirits of those who have been killed because of her face, she fears, will glare at her forever and gloat over everything that does her harm. Moreover, the relatives of the dead will beg their gods to afflict her with misfortunes, 'and the gods will become so hostile that I shall be condemned to a cruel death'.[76] When Arcita wins the tournament, Emilia ceases to care about Palemone and genuinely falls in love with Arcita: 'she already told herself that she was espoused to Arcita, and already she secretly felt unaccustomed love for him, and already she prayed often to the gods for her lord. Now she looked at him with new desire as she praised everything that he did'.[77] After his accident, she cries out against the gods who have bereft her of her happiness, which was all too brief.[78]

By contrast, Chaucer's Emelye appears as negative and shadowy: always in the background, she seems to accept meekly her role as prize in a trial of strength. However, far from destroying his heroine's character, Chaucer created it afresh: Emelye's paganism is stressed, and this seems to be the key to her character. Chaucer invented a description of the temple of Diana to parallel the descriptions of the shrines of Venus and Mars. This is part of the process by which Emilia's heathen piety was made as substantial as that of any of the male characters in *The Knight's Tale*.

The story of Nectanabus as told by Vincent of Beauvais and Ralph Higden (paraphrased above on pp. 63–4) reveals the extent to which, according to late-medieval scholars of antiquity, pagan peoples had believed in the inevitability of fate. In his very attempt to reject the notion of a fixed fate, Alexander sealed the fate of the man who was his real father. 'No man may flee his destinee', exclaims the dying astrologer, 'for y knewe by myn arte þat myne awne sonne scholde by cause of my dethe'. Similarly, Emelye believes that no-one can escape his or her destiny. Faced with the equal loves of her two suitors, she is concerned to discover if

> 'my destynee be shapen so
> That I shal nedes have oon of hem two . . .'
>
> (I, 2323–4)

—and Diana leaves her in no doubt that the gods have made an irrevocable decision:

> 'Among the goddes hye it is affermed,
> And by eterne word writen and confermed,
> Thou shalt ben wedded unto oon of tho
> That han for thee so muchel care and wo . . .'
>
> (I, 2349–52)

Unlike Boccaccio's Emilia, Emelye never cries out against her gods: as a virtuous pagan, she accepts their will. The fact that (to a Christian) Diana is an unworthy object of worship is not her fault: historically speaking, Emelye was quite justified.

'I putte me in thy proteccioun,
Dyane, and in thy disposicioun'.

(I, 2363-4)

Such perfect faith must impress even those who cannot share it; such trust in the divine will is of the superlative kind that (in the view of the classicizers) should put many a Christian to shame.

Attempts to analyse Emelye simply in terms of *fin' amors* are therefore misguided: she could hardly be more different from, for example, the heroine of *Le Roman de la Rose* who exercises supreme power over her lover, and has the sole responsibility for deciding the outcome of his suit. Chaucer was concerned to portray not a fourteenth-century courtly lady but an 'ancient' pagan, and, as we are reminded in *Troilus*, 'ancient' and 'modern' methods of pursuing a love-suit can be dissimilar:

for to wynnen love in sondry ages,
In sondry londes, sondry ben usages. . . .

For every wight which that to Rome went
Halt nat o path, or alwey o manere . . .

(II, 27-37)

Emelye's passivity becomes comprehensible only if it is placed in its historical perspective and related to her fatalism.

This passivity is rendered more acceptable to us because of Chaucer's narrative technique in *The Knight's Tale*: the pagans are allowed to think and speak for themselves, to define their pagan standards without explicit criticism. The double standard of *Troilus and Criseyde* encourages us to judge Criseyde more critically, and of course we have more to criticize her for, every possible excuse having been made for her behaviour. In that poem, people are shown to be responsible for their actions, irrespective of what they themselves might believe to the contrary. Therefore, Criseyde's faithlessness cannot be blamed on fate; her 'To Diomede algate I wol be trewe' is pathetic rather than noble. By contrast, we are not made aware that Emelye has any freedom of action, other than the freedom to ennoble what must be by accepting it bravely.

Indeed, fatalism is the norm in the 'closed' pagan world of *The Knight's Tale*, and the monotheistic vision attained by Theseus at the end of the poem is the exception that proves the rule. In general, Theseus seems to be polytheistic— the 'rede statue of Mars' adorns his banner (975-6) and he can swear by 'myghty Mars' (1747)—and therefore his final speech should perhaps, technically speaking, be regarded as a statement concerning Jupiter as the greatest of the pagan gods rather than as a single omnipotent god, although its indubitable monotheism is, quite clearly, meant to be understood as an enlightened pagan anticipation of Christian belief. Theseus, although not in the same intellectual league as Socrates and Plato (who were supposed to have rejected polytheism utterly), resembles those Stoic philosophers who, according to Bradwardine, identified fate with the dictates of Jove, their greatest god, and regarded fate as 'the effecting of the divine will' (cf. pp. 43-4 above). The young pagans in Chaucer's poem, however, do not get so far, since they believe that men are predetermined by the power of the stars and conceive of fate in terms of a fixed order of events. The necessity of which Emelye, Arcite and Palamon make virtue is the absolute necessity of which Troilus spoke in book IV of *Troilus and Criseyde*:

> 'al that comth, comth by necessitee:
> Thus to ben lorn, it is my destinee'.
> (IV, 958–9)

Perhaps Theseus's implicit belief in conditional necessity, judged by the standards of his day, is somewhat optimistic, although of course it is the hope for the future, the theory of divine control which one day history will prove to be the right one.

As in *Troilus*, in *The Knight's Tale* the pagan deities are assimilated to the planets which bear their names, and belief in planetary influences and astral determinism is inextricably linked with polytheism. The god Saturn causes Arcite's death yet, earlier in the poem, Arcite blames the misfortunes which Palamon and he have to suffer on fortune and the wicked aspect of the planet Saturn:

> 'Fortune hath yeven us this adversitee.
> Som wikke aspect or disposicioun
> Of Saturne, by som constellacioun,
> Hath yeven us this . . .'
> (I, 1086–9)

Arcite performs 'his sacrifice, / With alle the rytes of his payen wyse', in the temple of the planet-god Mars (2368–70); Palamon does likewise in the temple of the planet-god Venus. Yet the fact that they are deeply embrangled in 'observaunces of judicial matere and rytes of payens' does not imply that they lack virtue in some way; there is no suggestion that their worship of false gods is a reflection of moral falsity, as was the case with the dubious piety of Calkas in *Troilus*. Indeed, Arcite and Palamon are presented with considerable sympathy. Chaucer avoided all mention of Arcite's faithlessness to Anelida (which forms the subject of his short poem *Anelida and Arcite*): obviously he did not wish the character in *The Knight's Tale* to be accused of moral turpitude, or the honesty of his love for Emelye to be questioned.

Because the cousins are presented as essentially virtuous, their reservations about the standard religious and philosophical beliefs of their time carry considerable weight. For all their trust in Mars and Venus respectively, Arcite and Palamon incline towards the belief that the gods kill men for their sport. Palamon, left alone in prison when Arcite is freed, cries out against the cruel gods who lead mankind like sheep to the slaughter:

> Thanne seyde he, 'O crueel goddes that governe
> This world with byndyng of youre word eterne, . . .
> What is mankynde moore unto you holde
> Than is the sheep that rouketh in the folde?
> For slayn is man right as another beest . . .'
> (I, 1303–9)

Men without guilt are often tormented:

> 'What governance is in this prescience,
> That giltelees tormenteth innocence?'
>
> (1313–4)

Here one is reminded of the commonplace medieval theory that the pagan gods were actually demons, who purposed no good to mankind. Palamon proceeds to claim that the gods Saturn and Juno, 'jalous and eek wood', have destroyed Thebes and now seek to destroy him (1328–31). Similarly, Arcite complains about Juno and 'felle Mars' (1540–62). Forced to leave Athens and Emelye, he laments that fortune has turned the dice in favour of Palamon, then muses that the 'purveiaunce of God' or fortune often gives men good or ill in disguise (1234–65), concluding that

> 'We seken faste after felicitee,
> But we goon wrong ful often, trewely'.
>
> (1266–7)

The Boethian allusion is obvious: in pursuing earthly beauty in the form of Emelye, the lovers are seeking a kind of false felicity which falls far short of the ultimate end of true happiness.

In this way, Chaucer characterises his benighted pagans, walking by the best light they have, striving for felicity but not finding it, wasting their devotions on false gods. The implicit Christian standard in *The Knight's Tale* is thereby indicated, and a focus provided for Christian distrust of the 'rytes of payens'. Particularly striking is the cousins' impression that the gods act arbitrarily and without a fixed standard of justice. This suspicion proves to have been well-founded, as an examination of their callous treatment of Arcite will indicate.

IV   'GODDES SPEKEN IN AMPHIBOLOGIES':
THE AMBIGUOUS ORACLE

Boccaccio was more interested in Arcita than in Palemone—a fitting sub-title for *Il Teseida* would be, 'The Death of Arcita'. Arcita sees Emilia first, and Boccaccio seems to think that he deserved her most. Moreover, Arcita's appeal to Mars comes first in Boccaccio's sequence of prayers to the pagan gods. By contrast, Chaucer's Palamon sees Emelye first, his prayer to Venus comes first, and the story is referred to as 'Palamon and Emelye' (I, 3107). However, these should be taken as hints of Palamon's ultimate victory, and not mistaken for an attempt to establish the primacy of Palamon's character. Palamon and Arcite may have different personalities (as has been argued above) but they are equally honourable and brave as knights, equally ardent as lovers, and equally

135

limited as pagans. Even the most wise Theseus cannot judge which is the more worthy of Emelye:

> 'Ech of you bothe is worthy, doutelees,
> To wedden whan tyme is . . .'
>
> (I, 1831–2)

There is no suggestion that Palamon was the most deserving, or indeed that Emelye got the man who loved her most. The cousins are equally worthy men—and that, I suggest, is precisely Chaucer's point. Had Palamon deserved Emelye more than Arcite, one could have argued that the pagan gods had acted properly and justly in judging that he should have her. But there is no divine justice in *The Knight's Tale*: the pagan gods act arbitrarily and capriciously, and they have their favourites.[79] Arcite loses his life and his lady simply because he prayed to the wrong god, and because Saturn had a grudge against his race. Palamon wins Emelye because he had the good luck—one can hardly call it good judgment—and the personality to pray to Venus.

It might be objected that, technically speaking, Mars and Saturn are within their rights: after all, Arcite asked for victory, not for Emelye. But it is obvious that Arcite is interested in victory not for its own sake, but as a means to an end, namely, the winning of Emelye. This is made very clear in his address to Mars:

> 'wel I woot, er she me mercy heete,
> I moot with strengthe wynne hire in the place,
> And, wel I woot, withouten help or grace
> Of thee, ne may my strengthe noght availle.
> Thanne help me, lord, tomorwe in my bataille . . .'
>
> (I, 2398–402)

Thus the gods' legalism is both mean and misleading. They fail to provide Arcite with full information concerning his future; they are guilty, at least, of what a Christian would call a sin of omission. We already have noted the common late-medieval conviction (as held by Vincent of Beauvais, Holcot and others) that the gentile gods, who were really demons, warned the 'ancient' pagans about certain future events in order to lead them to wreck and ruin (cf. pp. 33–7 and 81 above). The intimation of victory given to Arcite in the temple of Mars (2427–33) should perhaps be regarded in this light. From the image of Mars comes the mumbled word, 'Victorie!', which Arcite naturally interprets as meaning total victory, including the possession of Emelye. It transpires that he had been granted mere victory in battle.

Our understanding of this episode, which largely is Chaucer's invention, is crucial for our understanding of *The Knight's Tale* as a whole. In *Il Teseida*, Boccaccio recounts how Arcite's prayer arrives at the heavenly house of Mars, whereupon the god makes his way to the earthly temple in which his devotee is praying.[80] As soon as the temple hears its sovereign god, it begins to tremble and its gates begin to roar, so that Arcita is very much afraid. The votive fires which he has kindled burn with a brighter glow, the earth emits a marvellous aroma and the smoke of the incense draws near the image erected in honour of Mars. The armour on this statue moves of its own accord and resounds with sweet music, and 'signs' are given to 'wondering Arcita' that his prayer has been heard. And so, Boccaccio continues, the young man rests content with the thought of achieving victory. He remains in the temple that night and receives other reassuring signs. Chaucer, it would seem, has made the response of Mars more definite and ultimately more damning as far as the character of the god is concerned. He seems to have been influenced by the commonplace of medieval classicism that demon-gods often deceived men through the agency of oracles and speaking images.[81]

In Trevet's commentary on *De Consolatione Philosophiae* Chaucer would have read the tale of how King Croesus had consulted the Delphic oracle concerning his projected war with Persia.[82] Apollo's answer was ambiguous: 'If Croesus crosses the Alys, a great kingdom will fall'. Croesus, reassured by this prediction, crossed the river Alys, and a great kingdom did fall—his own. The answer which Arcite receives from Mars is ambiguous in the same way. We are reminded of Criseyde's greatest theological insight:

> 'goddes speken in amphibologies,
> And, for a sooth, they tellen twenty lyes'.
>   (IV, 1406–7)

As was suggested in our previous chapter, here she has in mind Apollo, who was notorious for his ambiguous answers. Apollo is the special god of her father, Calkas, and it is significant that he too has a reputation for dissimulation—like god, like prophet. Diomede, skeptical of Calkas's prediction concerning the fall of Troy, complains that this dubious prophet may be leading the Greeks

> 'with ambages,
> That is to seyn, with double wordes slye,
> Swiche as men clepen a word with two visages . . .'
>   (V, 897–9)

Arcite is misled by what might be regarded as a 'double worde slye': Mars's word 'Victorie!' certainly has 'two visages'; the god of war is as deceitful as the demon of Delphi.[83]

In Chapter II it was explained that stories of deceptive pagan oracles occur in a wide variety of medieval works: in standard reference books like Vincent of Beauvais' *Speculum Historiale*, Jacob of Voragine's *Legenda Aurea* and Higden's *Polychronicon*, in Latin versions of the Troy legend such as Guido delle Colonne's *Historia Destructionis Troiae* and Joseph of Exeter's *De Bello Trojano*, and in Old French romances with an antique setting like the anonymous *Roman de Thebes* and Benoît de Sainte-Maure's *Roman de Troie*. I shall take as representative two episodes from John Lydgate's *Troy Book* and *Siege of Thebes*, these being free translations of Guido's *Historia* and the *Roman de Thebes* respectively.

In *The Troy Book*, IV, 6930–7035 Lydgate curses the false gods for not punishing the Greeks for their murder of Hecuba and Polyxena.[84] Those statues of wood and stone to which the pious Trojans prayed were inhabited by Satan, the old snake himself, who sought to lead them astray.

137

þat an evele chaunce
Come to þeis false goddes euerychoon!
And her statues of stokkes & of stoon,
In whiche þe serpent & þe olde snake,
Sathan hym silf, gan his dwellinge make;
And fraudently folkes to illude,
Ful sotilly kan hym silfe include
In ymagis, for to make his hold,
þat forged bene of siluer & of gold,—
þat by errour of false illusioun,
He hath y-brou3t to confusioun,
þoru3 myscreaunce, þe worþi kynde of man,
Siþen tyme þat aldirfirst be-gan
þe false honour of ydolatrie
And þe worship vn-to mawmetrie. . .

(IV, 6930–44)

All the pagan deities, Lydgate continues, sprang from the devil, as David bears witness in the Psalter where he writes expressly that 'þe goddes of paganysme rytes' are all fiends. Those who trust in them shall endure great mischief in this life and be damned in the next. In *The Siege of Thebes* our attention is focused on one idol in particular, the statue of Apollo which, although it stands in a splendid chariot of bright gold, is inhabited by an unclean spirit which

Be fraude only / and fals collusioun,
Answere gaf / to euery questioun,
Bryngyng the puple in ful gret errour,
Such as to hym dyden fals honour
Be Rytys vsed in the olde dawes
Aftere custome / of paganysmes lawes.

(I, 539–44)[85]

In both these episodes Lydgate emphasizes the contrast between the pagans' piety and the wickedness of the gods to whom it is directed. Edippus (=Oedipus) prays devoutly 'with full humble chere' and 'gret deuocioun' to Apollo, beseeching him on his knees for any sign whereby he might learn his lineage. The invisible fiend promptly orders him 'with a vois dredful and horrible' to go to Thebes, thereby setting him on the road to parricide, incest, madness and death (*Siege of Thebes*, I, 545–57). Similarly, Troy expected to prosper by the help of its gods,

Whom þei wer wont to honour & to serue
With Cerymonyes & with sacrifise

(IV, 7024–5)

Instead the town was destroyed, thus manifesting the result of pagan faith:

Here may 3 sen how þe venym bites,
At þe ende, of swiche olde rytes,
By evidence of þis noble toun.

(IV, 7029–31)

The great piety of Chaucer's pagans is striking also: each of the young people fervently worships his or her special god. Yet all this ardent devotion would seem to be misplaced, in view of the suffering which ensues. Like Edippus and the Trojans, they are deceived and deluded. Lydgate's rhetorical question—which may well reflect his understanding of the *Troilus* epilogue—is as relevant to them as it is to the hapless and helpless Trojans:

> What may now helpe her frauded fantasie
> Of al her olde false ydolatrie?
> Allas, allas! þei bouȝt it al to sore.
> *(The Troy Book,* IV, 7033–5)

This suggestion concerning the malevolence of the pagan deities seems to be substantiated by the way in which Chaucer handled the 'assembly of the gods' episode. Boccaccio had said simply that a new strife arose in the heavens between Venus and Mars, but the gods found a way to content both prayers:

> e si ne nacque in ciel novella lite
> intra Venere e Marte, ma trovata
> da lor fu via con maestrevol arte
> di far contenti i prieghi d'ogni parte.
> (VII, 67)[86]

Chaucer substitutes an argument among the gods, briefly alluding to Jupiter in his traditional role of peacemaker:

> And right anon swich strif ther is bigonne,
> For thilke grauntyng, in the hevene above,
> Bitwixe Venus, the goddesse of love,
> And Mars, the stierne god armypotente,
> That Juppiter was bisy it to stente . . .
> (I, 2438–42)

Significantly, it is 'pale Saturnus the colde', and not the benevolent Jupiter, who finds 'in his olde experience an art' which enables him to please the haggling gods (2443–6). We are left in no doubt concerning what kind of 'experience' Saturn has:

> 'Myn is the drenchyng in the see so wan;
> Myn is the prison in the derke cote;
> Myn is the stranglyng and hangyng by the throte,
> The murmure and the cherles rebellyng,
> The groynynge, and the pryvee empoysonyng . . .'
>
> (I, 2456–60)

Chaucer seems to have been indebted to the traditional description of Saturn as a malicious planet and hence a thoroughly unpleasant planet-god. For example, in Trevisa's translation of *De Proprietatibus Rerum* we read that

Saturnus is an yuel-willid planete, colde and drye, a ny3t planete, and heuy; and þerfore by fablis he is ipeyntid as an olde man. . . . And is pale in colour oþir wan as leed, and hath tweye dedliche qualitees, cooldnes and drynes. And þerfore a childe and oþir brood þat is conceyued and comeþ forþ vndir his lordschipe dyeþ oþir haþ wel yuel qualitees, for . . . he makþ a man brown and foule, mysdoynge, slowh and heuy, elynge and sory, seldome glade and merye oþir lau3hynge. . . . And he loueþ stink-inge beestis and vnclene, and soure þingis and scharpe, for in here complexioun melancolik humour haþ maistrie. . . . Vndir him is con-teyned lyf, buldinge, lore, and coolde place and drye. In dome and iugement he tokeneþ sorowe and wo and elyngenes.[87].

Bersuire repeats this account in the fifth book of his *Reductorium Morale*; in the fifteenth book (the *Ovidius Moralizatus*) he provides a moral allegory of Saturn as an old and depraved man.[88] Alain de Lille says that in the abode of Saturn, grief, groans, tears, discord, terror, sadness, wanness, mourning and injustice hold sway.[89] It would seem, then, that any course of action proposed by this unfortunate figure can be expected to be nasty and unjust.[90]

However, there was another (and less common) medieval tradition relating to Saturn which saw him in a very good light. Following Macrobius, Alexander Neckham credited him with wisdom: 'Saturn is rightly described as an old man by the philosophers for old men are of mature judgment'.[91] In his *Fulgentius Metaforalis*, John Ridevall interpreted Saturn as prudence and his four chil-as the virtues which attend prudence.[92] Jupiter represents the harmony of all the moral goods; Juno, the memory of past things; Neptune, the understand-ing and ordering of present things; and Pluto, the providence of future things. Bersuire incorporated this account into the second recension of his *Ovidius Moralizatus*, the version that Chaucer knew.[93].

Some critics, seeking to demonstrate that this 'good' tradition is dominant in Chaucer's depiction of Saturn, have focused their attention on lines 2443–52, where the age and wisdom of the planet-god are apparently praised:

> the pale Saturnus the colde,
> That knew so manye of aventures olde,
> Foond in his olde experience an art
> That he ful soone hath plesed every part.
> As sooth is seyd, elde hath greet avantage;
> In elde is bothe wysdom and usage;
> Men may the olde atrenne, and noght atrede.

But in context these words are heavily ironic, almost to the point of sarcasm. The long catalogue of horrid 'aventures olde' produced by the malevolent agency of the planet-god (2453–69) condemns him out of his own mouth—such is the 'wysdom and usage' of Saturn! In the following lines the knight remarks that

> Saturne anon, to stynten strif and drede,
> Al be it that it is agayn his kynde,
> Of al this strif he gan remedie fynde.
> (2450–2)

This has been interpreted as a declaration that Saturn is putting aside his normally nasty nature to produce something positive and constructive for once, a solution which will satisfy all parties (except the human testees, of course).[94] In my opinion, it continues the irony established in lines 2443–52, thereby warning the reader that Saturn's 'remedie' will be a medicine of the type that cures the ailment by killing the patient. After all, it is Jupiter's 'kynde' to 'stynten strif and drede'; yet the Jupiter of *The Knight's Tale* is a moral coward who, after a feeble attempt at peacemaking, relinquishes his proper role to his mischief-making father. It is possible, I suppose, to argue that the 'good tradition' relating to Saturn may have influenced the portrayal of the other aged father figure in the poem, namely Egeus,[95] whose speech in lines 2836–51 exemplifies all the virtues which (according to Ridevall and Bersuire) attend prudence: the harmony of all moral goods, the memory of past things, the understanding and ordering of present things, and the providence of future things. But the essence of Chaucer's Saturn is the common astrological 'picture' of the wicked old man.

In *The Knight's Tale* Saturn acts true to this type. He passes a death-sentence on Arcite, which he carries out himself: it is he (and not Venus, as in the *Teseida*) who asks Pluto to send the infernal fury which startles Arcite's horse (2684–91).[96] Saturn has no interest in justice or human merit; his concern is to reconcile the gods at whatever expense to human beings, and to indulge his ancient malice against Thebans (clearly intimated in lines 1328–31; cf. 1087–90). According to the astrologers, Jupiter constantly abates the malice of Saturn; in *The Knight's Tale*, Saturn seems to be abating the 'honeste' of Jupiter. 'Juppiter, the kyng' is not in such benevolent control of the pantheon as Theseus's depiction of him would suggest. Perhaps the reader is expected to have the reaction which Chaucer made explicit at the end of *Troilus and Criseyde*:

> Lo here, of payens corsed olde rites,
> Lo here, what alle hire goddes may availle;
> Lo here, thise wrecched worldes appetites;
> Lo here, the fyn and guerdoun for travaille
> Of Jove, Appollo, of Mars, of swich rascaille!
> (V, 1849–53)

It would seem then, that while Chaucer's Knight dislikes and distrusts the pagan gods, he has considerable respect and sympathy for the noble paganism of his characters, especially that of Theseus. We see into the heathen heaven— a privilege denied us in *Troilus*—and receive first-hand information about the disorganized haggling, the petty spites and the self interest, of its denizens. The difference between what the pagans think their gods are like and what they are really like is quite startling, and the gods fare very badly from the comparison. Quite clearly, the pagans deserve better gods than the ones they worship, as is most evident in the case of Theseus's reverence for Jupiter. It is as if he has created his god in his own image. Theseus possesses the qualities of 'witte and wisdome and resoun' in abundance, and naturally ascribes them to Jupiter; he wields power and exercises control over the pagan world of the poem, and believes that his god has such power and control. This noble view of Jupiter is very flattering to the god, but it does Theseus considerable credit: only an extremely noble pagan could attain such an enlightened view of deity.

For the regal 'Juppiter' of Theseus's speech does exist: he may be identified not with the ether or with a demon, but with the one true God who is known more fully to Christians. Bersuire interpreted the traditional 'picture' of Jupiter as an allegory of the Almighty;[97] Christians may regard Theseus's depiction of the 'prince and cause of alle thyng' as an incomplete but substantially correct description of their God. If ever a good pagan merited salvation, it is Theseus. Perhaps Chaucer wished us to make the inference.

However, although we may suspect that Chaucer regarded Theseus as a 'friend of God', there is no firm confirmation of this provided in the poem. The Knight also avoids discussing the issue of the fate of Arcite's soul, claiming that he has neither the knowledge nor the will to do so. Besides, in the register (i.e., the table of contents) of the authoritative book he is following, there is nothing mentioned about souls—an oblique way of saying that his source does not treat of the subject.[98]

> His spirit chaunged hous and wente ther,
> As I cam nevere, I kan nat tellen wher.
> Therfore I stynte, I nam no divinistre;
> Of soules fynde I nat in this registre,
> Ne me ne list thilke opinions to telle
> Of hem, though that they writen wher they dwelle.
> Arcite is coold, ther Mars his soule gye!
>
> (I, 2809-15)

As in *Troilus and Criseyde*, in *The Knight's Tale* Chaucer is preoccupied with what his pagan characters achieved during their lives, and it is quite clear that Theseus has achieved the most.

It has been said that Boccaccio's Teseo is 'closer to the ideal governor of a republic than to the traditional ruler of a medieval kingdom'.[99] In fact, this description fits Chaucer's hero much more exactly. Teseo is first and foremost a conqueror whose greatest delight is in fighting. Theseus, on the other hand, is as accomplished in philosophy (metaphysical, ethical and political) as he is in military matters, a suggestion which may be substantiated from the second prologue to Holcot's commentary on that Biblical 'Mirror for Princes', the Book of Wisdom. According to Holcot, the objective of wisdom is to dispose men in order and harmony.[100] Cicero speaks of a time before law and order were invented, when men lived like beasts, doing nothing by the guidance of reason but relying chiefly on physical strength. Then a great and wise man appeared, who assembled and gathered these rude men in accordance with a plan. When, through reason and eloquence, he made them listen to him, 'he transformed them from wild savages into a kind and gentle folk'. The same point was made, Holcot continues, by those poets who created the fable of Orpheus. As Boethius says in *De Consolatione Philosophiae* III pr. 12, he was so skilled a harpist that he could make the rivers stand still and the woods move, the hind to come together with the lion, and the hare with the hound. Orpheus really designates wise men (*sapientes*) whose task it is to reconcile in civilization men who are vicious and divided among themselves.[101] Holcot concludes this argument with Boethius's summary of the doctrine of Plato that 'those states would be happy where philosophers were kings or their governors were philosophers'. Philosophers 'must involve themselves in political affairs, lest the rule of nations be left to the base and wicked, bringing ruin and destruction on the good' (I pr. 4, 18–25).[102] Without wishing to imply that life in the ancient world depicted in *The Knight's Tale* is brutish (although it can be nasty and short), it may be pointed out that Chaucer's Theseus possesses in large measure all the essential qualities here commended by Holcot: he imposes law and order on anarchy and potential chaos, brings reason to bear on destructive passions, reconciles warring factions, and in general makes virtue of necessity. The state of Athens can be happy because its king is a philosopher, a *sapiens* in the subject-areas of ethics, politics and even metaphysics.

Chaucer's 'medievalization' of Boccaccio was carried out with a large measure of consistency, and I have sought to demonstrate that at least some of the principles at work may be illuminated through investigation of the attitudes to pagan antiquity which were current in fourteenth-century England. In such theological, encyclopaedic and historical works as Chaucer and his contemporaries read, one may find the basis for an approach to *Troilus and Criseyde* and *The Knight's Tale* which takes stock both of Chaucer's celebration of the achievements of good pagans and his fundamental detachment from such pagan limitations as the 'observaunces of judicial matere' and 'corsed olde rytes'. As a result of this inquiry, it should be recognized that the paganism in these poems is not mere background and setting, but an essential aspect of their overall meaning.

APPENDIX

Translation of Extracts from Trevet's Commentary on Boethius, De Consolatione Philosophiae

Translated by Edward Bower from the (unfinished) edition of the Latin text by E. T. Silk. Line references are to the edition of the *De Consolatione Philosophiae* in *Boethius: The Theological Tractates and The Consolation of Philosophy*, ed. H. F. Stewart, E. K. Rand and S. J. Tester, Loeb Classical Library (Cambridge, Mass., rev. ed. 1973).

I
TREVET'S COMMENTARY ON DE CONSOLATIONE PHILOSOPHIAE
II met. 8 (complete)

THAT THE WORLD The eighth and last metrum of this second book, called glyconic (which has been discussed above in the first book, sixth metrum). Because Philosophy had said above that friends are the most precious kind of riches, arising from this in this metrum he commends love; firstly divine love, showing how the harmony of the world is brought about by it; secondly the love of men, teaching how human friendship is brought about by it [22] HE BY SACRED. So he says first [14] LOVE RULING LAND AND SEA AND REIGNING IN HEAVEN that is divine love by which he [i.e. God] brings forth and rules his creatures [13] MAKES FIRM THIS NEXUS that is the harmony of things [1] THAT THE WORLD IN SETTLED CERTAINTY that is in a sure compact [2] BRINGS ABOUT ITS HARMONIOUS CHANGES viz. according to the four seasons of the year and the alternation of day and night [3] THAT THE WARRING SEEDS i.e. the elements of which created things are made as if from seeds [4] KEEP PERPETUAL COMPACT viz. in accordance with reciprocal generation [5] THAT PHOEBUS i.e. the sun WITH HIS GOLDEN CHARIOT BRINGS FORTH THE ROSEATE DAY this is set forth above in the third metrum [7] THAT PHOEBE i.e. the moon SHOULD RULE THE NIGHTS WHICH HESPERUS HAS DRAWN FORTH Hesperus is said to draw forth the night because it appears at the beginning of the night, as mentioned above in the first book, fifth metrum [9] THAT THE EAGER SEA viz. eager to get out as it seems to be when it is flowing [10] MAY KEEP THE WAVES IN CHECK WITHIN FIXED BOUNDS [11] LEST IT BE ABLE TO STRETCH i.e. extend ITS BROAD LIMITS OVER THE WIDE-RANGING EARTH as if to say so that it may not completely cover the earth. [16] IT viz. divine love IF IT RELAX

THE REINS i.e. the system of control by which things are curbed within fixed limits [17] WHATEVER NOW LOVES AND IS LOVED i.e. is bound together in harmony; he puts 'love' for 'harmony', for 'love' is not the appropriate word in connection with non-rational things [18] WILL AT ONCE MAKE WAR AND MAY STRIVE i.e. will strive TO BREAK UP THE FABRIC viz. of the world [19] WHICH NOW IN FAITHFUL ALLIANCE i.e. in a harmonious compact [20] THEY URGE ON IN ITS FAIR MOTIONS i.e. make it move in an ordered manner.

Then when he says [22] HERE IN SACRED he shows how by love human friendship is formed, saying HE i.e. love BINDS AND HOLDS PEOPLE ALSO YOKED TOGETHER IN SACRED BOND i.e. of friendship and [24] HE i.e. love SEALS THE SACRED BOND i.e. the sacrament OF MAR-RIAGE WITH CHASTE LOVES viz. of husband and wife [26] HE ALSO viz. love DICTATES HIS LAWS i.e. imposes the laws of friendship ON LOYAL COMRADES. And because all this results from divine love as its origin he therefore adds [28] O HAPPY RACE OF MEN viz. I say that they would be [i.e. happy] [29] IF LOVE BY WHICH HEAVEN IS RULED i.e. divine love which causes harmony in heavenly things WERE TO RULE YOUR HEARTS viz. by causing in them the harmony of friendship.

II
TREVET'S COMMENTARY ON
DE CONSOLATIONE
PHILOSOPHIAE
V pr. 3 AND V pr. 4 (extracts)

V pr. 3

THEN I The third prose, in which he raises objections to what has been said, showing that free choice and providence cannot exist together. It is divided into two parts, in the first of which he shows the incompatibility of providence and free choice. In the second on this question he puts the exclamation in the third metrum as follows: [met. 3, 1] WHAT DISCORDANT. On the first point he does two things. First he intimates that what has been said is open to doubt. Secondly he states the reason for that doubt as follows: [4] TOO MUCH, I SAY. On the first, he proceeds as follows: first Boethius intimates that he is in doubt by reason of what has been said, saying [1] THEN, i.e. when Philosophy has finally finished speaking LOOK that is behold I SAY I AM AGAIN CONFOUNDED BY A STILL MORE DIFFICULT PROBLEM for a man sometimes encounters a greater problem in expounding truth than in expounding falsehood. Accordingly to avoid difficulty many abandon truth and state what is false, as is clear in the case of Zeno, who wishing to avoid the difficulty about traversing infinity denied the existence of motion, as is made clear by the philosopher [Aristotle] in the sixth and eighth books of the *Physics*. Secondly Philosophy asks what this doubt is, saying [2] WHAT, SHE SAYS, IS THAT? i.e. that ambiguity FOR I ALREADY CONJECTURE i.e. foresee WHAT PERTURBS i.e. disturbs YOU. Philosophy here conjectures from a matter which commonly arises, because commonly those who talk about providence and free choice express doubts about their compatibility. Then when he says [4] INQUAM Boethius expresses his own doubt, showing that providence and free will are not compatible. On this point he does two things; first he rejects their compatibility, secondly he excludes the ways by which some have sought to defend providence [65] WHAT THEREFORE? On the first he makes three points, the second beginning [52] FURTHERMORE, AS WHEN; the third [55] FINALLY. On the first point he does two things; first he states the point; secondly he excludes a solution which can be given as follows: [16] NOR DO I APPROVE. So, expressing his doubt Boethius says [4] IT SEEMS, I SAY, TO BE TOO INCONSISTENT AND INCOMPATIBLE FOR GOD TO FORESEE EVERYTHING AND FOR ANY FREEDOM OF CHOICE TO EXIST.

That those two things are inconsistent and incompatible he goes on to prove immediately, saying [6] FOR IF GOD FORESEES ALL AND CAN IN NO WAY BE IN ERROR, IT IS NECESSARY FOR THAT TO HAPPEN WHICH PROVIDENCE FORESEES IS TO HAPPEN because if it did not happen, providence would be in error. [8] WHEREFORE IF FROM ETERNITY HE FOREKNOWS NOT ONLY i.e. not solely THE ACTIONS OF MEN BUT ALSO THEIR COUNSELS AND WILLS, THERE WILL BE NO FREEDOM OF WILL sc. because everything happens of necessity; for freedom does not exist in respect of things which happen of necessity. That God knows beforehand by his providence all voluntary acts is clear from what has already been said, wherefore he sets this down as plain fact [10] FOR NO OTHER ACTION NOR ANY WILL i.e. voluntary action WILL BE ABLE TO EXIST EXCEPT THOSE WHICH INFALLIBLE DIVINE PROVIDENCE HAS PRESAGED i.e. foreknown, nor can it turn out otherwise than has been foreseen. [13] FOR IF THEY COULD BE TURNED ASIDE IN ANOTHER DIRECTION sc. to happen differently THAN WAS FORESEEN, THERE WILL BE NO LONGER FIRM FOREKNOWLEDGE OF THE FUTURE BUT RATHER UNCERTAIN OPINION because there is knowledge of those things which cannot be otherwise, as is made clear by the philosopher [Aristotle] in the first book of the *Posterior Analytics*, but opinion of things which can be as they are but can also be otherwise WHICH I JUDGE IT TO BE IMPIOUS TO BELIEVE OF GOD because this would detract greatly from the nobility of his understanding; so foreknowledge and freedom of will cannot exist together.

Then when he says [16] FOR NEITHER THAT (REASON) he excludes one answer which can be given, and does two things in this connection; first he gives the answer; then he excludes it as follows: [25] AS IF INDEED. He says therefore [16] FOR I DO NOT ACCEPT i.e. approve THAT ANSWER BY WHICH SOME BELIEVE THAT THEY CAN LOOSEN THE KNOT i.e. the difficulty OF THE QUESTION. [18] FOR THEY SAY THAT A THING WILL NOT COME ABOUT BECAUSE PROVIDENCE HAS FORESEEN THAT IT WILL HAPPEN, BUT RATHER ON THE CONTRARY, SINCE A THING i.e. anything IS GOING TO HAPPEN IT CANNOT ESCAPE THE NOTICE OF DIVINE PROVIDENCE, as if to say that the happening of events is the cause of foreknowledge and therefore the necessity of foreknowledge must be deduced from the occurrence of the event and not vice versa, and this is what he means by saying IN THIS WAY THE NECESSITY sc. that which is deduced about the happening of the event

IS TRANSFERRED TO THE OPPOSITE SIDE sc. that it should be concluded about the foreknowledge, whence he adds [23] AND IT IS NOT NECESSARY THAT THE THINGS FORESEEN SHOULD HAPPEN, BUT THE THINGS WHICH ARE TO HAPPEN MUST BE FORESEEN. Then when he says [25] AS IF INDEED he excludes this answer. Here we should reflect that this seems to have been the answer of Origen, who says in expounding the Letter to the Romans: a thing will not happen because God knows it will happen, but because it will happen it is therefore known by God before it can happen. This can be understood in two ways: either that the occurrence of the event is the cause of the foreknowledge in the sense that one is a consequence of the other and so the answer is true but not adequate; or in the sense that the event is the cause of the foreknowledge in respect of its existence, and so it is false, and in this sense it is disapproved of here by Boethius. Inasmuch as Origen denies that God's knowledge is the cause of the occurrence of the event, we must understand this of knowledge taken in the precise sense, without the assumption of will. So he excludes this answer as understood in this mistaken sense. In this connection he does two things; first he says that it has no relevance to the purpose of the present doubt; secondly, he shows that it is untrue, in the following passage [46] NOW INDEED.

He says therefore [25] AS IF THE ISSUE WERE i.e. the answer proceeds as if the problem lay in the question WHICH IS THE CAUSE OF WHICH THING: IS THE FOREKNOWLEDGE THE CAUSE OF THE NECESSITY OF FUTURE EVENTS, OR IS THE NECESSITY OF FUTURE EVENTS THE CAUSE OF THE FOREKNOWLEDGE? but it is not our intention to ask this AND NOT THAT i.e. the reply proceeds as if WE WERE NOT TRYING TO DEMONSTRATE THE FOLLOWING sc. THAT IT IS NECESSARY THAT THINGS KNOWN BEFOREHAND SHOULD HAPPEN WHATEVER THE CAUSAL SEQUENCE MAY BE and yet this is what we have in mind EVEN IF i.e. although THE FOREKNOWLEDGE DOES NOT SEEM TO INVOLVE FOR FUTURE EVENTS THE NECESSITY OF HAPPENING. And to make the intention plainer he makes it clear by an example, saying [31] FOR INDEED IF A PERSON IS SITTING DOWN, THE OPINION WHICH CONJECTURES THAT HE IS SITTING DOWN MUST BE TRUE, AND VICE VERSA sc. just as, given the sitting, we conclude that the opinion is necessarily true, so on the contrary, given the truth of the opinion, we conclude that there is necessity as far as the sitting is concerned, because if THE OPINION THAT HE IS SITTING IS TRUE OF A PERSON, HE MUST IN FACT BE SITTING. [35] IN EITHER CASE THEREFORE sc. in the opinion and in the sitter THERE IS NECESSITY; IN THE ONE i.e. the sitter THAT sc. the necessity OF SITTING, IN THE OTHER sc. the opinion THAT OF BEING TRUE sc. the necessity. [36] BUT A PERSON IS NOT SITTING BECAUSE THE OPINION IS TRUE, i.e. the truth of the opinion is not the cause of the sitting but vice versa, whence he adds [37] BUT THIS sc. the opinion IS TRUE RATHER SINCE THE SITTING DOWN OF A PERSON HAS PRECEDED IT sc. in the order of causation. [39] AND SO ALTHOUGH THE CAUSE OF THE TRUTH PROCEEDS FROM THE ONE PART, YET THERE IS A COMMON NECESSITY IN BOTH PARTS. And it is appropriate to argue in the same way about providence in the case of things which are foreseen, whence he says [41] IT IS OPEN TO ARGUE i.e. it is clearly possible by rational argument to draw conclusions SIMILARLY ABOUT PROVIDENCE AND FUTURE EVENTS. [42] FOR EVEN IF i.e. although THEY ARE FORESEEN MERELY BECAUSE THEY ARE GOING TO HAPPEN so that causality does not arise from providence, whence he says THEY DO NOT IN FACT HAPPEN BECAUSE THEY ARE FORESEEN, NEVERTHELESS HOWEVER IT IS NECESSARY FOR WHAT IS TO COME TO BE FORESEEN BY GOD, OR FOR WHAT IS FORESEEN TO HAPPEN, because there is necessity in both parts, though causality only in one WHICH ALONE IS ENOUGH TO ELIMIN-ATE FREEDOM OF CHOICE.

Then when he says [46] NOW INDEED HOW he shows that that answer contains within itself some falsity, sc. because it posits that something temporal is the cause of something eternal, whence he says NOW INDEED HOW PREPOSTEROUS IT IS sc. it clearly is THAT THE OCCURRENCE OF TEMPORAL THINGS SHOULD BE SAID TO BE THE CAUSE OF ETERNAL FOREKNOWLEDGE, but this is stated in that answer. Where-fore he adds [48] BUT TO THINK THAT GOD FORESEES THE FU-TURE BECAUSE IT IS GOING TO HAPPEN—WHAT IS THIS BUT TO THINK THAT THINGS WHICH HAVE HAPPENED IN THE PAST ARE THE CAUSE OF SUPREME PROVIDENCE? as if they were identical. Then when he says [52] FURTHERMORE he adds a second reason to the principal argument and argues from proportion saying FURTHERMORE sc. in addition to what has been said we must add this reason JUST AS WHEN I KNOW SOMETHING EXISTS IT MUST IN FACT EXIST because the relationship of the knowledge of the present to that present is the same as the knowledge of the future to that future, so therefore it comes about that the happening of something known beforehand cannot be avoided.

V pr. 4

THEN SHE The fourth prose of the fifth book in which Philosophy begins to resolve that doubt of Boethius, and this part is divided into two; in the first of these she points out a difficulty involved in that doubt, in the second she begins to resolve that doubt as follows: [10] WHICH THUS AT LAST. In connection with the first she does two things; first she shows the difficulty of this doubt, secondly she assigns a reason for the difficulty as follows: [6] OF WHICH OBSCURITY. She therefore makes the difficulty of this doubt clear first of all by showing that for men to be troubled by this difficulty is not a new thing but an old one, saying [1] THEN SHE sc. Philosophy SAYS, THIS COM-PLAINT ABOUT PROVIDENCE IS AN OLD ONE. Secondly she shows the difficulty of this by the fact that great men who treated it were unable to resolve it. Hence he says that THIS COMPLAINT WAS VIGOROUSLY PURSUED i.e. discussed BY M. TULLIUS saying WHEN HE DISTRI-BUTED DIVINATION sc. in the book *On Divination* where he divides divination into many species; and not only this but A MATTER INVESTI-GATED VERY LONG AND VERY DEEPLY BY YOURSELF ALSO, BUT BY NO MEANS i.e. nowhere DELIGENTLY AND DECIDEDLY ENOUGH EXPLAINED BY ANY OF YOU SO FAR, in fact Tullius being unable to resolve that difficulty flatly denies providence and foreknowledge of the future by God in the above mentioned book. And this was so that he could keep (free choice). Then when she says [6] OF WHICH OBSCURITY she assigns a reason for this difficulty saying OF WHICH OBSCURITY i.e. problem or difficulty THE CAUSE IS THAT THE ACTION OF HUMAN REASON CANNOT APPROACH i.e. be applied to the comprehension of THE SIMPLICITY OF THE DIVINE FOREKNOWLEDGE, WHICH sc. the simplicity of the divine foreknowledge IF IT COULD BE CONCEIVED IN ANY WAY, WILL LEAVE NO DOUBT REMAINING. Then when she says [10] WHICH THUS she begins to resolve the difficulty. In this connection she does two things; first she sets out the way by which she intends to proceed on the resolution of this doubt; in the second part she pursues the subject in accordance with the method thus set out [11] I ASK. The method of procedure is that first, after the manner of a disputation, she discusses the matter put forward by Boethius, and secondly as if making a determination [i.e. making an authoritative statement of the correct doctrine] she resolves the matter.

ABBREVIATIONS

AHDLMA	*Archives d'histoire doctrinale et littéraire du moyen âge*
Bersuire, *Reductorium Morale*	Petrus Berchorius, *Reductorium Morale* (Venice, 1583)
Bersuire, *Ovidius Moralizatus*, ed. Engels	*Petrus Berchorius: Reductorium Morale, lib. xv: Ovidius Moralizatus, cap. i: De Formis Figurisque Deorum*, ed. J. Engels, Werkmaterial iii (Utrecht, 1966)
Bradwardine, Thomas	*De Causa Dei contra Pelagium et de virtute causarum ad suos Mertonenses*, ed. H. Savile (London, 1618)
Chaucer: Works	*The Works of Geoffrey Chaucer*, ed. F. N. Robinson, 2nd ed. (London, 1957)
EETS ES	Early English Text Society, Extra Series
EETS OS	Early English Text Society, Original Series
ELH	*English Literary History*
Holcot, *Sap. Sal. praelectiones*	Robert Holcot, *Sapientiae Regis Salamonis praelectiones* (Basel, 1586)
JEGP	*Journal of English and Germanic Philology*
John of Wales, *Communiloquium*	*Summa de regimine vite humane s. margarita doctrorum* (Lyon, 1511), fols 1ʳ–139ᵛ.
John of Wales, *Compendiloquium*	*Florilegium de Vita et Dictis Philosophorum et Breviloquium de Sapientia Sanctorum*, ed. Luke Wadding (Rome, 1655), pp. 19–426
JWCI	*Journal of the Warburg and Courtauld Institutes*
Migne, *PL*	*Patrologia Latina*, ed. J.-P. Migne (Paris, 1844–64)
MLQ	*Modern Language Quarterly*
MP	*Modern Philology*
MS	*Mediaeval Studies*
PBB	*Beiträge zur Geschichte der deutschen Sprache und Literatur*
PMLA	*Publications of the Modern Language Association of America*
Polychronicon Ranulphi	*Polychronicon Ranulphi Higden; together with the English translations of John Trevisa*

	and of an unknown writer of the fifteenth century, ed. C. Babington and J. R. Lumby (London, 1865–86)
RES	*Review of English Studies*
Ridevall, *Fulgentius Metaforalis*	John Ridevall, *Fulgentius Metaforalis*, ed. H. Liebeschütz, Studien der Bibliothek Warburg, iv (Leipzig, 1926)
RSPT	*Revue des sciences philosophiques et théologiques*
SP	*Studies in Philology*
Trevet, commentary on Boethius	Nicholas Trevet, commentary on the *De Consolatione Philosophiae* of Boethius; unfinished edition by the late E. T. Silk
Vincent of Beauvais, *Speculum Maius*	Vincent of Beauvais, *Speculum Maius* (Venice, 1591)

NOTES

INTRODUCTION

1 *La Chanson de Roland*, 1015 (ed. C. Segre, Documenti di Filologia, xvi, (Milan and Naples, 1971), 190).
2 *Le Roman de la Rose*, 7061–2 (ed. E. Langlois (Paris, 1914–24), iii, 28; trans. C. Dahlberg, *The Romance of the Rose by Guillaume de Lorris and Jean de Meun* (Princeton, New Jersey, 1971), pp. 134–5).
3 This is argued in Chapter 4 of my forthcoming book *Medieval Theory of Authorship: Scholastic Literary Attitudes in the Later Middle Ages.*
4 In the later Middle Ages the term *antiqui* could designate the 'ancient' writers of Greco–Latin antiquity as opposed to 'modern' Christians, those 'ancient' people who lived before the time of Christ as opposed to those who live after it, or the 'ancient' Church Fathers as opposed to 'modern' medieval writers. Throughout this book *'antiqui'* and *'moderni'* are used in the first two senses only. For discussion see M.-D. Chenu, *'Antiqui, Moderni'*, *RSPT*, xvii (1928), 82–94. In scholasticism a more specialised sense developed, whereby *'antiqui'* could refer to previous generations of scholars, while *'moderni'* referred to the scholars of one's own generation. When designating one's opponents, *'moderni'* could have a derogatory connotation: see Philotheus Boehner, *Collected Articles on Ockham*, ed. E. M. Buytaert, Franciscan Institute Publications, Philosophy Series, xii (New York, 1958), 40–1; cf. Janet Coleman, *Piers Plowman and the 'Moderni'*, Letture di pensiero e d'arte (Rome, 1981).
5 See D. Comparetti, *Vergil in the Middle Ages*, trans. E. F. M. Benecke (London, 1895), pp. 99–103; cf. pp. 219–31, on Dante's attitude to Virgil.
6 *The Oxford Book of Medieval Latin Verse*, ed. F. J. E. Raby (Oxford, 1959), p. 392. For commonplace medieval attitudes to sibyls see Vincent of Beauvais, *Speculum Historiale*, ii.100 (*Speculum Maius*, iv, fol. 28ʳ).
7 See *Giles of Rome, De Erroribus Philosophorum*, ed. J. Koch and trans. J. O. Riedl (Milwaukee, 1944).
8 In the case of *Patience* I am thinking of lines 165–240, in which Jonah converts the pagan seafarers to monotheism: see *Patience*, ed. J. J. Anderson (Manchester, 1969), 36–9. *St Erkenwald, The Travels of Sir John Mandeville, Patience, Alexander B, The Awntyrs of Arthure, Piers Plowman* and (briefly) *Troilus and Criseyde* are discussed in respect of their literary paganism by T. G. Hahn, *God's Friends: Virtuous Heathen in Later Medieval Thought and English Literature* (Ph.d. thesis, University of California, Los Angeles, 1974).
9 Hahn, *God's Friends*, p. 152.
10 *Biblia Sacra cum Glossa Ordinaria et Postilla Nicolai Lyrani* (Lyon, 1589), iii, cols 1917–8.
11 For the anonymous *Liber Philosophorum* see *The Dicts and Sayings of the Philosophers*, ed. C. F. Bühler, EETS OS ccii (London, 1941), pp. x–xi; for Burley see the edition by H. Knust (Tübingen, 1886). Full references to the other works mentioned here may be found in my table of Abbreviations.
12 For discussion see D. L. Douie, *Archbishop Pecham* (Oxford, 1952), pp. 272–301; F. Van Steenberghen, *Aristotle in the West: The Origins of Latin Aristotelianism*, trans. L. Johnston (Louvain, 1955), pp. 230–8; G. Leff, *Paris and Oxford Universi-*

ties in the Thirteenth and Fourteenth Centuries (New York, 1968), pp. 222–40; and especially R. Hissette, *Enquête sur les 219 articles condamnés à Paris le 7 Mars 1277*, Philosophes Médiévaux, xxii (Louvain and Paris, 1977).

13 *The Medieval Attitude toward Astrology, particularly in England*, Yale Studies in English, lx (New Haven, 1920), pp. 145, 148. For a sensible approach to the problem see Chauncey Wood's chapter on 'Chaucer's Attitude toward Astrology' in his *Chaucer and the Country of the Stars* (Princeton, 1970), pp. 3–50.

14 The literature on late-medieval nominalism is vast. For the purposes of this study, the following have been especially helpful: P. Vignaux, *Justification et prédestination au XIVᵉ siècle* (Paris, 1934), and *Nominalisme au XIVe siècle* (Montreal and Paris, 1948); the compendium of William of Ockham's theological ideas (perhaps assembled by Robert Holcot) edited by L. Baudry as *Le 'Tractatus de principiis theologiae' attribué à Guillaume d'Occam* (Paris, 1936); R. Guelley, *Philosophie et théologie chez Guillaume d'Ockham* (Louvain and Paris, 1947); L. Baudry, *Lexique philosophique de Guillaume d'Occam* (Paris, 1957); H. A. Oberman, *The Harvest of Medieval Theology: Gabriel Biel and Late Medieval Nominalism* (Grand Rapids, Michigan, 1967); *William of Ockham: Predestination, God's Foreknowledge, and Future Contingents*, trans. M. M. Adams and N. Kretzmann (New York, 1969); Gordon Leff, *William of Ockham* (Manchester, 1975).

15 See p. 11.

16 *The Scale of Perfection*, ii.3, ed. S. S. Hussey, *An Edition, from the Manuscripts, of Book ii of Walter Hilton's Scale of Perfection* (Ph.d. thesis, University of London, 1962), pp. 7–9.

17 Note the striking verbal parallels between this passage and the statement made by Langland's Ymaginatif (which arises out of his defence of the proposition that the good pagan Trajan is saved) to the effect that God will recognise the 'truþe' of the man who observes the best law available to him:

> 'Ac truþe þat trespased neuere ne trauersed ayeins his lawe,
> But lyueþ as his lawe techeþ and leueþ þer be no bettre,
> And if þer were he wolde amende, and in swich wille deieþ —
> Ne wolde neuere trewe god but [trewe] truþe were allowed'.

Piers Plowman, B-text, XII, 287–90, ed. G. Kane and E. T. Donaldson (London, 1975), p. 483. Clearly, Ymaginatif and Hilton are referring to the same doctrine. John Trevisa agreed with Hilton rather than with Ymaginatif: see above p. 55.

18 For discussion see above pp. 11, 55–9. There have been several attempts to relate some of Chaucer's ideas and attitudes to late-medieval nominalism and so-called skepticism, notably Sheila Delany, *Chaucer's House of Fame: The Poetics of Skeptical Fideism* (Chicago and London, 1972); John Gardner, *The Poetry of Chaucer* (Carbondale, Illinois, 1977), pp. ix, xvii, xviii, 43, 156, 254, 298, 316, 337; R. A. Peck, 'Chaucer and the Nominalist Questions', *Speculum*, liii (1978), 745–60. No specific and indubitable instances of nominalist influence on Chaucer have, however, been provided as yet; we are offered analogies of the most general kind. Most of the scholastic texts cited in such discussions fail to meet the two aspects of the criterion of historical plausibility described on pp. 9–10 above. In view of the danger of solipsism, it seems prudent, at the outset, to investigate thoroughly the philosophical ideas in known Chaucer sources, to determine how adequate they are for our interpretative needs. Only when this is done—and we have a long way to go—should we turn to tangential texts or to the 'general intellectual climate of the age' (assuming that such a thing exists, and, if so, that we can agree on its nature—which seems highly unlikely).

19 *The Oxford Dictionary of the Christian Church*, ed. F. L. Cross, 2nd ed. (Oxford, 1974), s,v. 'Saracens', p. 1236.

20 Thomas Aquinas became aware of the importance of the missionary efforts in Spain

and North Africa, perhaps due to Raymond of Peñafort, who after serving as Master General of the Order of Preachers for two years (1238–40), resigned to work in Barcelona. According to tradition, it was in response to Raymond's request that he wrote 'a work against the errors of the infidels that would both take away the thick atmosphere of darkness, and unfold the doctrine of true light to those willing to believe'. This work, the *Summa contra Gentiles* (1259–64), was intended for experienced missionaries rather than beginners; it may also have been intended to counter the errors of the Parisian 'Gentiles', i.e. those contemporaries of Aquinas who had been led astray by Arabic philosophers. See J. A. Weisheipl, *Friar Thomas d'Aquino* (Oxford, 1975), pp. 130–3; M.-D. Chenu, *Toward understanding St Thomas*, trans. A.-M. Landry and D. Hughes (Chicago, 1964), pp. 288–92.

21 See R. W. Southern, *Western Views of Islam in the Middle Ages* (Cambridge, Mass., 1962), p. 73; cf. Coleman, *Piers Plowman and the 'Moderni'*, pp. 115–6.

22 *De Causa Dei*, i.1, corollarium 16 (ed. Savile, p. 12); cf. *The Travels of Marco Polo*, ch. 2, trans. R. E. Latham (Harmondsworth, 1958), p. 68.

23 See the useful summary in J. F. Poag, *Wolfram von Eschenbach* (New York, 1972), pp. 102, 104–5.

24 See Carl Lofmark, *Rennewart in Wolfram's 'Willehalm'* (Cambridge, 1972), pp. 129–35, esp. p. 135.

25 I have taken the term 'historial' poet from C. S. Lewis, 'What Chaucer really did to *Il Filostrato*', rept. in *Chaucer Criticism*, ed. R. J. Schoeck and Jerome Taylor (Notre Dame, Indiana, 1960–1), ii, 16–33 (pp. 19–21).

26 *Sir Philip Sidney: An Apology for Poetry*, ed. G. Shepherd (London, 1965), p. 111.

27 L. B. Wright, *Middle Class Culture in Elizabethan England* (London, 1964), p. 297.

CHAPTER 1

1 E. D. Hirsch, *The Aims of Interpretation* (Chicago and London, 1976), pp. 7–8.

2 For the concept of 'alterity' see H. R. Jauss, *Alterität und Modernität der mittelalterlichen Literatur* (Munich, 1977); also his article 'The Alterity and Modernity of Medieval Literature', *New Literary History*, x (1979), 385–90. See further the important reservations expressed by John Burrow, 'The Alterity of Medieval Literature', *ibid.*, pp. 385–90.

3 The following few pages constitute a reworking of part of my paper 'Chaucer and Comparative Literary Theory', in *New Perspectives in Chaucer Criticism*, ed. D. M. Rose (Norman, Oklahoma, 1981), pp. 53–69.

4 Hirsch, *The Aims of Interpretation*, p. 41.

5 See Chenu, *Toward Understanding St Thomas*, p. 144; P. C. Spicq, *Esquisse d'une histoire de l'exégèse latine au moyen âge*, Bibliothèque Thomiste, xxvi (Paris, 1944), p. 250.

6 A useful review of Boccaccio's influence on Chaucer and up-to-date Bibliography are included in N. R. Havely, *Chaucer's Boccaccio*, Chaucer Studies, iii (Woodbridge, 1980). R. A. Pratt has suggested that Chaucer used a French translation of *Il Filostrato*: 'Chaucer and *Le Roman de Troyle et de Criseida*', *SP*, liii (1956), 509–39. However, Louis de Beauvau, its putative author, wrote much later than Chaucer.

7 On the nature of these works, and their influence on Chaucer, see especially K. Young, *The Origin and Development of the Story of Troilus and Criseyde* (London, 1908); G. L. Kittredge, 'Chaucer's Lollius', *Harvard Studies in Classical Philology*, xxviii (1917), 47–133; R. K. Root, 'Chaucer's Dares', *MP*, xv (1917), 1–22, and the excellent notes in his edition of *Troilus and Criseyde* (Princeton, 1945); J. C. McGalliard, *Classical Mythology in certain Mediaeval Treatments of the Legends of Troy, Thebes, and Aeneas: A Study in the Literary Paganism of the Middle Ages*

(Ph.d. thesis, Harvard University, 1930); E. B. Atwood, *English Versions of the Historia Trojana* (Ph.d. thesis, University of Virginia, 1932); R. M. Lumiansky, 'The Story of Troilus and Briseida according to Benoît and Guido', *Speculum*, xxix (1954), 727–33; W. B. Wigginton, *The Nature and Significance of the Late Medieval Troy Story: A Study of Guido delle Colonne's Historia Destructionis Troiae* (Ph.d. thesis, Rutgers University, 1965); C. David Benson, *The History of Troy in Middle English Literature* (Woodbridge, 1980).

8 On Benoît's *Roman* as a *roman d'antiquité* see especially Mary F. Baskerville, *Two Studies in the Redaction of the Medieval Troy Story: Guido delle Colonne's Historia Destructionis Troiae and the Alliterative Destruction of Troy* (Ph.d. thesis, Columbia University, 1978), pp. 7–9.

9 See K. O. Petersen, 'Chaucer and Trivet', *PMLA*, xviii (1903), 173–93; B. L. Jefferson, *Chaucer and the 'Consolation of Philosophy' of Boethius* (Princeton, 1917), pp. 1–15; E. T. Silk, *Cambridge MS Ii.3.21 and the Relation of Chaucer's Boethius to Trivet and Jean de Meung* (Ph.d. thesis, Yale University, 1930), pp. 5–19; V. L. Dedeck-Héry, 'Jean de Meun et Chaucer: traducteurs de la Consolation de Boèce', *PMLA*, xlii (1937), 967–91; A. J. Minnis, 'Aspects of the Medieval French and English Traditions of the *De Consolatione Philosophiae*', in *Boethius: His Life, Thought and Influence*, ed. M. T. Gibson (Oxford, 1981), pp. 312–61, esp. p. 341.

10 Cf. Chapter 3 of my forthcoming book *Medieval Theory of Authorship*.

11 I consulted the second redaction of this work, in London, British Library, MS Royal 15.B.III.

12 See M.-D. Chenu, 'Les "philosophes" dans la philosophie chrétienne médiévale', *RSPT*, xxvi (1937), 27–40; the Introduction to *Aquinas: Division and Methods of the Sciences*, trans. A. Maurer, 3rd ed. (Toronto, 1963); J. A. Weisheipl, 'Classification of the Sciences in Medieval Thought', *MS*, xxvii (1965), 54–90, esp. pp. 72–90; M.-D. Chenu, *La Théologie comme science au XIIIe siècle*, 3rd ed., Bibliothèque Thomiste, xxxiii (Paris, 1969), 71–80; U. Köpf, *Die Anfänge der theologischen Wissenschaftstheorie im 13. Jahrhundert*, Beiträge zur historischen Theologie, xlix (Tübingen, 1974), pp. 37–44.

13 D. A. Callus, 'The Function of the Philosopher in Thirteenth-Century Oxford', *Miscellanea Mediaevalia*, iii (Berlin, 1964), 153–62 (p. 155).

14 In II Sent. dist. xiii a.12, quoted by Callus, p. 159.

15 *Compendiloquium*, pars i, cap. 2 (ed. Wadding, p. 38).

16 The *Speculum Morale*, a compilation drawn largely from the works of St Thomas Aquinas, was a later addition. On Chaucer's knowledge of the *Speculum Maius* see Pauline Aiken's series of articles in *Speculum*, x (1935), 281–7; *SP*, xxxiii (1936), 40–4; *Speculum*, xiii (1938), 232–36; *SP*, xxxv (1938), 1–9; *Speculum*, xvii (1942), 56–68; *SP*, xli (1944), 371–89; also W. K. Wimsatt, 'Vincent of Beauvais and Chaucer's Cleopatra and Croesus', *Speculum*, xii (1937), 375–81. In the G prologue to the *Legend of Good Women*, line 307, the God of Love refers to Vincent's 'Estoryal Myrour' as a book that Chaucer actually owns: *Chaucer: Works*, p. 490.

17 See R. A. Pratt, 'Chaucer and the Hand that Fed Him', *Speculum*, xli (1966), 619–42.

18 K. O. Petersen, *Sources of the Nonnes Preestes Tale*, Radcliffe College Monographs, x (Boston, 1896); R. A. Pratt, 'Some Latin Sources of the Nonnes Preest on Dreams', *Speculum*, lii (1977), 538–70.

19 See especially M. Twycross, *The Medieval Anadyomene: A Study in Chaucer's Mythography*, Medium Ævum Monographs, New Series, i (1972).

20 For this use of the term 'classicizing' cf. Beryl Smalley, *English Friars and Antiquity in the Early Fourteenth Century* (Oxford, 1960), pp. 1–8.

21 See H. A. Oberman and J. A. Weisheipl, 'The *Sermo Epinicius* ascribed to Thomas Bradwardine (1346)', *AHDLMA*, xxv (1958), 295–329.

22 The differences of interest and emphasis which can occur are well illustrated by fourteenth-century interpretations of Augustine's *De Civitate Dei*. As J. P. McCall

says, if Chaucer 'had read Augustine with a classicizing gloss by one of the fourteenth-century English friars, he would have come away with a strong sense of Augustine's distinction between Christian and pagan (natural) theology and of the commentators' awareness of certain striking similarities between Christian and pagan peoples, between old Troy and new Troy (London), and between the ways that men and women of old (even gods and goddesses) fell in love, or prayed, or partied, or jealously defended their honour—like men and women of fourteenth-century England': *Chaucer among the Gods: The Poetics of Classical Myth* (Pennsylvania State University Press, 1979), p. 16. For examples of such classicizing glosses see Smalley, *English Friars and Antiquity*, pp. 99–100, 103–4, 130.

23 For discussion see R. H. Green, 'Dante's "Allegory of the Poets" and the Mediaeval Theory of Poetic Fiction', *Comparative Literature*, ix (1957), 118–28. See further Ian Bishop, *Pearl in its Setting* (Oxford, 1968), pp. 51–5.

24 *Il Convivio*, ii.1 (ed. B. Cordati (Turin, 1968), pp. 49–51).

25 See Chapter 1 of my forthcoming book *Medieval Theory of Authorship*.

26 *The Holy Bible: made from the Latin Vulgate by John Wycliffe and his Followers*, ed. J. Forshall and F. Madden (Oxford, 1950), i, 52–3; cf. Nicholas of Lyre's first prologue to his *Postilla Litteralis* in *Biblia Sacra*, i, unfol.

27 *Dantis Alagherii Epistolae*, ed. P. Toynbee, 2nd ed. by C. G. Hardie (Oxford, 1966), pp. 173–4; 199–200. See further B. Sandkühler, *Die frühen Dantekommentare und ihr Verhältnis zur mittelalterlichen Kommentartradition*, Münchner Romanistische Arbeiten, xix (Munich, 1967); L. Jenaro–MacLennan, *The Trecento Commentaries on the Divina Commedia and the Epistle to Cangrande* (Oxford, 1974).

28 Cf. *Boccaccio on Poetry*, ed. C. O. Osgood, The Library of Liberal Arts (Indianapolis and New York, 1956), p. xviii.

29 Cf. R. Klibansky, E. Panofsky and F. Saxl, *Saturn and Melancholy* (London, 1964), p. 173; also McCall, *Chaucer among the Gods*, p. 13. For twelfth-century precedents to Bersuire's practice see McCall, p. 11.

30 Bersuire, *Ovidius Moralizatus*, ed. Engels, p. 5.

31 Ibid., p. 2.

32 Ibid., p. 5.

33 For a good introduction to this subject see Daniel Cooke, 'Euhemerism: A Mediaeval Interpretation of Classical Paganism', *Speculum*, ii (1927), 396–410.

34 *Ovidius Moralizatus*, ed. Engels, p. 6.

35 Ibid., pp. 6–10.

36 Cf. the description of John Ridevall's moralizing technique in J. B. Allen, 'Commentary as Criticism: The Text, Influence and Literary Theory of the "Fulgentius Metaphored" of John Ridevall', in *Acta Conventus Neo-Latini Amstelodamensis: Proceedings of the Second International Congress of Neo-Latin Studies, Amsterdam 19–24 August 1973*, ed. P. Tuynman *et al.* (Munich, 1979), 25–47 (pp. 32–4).

37 On the decline of allegorical exegesis see especially B. Smalley, *The Study of the Bible in the Middle Ages* (Oxford, 1952), pp. 281–355.

38 See A. J. Minnis, '"Authorial Role" and "Literary Form" in Late-Medieval Scriptural Exegesis', *PBB*, xcix (1977), 37–65 (p. 40); cf. Aquinas as cited by Spicq, *Esquisse*, p. 251.

39 Cf. Smalley, *Study of the Bible*, pp. 292–3.

40 Ibid., pp. 300–1; Spicq, *Esquisse*, pp. 279–81.

41 For Aquinas's well-known distinction between significative words and significative things see *Summa Theologiae*, I^a 1, 10, responsio ((London and New York, Blackfriars ed., 1963–), i, 40).

42 *Prologus secundus de intentione auctoris* (*Biblia Sacra*, i, unfol.).

43 See the useful summary description of Robertson's approach in A. R. Kaminsky, *Chaucer's Troilus and Criseyde and the Critics* (Ohio University Press, 1980), pp. 32–3.

44 D. W. Robertson, 'Chaucerian Tragedy', rpt. in *Chaucer Criticism*, ed. Schoeck and Taylor, ii, 86–121 (p. 97).

45 D. W Robertson, *A Preface to Chaucer* (Princeton, 1962), p. 110. For a milder version of this view see McCall, *Chaucer among the Gods*, pp. 84–6.

46 This can be regarded as a general rule for all the English writers of Chaucer's day. There may be one exception, the eccentric *Testament of Love* by Thomas Usk. At the end of this work Usk spells out the significance of the 'lady precious Margarit' who has figured throughout: 'Margarite, a woman, betokeneth grace, lerning, or wisdom, or els holy church'. See *Supplement to the Works of Geoffrey Chaucer, vol. vii: Chaucerian and Other Pieces*, ed. W. W. Skeat (Oxford, 1897), p. 145. This appears to be a development of the usual technique of fable-moralization, with Scriptural exegesis in mind. It should be emphasized that there is no attempt to conceal allegorical meaning in the *Testament*: on the contrary, Usk was determined to make it perfectly clear to all and sundry. Cf. note 72 below.

47 Cf. A. J. Minnis, 'The Influence of Academic Prologues on the Prologues and Literary Attitudes of Late-Medieval English Writers', *MS*, xliii (1981), 342–83 (pp. 381–2).

48 Cf. A. J. Minnis, 'Literary Theory in Discussions of *Formae Tractandi* by Medieval Theologians', *New Literary History*, xi (1979/80), 133–45 (pp. 140–1).

49 See the passage from Auriol's *Compendium totius Biblie* printed by Minnis, '"Authorial Role" and "Literary Form"', p. 58.

50 Ulrich of Strassburg, *Liber de summo bono*, i, tr.2, cap. 9 (ed. J. Daguillon, *Ulrich de Strasbourg, O.P., La Summa de Bono, livre i*, Bibliothèque Thomiste, xii (Paris, 1930), p. 52); Bersuire, *Ovidius Moralizatus*, ed. Engels, pp. 2–3; Thomas of Ireland, *Manipulus Florum*, printed as *Flores omnium pene doctorum . . . alphabetico ordine digesti* (Paris, 1556), pp. 406–7.

51 *Chaucerian and Other Pieces*, ed. Skeat, p. 3.

52 See Minnis, 'The Influence of Academic Prologues', pp. 359–63.

53 Cf. the general tenor of some of the remarks in McCall's *Chaucer among the Gods*, pp. 16–17, 43–4, 58. Our approaches and interests, however, are quite different.

54 On this twelfth-century practice see Peter Dronke, *Fabula: Explorations into the Uses of Myth in Medieval Platonism* (Leiden and Köln, 1974); W. Wetherbee, *Platonism and Poetry in the Twelfth Century* (Princeton, 1972).

55 Cf. H. R. Jauss, 'La transformation de la forme allégorique entre 1180 et 1240: d'Alain de Lille à Guillaume de Lorris', in *L'humanisme médiéval dans les littératures romanes*, Centre de Philologie et de Littératures Romanes de l'Université de Strasbourg, Actes et Colloques, iii (Paris, 1964), 107–46 (p. 146).

56 MS Royal 15.B.III, fol. 122ʳ.

57 *Roman de la Rose*, ed. Langlois, ii, 261; trans. Dahlberg, p. 113.

58 *Roman de la Rose*, ed. Langlois, iii, 32–3; trans. Dahlberg, p. 136.

59 Cf. Minnis, 'Medieval French and English Traditions of the *De Consolatione Philosophiae*', pp. 314–5.

60 It should, however, be mentioned that historical interpretation does figure in the *Ovide Moralisé*: see P. Demats, *Fabula: Trois études de mythographie antique et médiévale*, Publications romanes et françaises, cxxii (Geneva, 1973), 101–3. Bersuire, on the other hand, largely ignored the literal sense: see above p. 14.

61 *Ovide Moralisé*, vol. iv, ed. C. de Boer, Verhandelingen der Koninkijke Akademie van Wetenschappen te Amsterdam, Afdeeling Letterkunde, deel xxxvii (Amsterdam, 1936), 198–219. On Chaucer's knowledge of the *Ovide Moralisé* see J. L. Lowes, 'Chaucer and the *Ovide Moralisé*', *PMLA*, xxxiii (1918), 302–25; S. B. Meech, 'Chaucer and the *Ovide Moralisé*: A Further Study', ibid., xlv (1931), 182–204; J. Wimsatt, 'The Sources of Chaucer's "Seys and Alcyone"', *Medium Ævum*, xxxvi (1967), 231–41; S. Delaney, 'Chaucer's *House of Fame* and the *Ovide Moralisé*', *Comparative Literature*, xx (1968), 254–64.

62 *The English Works of John Gower*, vol. i, ed. G. C. Macaulay, EETS ES lxxxi (Oxford, 1900), 384.
63 See A. J. Minnis, 'A Note on Chaucer and the *Ovide Moralisé*', *Medium Ævum*, xlviii (1979), 254–7.
64 History was supposed to be divided into three great periods: the period of the natural law (from Adam until Moses), the period of the written law (from Moses until Christ), and the period of grace (from Christ until the end of the world). See *Peter Abelard: A Dialogue of a Philosopher with a Jew and a Christian*, trans. P. J. Payer, Pontifical Institute of Medieval Studies (Toronto, 1979), p. 1. Pagans who either had not heard of or had not accepted the Mosaic law 'or the law of Christ remained under the rule of natural law. The virtuous philosopher portrayed by Abelard is a man of the natural law who is seeking the salvation of his soul. This leads him into the debate with a Jew and a Christian, wherein he analyses their beliefs in accordance with the rule of reason.
65 *Ovide Moralisé*, vol. i, ed. de Boer, Verhandelingen . . . , deel xv (Amsterdam, 1915), 61.
66 See J. M. Steadman, 'Flattery and the *Moralitas* of the Nonnes Preestes Tale', *Medium Ævum*, xxviii (1959), 172–9, who argues that Chaucer concludes his tale 'with an explicit statement of its "moralite"', i.e. a warning against flattery. But Chaucer does *not* make this or any other 'moralite' explicit at the end of his story: all we have is the tantalizing statement that an (unspecified) 'moralite' *may* be taken from this fable. The Nun's Priest's warnings against pride are located at *The Canterbury Tales*, VII, 3325–30 and 3178–85; the warning against regarding sex as a panacea is implied in lines 3158–81.
67 Cf. S. Manning, 'The Nun's Priest's Morality and the Medieval Attitude towards Fables', *JEGP*, lix (1960), 403–16 (pp. 403, 416). A helpful review of critical opinion on the tale is included in D. Brewer, 'What is the *Nun's Priest's Tale* really about?', *Trames*, Coll. anglais, ii (1979), 9–23.
68 Cf. R. Hazelton, '*The Manciple's Tale*: Parody and Critique', *JEGP*, lxii (1963), 1–31.
69 *Historia Destructionis Troiae*, bk. xxxii (ed. N. E. Griffin, The Medieval Academy of America, Publication no. xxvi (Cambridge, Mass., 1936), pp. 248–9; trans. Mary E. Meek (Bloomington and London, 1974), pp. 239–40).
70 See Smalley, *English Friars and Antiquity*, pp. 110–8, 146–7, 165–83, 211, 215–6; cf. Twycross, *The Medieval Anadyomene*, pp. 18–21; also F. A. Yates, *The Art of Memory* (rept. Harmondsworth, 1969), pp. 105–8.
71 *Ovidius Moralizatus*, ed. Engels, pp. 15–16.
72 It should be added that, in late-medieval literature in general and Middle English Literature in particular, works which are allegorical in the moral or any other sense, declare themselves to be so in the most unequivocal of terms. Implicit meaning had to be made explicit in this way because there was no fixed system of allegorical equivalences which was universally accepted. The *Gesta Romanorum*, an anthology of moralized 'ancient' tales compiled for the benefit of preachers, makes this perfectly clear. Herein the moral allegories imposed on the stories of kings, emperors and knights are often unexpected and, indeed, sometimes quite eccentric. As S. Marchalonis puts it, 'it is difficult to imagine how the medieval reader or listener could arrive at the desired meaning without the application to each tale; if he could do so there would be no need for the application': 'Medieval Symbols and the *Gesta Romanorum*', *The Chaucer Review*, viii (1973), 311–19 (p. 318).
73 Cf. M. W. Bloomfield, 'Chaucer's Sense of History', *JEGP*, li (1952), 301–13 (p. 308, n. 17), from which I have borrowed a few phrases. See further his article : 'Distance and Predestination in *Troilus and Criseyde*', rpt. in *Chaucer Criticism*, ed. Schoeck and Taylor, ii, 196–210 (esp. p. 201); also Kittredge, 'Chaucer's Lollius', pp. 52–5. R. A. Pratt has suggested that Chaucer gained 'a sense of chronology, a

sense of the past, and a sense of history' from Nicholas Trevet's *Cronicles*: see 'Chaucer and *Les Cronicles* of Nicholas Trevet', *Studies in Language, Literature and Culture of the Middle Ages and Later*, ed. E. B. Atwood and A. A. Hill (Austin, 1969), pp. 303–11 (pp. 308–9). But, of course, Chaucer could have acquired these senses from Vincent's 'Estoryal Myrour' or indeed from many other medieval compilations. On the value of a fictitious pagan past to a philosophical poet see especially the perceptive remarks by R. B. Burlin, *Chaucerian Fiction* (Princeton, 1977), pp. 98–100, and J. D. Burnley, *Chaucer's Language and the Philosophers' Tradition*, Chaucer Studies, ii (Cambridge, 1979), 37–41, 79–80. However, in my opinion, Chaucer's presentation of his pagan characters is more historically accurate (to judge by the standards of his day) than Burnley would allow.

74 *Summa Britonis sive Guillelmi Britonis Expositiones Vocabulorum Biblie*, ed. L. W. Daly and B. A. Daly (Padova, 1975), i, p. xi.

75 Ibid., p. 25; cf. Isidore of Seville, *Etymologiae*, ed. W. M. Lindsay (Oxford, 1911), I.iv.1. Isidore's definition is included in, for example, Vincent of Beauvais, *Speculum Doctrinale*, iii.127 (*Speculum Maius*, ii, fol. 55ʳ).

76 *Summa Britonis*, ed. Daly, i, 251; cf. *Etymologiae*, I.xl.1. Isidore's definition is included in, for example, Vincent of Beauvais, *Speculum Doctrinale*, iii.113 (*Speculum Maius*, ii, fol. 53ʳ); Thomas of Ireland, *Manipulus Florum*, pp. 407–8.

77 *Rhetorica ad Herennium*, I.viii.13; *De Inventione*, I.xix.27; cf. Vincent of Beauvais, *Speculum Doctrinale*, iii.109 (*Speculum Maius*, ii, fol. 53ʳ).

78 See *The Trojan War: The Chronicles of Dictys of Crete and Dares the Phrygian*, trans. R. M. Frazer (Bloomington and London, 1966), pp. 20, 30, 133, 168.

79 Vincent of Beauvais, *Apologia actoris*, cap. i (ed. A.-D. v. den Brincken, 'Geschichsbetrachtung bei Vincenz von Beauvais', *Deutsches Archiv für Erforschung des Mittelalters*, xxxiv.2 (1978), 465–99). Cf. the discussion in Benson, *History of Troy in Middle English Literature*, pp. 9–12.

80 *Polychronicon Ranulphi*, I, 4–7.

81 *The Legend of Good Women*, F prologue, 26; G prologue, 26.

82 *Historia Destructionis Troiae*, prologus (ed. Griffin, p. 3; trans. Meek, p. 1). See further Benson's account of 'the eyewitness style' of Guido's *Historia*, in *History of Troy in Middle English Literature*, pp. 15–19.

83 *Roman de Troie*, 89–144 (ed. L. Constans (Paris, 1904–12), i, 6–9): Guido, *Historia Destructionis Troiae*, ed. Griffin, pp. 4, 273.

84 *Joseph of Exeter: The Iliad of Dares Phrygius*, trans. Gildas Roberts (Cape Town, 1970), pp. ix, 3.

85 *The Chronicles of Dictys and Dares*, trans. Frazer, p. 133.

86 *Yliados libri sex*, i, 24–6 (ed. L. Gompf, *Joseph Iscanus: Werke und Briefe*, Mittellateinische Studien und Texte, iv (Leiden and Köln, 1970), 78; trans. Roberts, p. 3).

87 *Historia Destructionis Troiae*, prologus (ed. Griffin, pp. 3–4; trans. Meek, pp. 1–2).

88 *Il Filostrato*, proemio, (ed. V. Branca, in *Tutte le opere di Giovanni Boccaccio*, ed. V. Branca, vol. ii, I Classici Mondadori (1964), p. 21; trans. R. K. Gordon, *The Story of Troilus* (New York, 1964), pp. xiv, 28).

89 *Chaucer Life-Records*, ed. M. N. Crow and C. C. Olson (Oxford, 1964), pp. 67–93, 344–7.

90 Cf. P. Boitani, *Chaucer and Boccaccio*, Medium Ævum Monographs, New Series, viii (Oxford, 1977), 7–9.

91 For references see Robinson's note in *Chaucer: Works*, p. 812.

92 Cf. Wigginton, *Nature and Significance of the Late Medieval Troy Story*, pp. 82–6.

93 Cf. Kittredge, 'Chaucer's Lollius', pp. 49–55.

94 *Historia Destructionis Troiae*, bk. xxxv (ed. Griffin, p. 276; trans. Meek, p. 265).

95 *Yliados libri sex*, vi, 965–7 (ed. Gompf, p. 211; trans. Roberts, pp. 86–7).

96 On this rhetorical device see F. Tupper, 'The Envy Theme in Prologues and Epilogues', *JEGP*, xvi (1917), 551–72.

97 There is no evidence that Chaucer knew the most avant-garde theory of tragedy in his day, that contained in Nicholas Trevet's commentary on Seneca's tragedies. For an interesting attempt to apply some of its principles to *Troilus and Criseyde* see John Norton-Smith, *Geoffrey Chaucer* (London and Boston, 1974), pp. 164–72, 187–8, 193. Much work remains to be done on medieval theory of tragedy. The way forward has been shown by the following studies: Paul G. Ruggiers, 'Notes towards a theory of Tragedy in Chaucer', *The Chaucer Review*, viii (1973), 89–99; J. B. Allen, 'Hermann the German's Averroistic Aristotle and Medieval Poetic Theory', *Mosaic*, ix/3 (1976), 67–81 (esp. pp. 69–71); H. A. Kelly, 'Aristotle–Averroes–Alemannus on Tragedy: The Influence of the "Poetics" on the Latin Middle Ages', *Viator*, x (1979), 161–209. Interesting discussion of *Troilus* as a Boethian tragedy is provided by M. E. McAlpine, *The Genre of Troilus and Criseyde* (Ithaca and London, 1978).

98 See Minnis, 'Medieval French and English Traditions of the *De Consolatione Philosophiae*', pp. 336–7.

99 Cf. Isidore, *Etymologiae*, XVIII.xliv. See further the definition of tragedy in Vincent of Beauvais: 'Tragedia vero poesis, a laeto principio in tristem finem definens'. *Speculum Doctrinale*, iii.109 (*Speculum Maius*, ii, fol. 53ʳ).

100 Cf. the discussion in R. A. Dwyer, *Boethian Fictions* (Cambridge, Mass., 1976), pp. 36–49.

101 See Wigginton, *Nature and Significance of the Late Medieval Troy Story*, pp. 112–9, 123, 130, who adds that, according to Albert of Stade's *Troilus* (1249), the 'fall of Troy was not a matter of blind fate' but 'was the direct result of moral depravity, and teaches a moral lesson'. Cf. Baskerville, *Two Studies in the Redaction of the Medieval Troy Story*, pp. 75–81; also McCall, *Chaucer among the Gods*, p. 94 and n. 16 on p. 175. For a different interpretation (namely, that Guido's *Historia* manifests a pessimistic view of fate and fortune as being 'distinctly and randomly malignant') see Benson, *History of Troy in Middle English Literature*, pp. 23–31. Unfortunately, Benson does not develop his insight that such a view of fate might have commended itself to Guido as being 'in harmony with the pagan perspective of Dares and Dictys' (p. 28).

102 *Yliados libri sex*, iv, 199–201 (ed. Gompf, p. 147; trans. Roberts, p. 44). On Guido's view of Helen see Baskerville, *Two Studies in the Redaction of the Medieval Troy Story*, p. 80.

103 See for example the criticism of Dalida in *The Monk's Tale*, VII, 2052–4, 2091–4.

104 See above pp. 88–89.

105 The extent to which this was an original stroke may be gauged from the example of a tragedy given in John of Garland's *Parisiana Poetria*, ch. 7 (ed. and trans. T. Lawler (New Haven and London, 1974), p. 137). Two washerwomen, we are told, furnish 'the services of laundry and copulation' for a band of sixty soldiers. 'But one was in love with one of the soldiers in the other washerwoman's group. She found out; a squabble developed between the washerwomen, and they came to blows. If fell out one night that the injured washerwoman found her rival sleeping with the solider she loved; and seeing them asleep, she took a sword and killed them both. Then, lest her crime be revealed in the morning, she secretly opened the castle and let in the enemy, who killed all the soldiers in the castle. . . . These are the characteristics of this tragedy: it is written in the high style; it deals with shameful and criminal actions; it begins in joy and ends in tears'. This is hardly a love-story, though one could say that there is love-interest, of a kind. The love-story which constitutes Chaucer's tragedy of *Troilus and Criseyde* is quite different in substance and kind.

106 *Teseida*, xi, st. 91 (ed. A. Roncaglia, Scrittori d'Italia, clxxxv (Bari, 1941), 340; trans. Havely, p. 147).

107 *The Poems and Fables of Robert Henryson*, ed. H. H. Wood (Edinburgh, 1958), p. 107.

1 *Compendiloquium*, Pars v, cap. 2 (ed. Wadding, pp. 292–3); cit. by W. A. Pantin, 'John of Wales and Medieval Humanism', in *Medieval Studies presented to Aubrey Gwynn* (Dublin, 1961), pp. 297–319 (p. 310). See further William of Ockham's view that there can be no perfect virtue without theological virtue, but there can be natural virtue which follows the precepts of right reason: Leff, *William of Ockham*, p. 491. By contrast, Bradwardine concluded that, since there is no true virtue in an infidel, they cannot carry out a really good action: *De Causa Dei*, i.39 (ed. Savile, p. 327); cf. G. Leff, *Bradwardine and the Pelagians*, Cambridge Studies in Medieval Life and Thought, New Series, v (Cambridge, 1957), p. 155.

2 *Compendiloquium*, pars ii, cap. 2 (ed. Wadding, p. 77); cf. John of Salisbury, *Policraticus*, iii.9 (ed. C. C. J. Webb (Oxford, 1909), i, 197–8; also Pantin, 'John of Wales', p. 309.

3 Vincent of Beauvais, *Speculum Doctrinale*, xix[=xvii], cap. 3 (*Speculum Maius*, ii, fol. 291ʳ), quoting Augustine, *De Civitate Dei*, vi.5. True or Christian theology is discussed in capi 27–9 (fol. 294ʳ). Cf. the comprehensive attack on all forms of polytheism in Bradwardine's *De Causa Dei*, i.1, coroll. pars 18 (ed. Savile, pp. 13–14). Bradwardine attacks idolatry in *De Causa Dei*, i.1, coroll. pars 21 (pp. 15–19).

4 *Etymologiae*, VIII.x.1

5 *Etymologiae*, VIII.x.2.

6 Guido, *Historia Destructionis Troiae*, bk. x (ed. Griffin, p. 94; trans. Meek, p. 91).

7 *Etymologiae*, VIII.x.4.

8 Hugutio, *Magnae Derivationes*, s.v. *pige* (Oxford, Bodleian Library, MS Bodley 376, fol. 152ʳ–152ᵛ); *Summa Britonis*, ed. Daly, ii, 514.

9 On this subject see especially Cooke, 'Euhemerism: A Medieval Interpretation of Classical Paganism'.

10 *Speculum Historiale*, i.102 (*Speculum Maius*, iv, fol. 13ᵛ); cf. *Speculum Doctrinale*, xix.6 (ii, fol. 291ʳ) which quotes *Etymologiae*, VIII.xi.1 (trans. as an appendix in K. N. Macfarlane, *Isidore of Seville's Treatise on the Pagan Gods* (Ph.d. thesis, University of Washington, 1978), p. 142.

11 *Speculum Historiale*, i.102, *Speculum Doctrinale*, xix.6, citing Isidore, *Etymologiae*, VIII.xi.2 (trans. Macfarlane, p. 142).

12 *Speculum Doctrinale*, xix.7 (*Speculum Maius*, ii, fol. 291ᵛ), following Isidore, *Etymologiae*, VIII.xi.29.

13 Holcot, *Sap. Sal. praelectiones*, lectio 155 (on Wisdom 13.2), p. 517 of the Basel edition. Cf. *Speculum Doctrinale*, xix.7 (*Speculum Maius*, ii, fol. 291ᵛ), quoting Isidore, *Etymologiae*, VIII.xi.29–41; also *Speculum Doctrinale*, xix.12 (ii, fol. 292ʳ). On the 'natural' interpretation, see further Augustine, *De Civitate Dei*, vi.8; Mythographus II, prohemium (ed. G. H. Bode, *Scriptores Rerum Mythicarum Latini Tres Romae nuper reperti* (Celle, 1834), p. 74).

14 *Etymologiae*, VIII.xi.29: 'this was wholly a fabrication of the poets, so that they might adorn their gods with figurative speech, although their stories confess them to have been damned and filled with an infamy of shame. For the place lies altogether open for fabrication, where truth has departed' (trans. Macfarlane, p. 148).

15 *Etymologiae*, III.lxxi.21.

16 *Historia Destructionis Troiae*, bk. x (ed. Griffin, p. 95; trans. Meek, p. 92). For an excellent discussion of the 'planet-gods' see M. A. Twycross, *The Representation of the Major Classical Divinities in the Works of Chaucer, Gower, Lydgate and Henryson* (B.Litt. thesis, University of Oxford, 1961), pp. 81–92.

17 Isidore states that 'demons substituted themselves to be worshipped' in place of dead men 'and persuaded those deceived and damned men to sacrifice to them': *Etymologiae*, VIII.xi.5 (trans. Macfarlane, p. 143). A little later Isidore repeats an

inaccurate yet appropriate etymology, that 'the word idol is derived from "fraud" (*dolus*), because the Devil conveyed to a created thing worship which is appropriate to a divine being': *Etymologiae*, VIII.xi.14 (trans. Macfarlane, p. 144).

18 *Historia Destructionis Troiae*, bk. x (ed. Griffin, pp. 93–6; trans. Meek, pp. 91–3). Cf. Peter Comestor, *Historia Scholastica*, pr. Migne, *PL*, cxcviii, col. 1090, and the briefer statement in Isidore, *Etymologiae*, VIII.xi.4–5, 23 (trans. Macfarlane, pp. 142–3, 146–7). Both Peter Comestor and Isidore are quoted in Vincent of Beauvais, *Speculum Doctrinale*, xix.5 (*Speculum Maius*, ii, 291ʳ). For the theory that Syrophanes of Egypt was the first to set up an idol see the references in note 45 below.

19 *Historia Destructionis Troiae*, bk. x (ed. Griffin, p. 97; trans. Meek, p. 94).

20 Isidore, *Etymologiae*, VIII.xi.15 (trans. Macfarlane, pp. 144–5), quoted in the *Summa Britonis*, i, 187, s.v. *demon*.

21 *Speculum Naturale*, ii.101 (*Speculum Maius*, i, fol. 25ᵛ); cf. *Speculum Doctrinale*, ix.117 (ii, fol. 157ʳ).

22 Cf. Isidore, *Etymologiae*, VIII.xi.16, quoted in *Summa Britonis*, i, 187, s.v. *demon*.

23 *Speculum Historiale*, i.10 (*Speculum Maius*, iv, fol. 2ᵛ).

24 *Speculum Morale*, lib. iii, dist. xvii, pars 3 (*Speculum Maius*, iii, fol. 198ᵛ).

25 Isidore, *Etymologiae*, VIII.xi.17 (trans. Macfarlane, p. 145).

26 For discussion see Minnis, 'Medieval French and English Traditions of the *De Consolatione Philosophiae*', pp. 335–6, cf. pp. 328–31. For the classical sources of this story see Joseph Fontenrose, *The Delphic Oracle: Its Responses and Operations, with a Catalogue of Responses* (Berkeley and Los Angeles, 1978), pp. 111–4, 302.

27 'Aio te, Aeacida, Romanos vincere posse': *Etymologiae*, I.xxxiv.13–16. See further the discussion of *equivocatio et amphibologia* in Vincent of Beauvais, *Speculum Doctrinale*, iii.92 (*Speculum Maius*, ii, fol. 51ʳ), and the account of medieval attitudes to Apollo in Twycross, *The Representation of the Major Classical Divinities*, pp. 275–80.

28 One may contrast another attitude to ambiguous predictions, represented by a section of Macrobius's commentary on the *Somnium Scipionis*, which Chaucer certainly knew. In the *Iliad* a dream sent from Zeus encouraged King Agamemnon to engage in battle with the enemy, yet he was heavily defeated:

> Must we say that the deity had sent him a deceitful vision? Not so, but because the Fates had already decreed such disaster for the Greeks, there was a hint concealed in the words of the dream which, if carefully heeded, could have enabled him at least to avoid calamity, and perhaps even to conquer. The divine command was to lead out the whole army, but he, thinking only of the command to fight, did not attend to the order to lead out the whole army and overlooked Achilles, who at that time was still smarting from a recent insult and had withdrawn his soldiers from battle. The king went forth to battle and sustained the defeat which was owing him, and thus absolved the deity from blame of falsehood by not following all of his commands.

Macrobius: Commentary on the Dream of Scipio, trans. W. H. Stahl (New York and London, 1952), pp. 118–9. A similar interpretation is offered of the Delian oracle's ambiguous statement to Aeneas concerning his destined kingdom (p. 119). Concerned as he was with the Christian truth which may be extracted from pagan fable, Macrobius felt obliged to defend divine revelations, whether pagan or Christian, from the charge of deceit: '*all* portents and dreams conform to the rule that their announcements, threats, or warnings of imminent adversity are always ambiguous' (p. 118; italics mine).

29 *Polychronicon Ranulphi*, viii, 134–9.

30 *Historia Destructionis Troiae*, bk. x (ed. Griffin, p. 93; trans. Meek, p. 91).

31 *Historia Destructionis Troiae*, bk. x (ed. Griffin, pp. 97–8; trans. Meek, pp. 94–5).

32 See the helpful discussion in Wigginton, *Nature and Significance of the Late Medieval Troy Story*, pp. 77–8.

33 *Sap. Sal. praelectiones*, lectio 160 (on Wisdom 13.17–19), p. 529.

34 *Yliados libri sex*, iv, 215–38 (ed. Gompf, pp. 147–8; trans. Roberts, p. 45).

35 *Le Roman de Troie en Prose*, ed. L. Constans and E. Faral, vol. i (Paris, 1922), p. 55. Cf. the reference in *Cleanness* to the 'stokkes and stones' which are worshipped as 'stoute goddes' by Belshazzar: *Cleanness*, 1337–44 (ed. J. J. Anderson (Manchester, 1977), p. 47).

36 *Sap. Sal. praelectiones*, lectio 159 (on Wisdom 13.11–16), pp. 526–8. Cf. Thomas Bradwardine, who points out that an image is a thing which is made; it is perishable, and needs to be supported physically. Man, beast, tree, sky, sun and moon are each and every one more perfect in nature than is the metal, wood, stone or mud of which an idol may be made. Since none of these is God, therefore an idol cannot be. *De Causa Dei*, i.1, coroll. 21 (ed. Savile, p. 15).

37 Lectio 160 (on Wisdom 13.17–19), pp. 528–30.

38 Lectio 158, pp. 524–5.

39 In III Lib. Sent., dist. ix, qu. i, art. ii, sol. 2, ad 3um. For a succinct account of these ideas, see Pamela de Wit, *The Visual Experience of Fifteenth-Century English Readers* (D. Phil. thesis, University of Oxford, 1977), pp. 12–17.

40 Cf. the arguments put forward by two contemporaries of Chaucer, John Deverose and Walter Hilton, in refuting Wycliffite iconoclasm, discussed by James Crompton, *Lollard Doctrine with special reference to the Controversy over Image Worship and Pilgrimages* (B. Litt. thesis, University of Oxford, 1948); also G. R. Owst, *Literature and Pulpit in Medieval England* (Oxford, 1966), pp. 137–9. In Hilton's *De Tolerandis Imaginibus* (London, British Library, MS Royal 11.B.X, fols 178ʳ–183ᵛ), a sharp contrast is made between pagan idolatry and Christian imagery. Christians do not imitate that gentile perversity whereby images depicting mere mortals were worshipped. Images in present-day churches are mnemonic signs of such real historical events as the incarnation and passion of Christ. When these images are adored the spiritual realities which they represent are the objects of worship, not the material objects themselves. God, speaking through Moses, prohibited the Children of Israel from making images of Him, because in that historical period neighbouring gentiles who had been 'seduced by illusions of demons' into idolatry could easily have misunderstood their function. Nowadays, of course, this problem does not exist, and Christians can utilise images with confidence.

41 Bradwardine adds that pagan idols were inhabited by evil spirits whereas Christian images are not inhabited by good spirits—why would any angel want to leave the supreme glories of heaven and angelic society for such a gross dwelling? Besides, if the consecration of an image could force an angel out of heaven into a material object, heaven would lose all its angels! *De Causa Dei*, i.1, coroll. 21 (ed. Savile, p. 17).

42 *Lydgate's DeGuilleville's Pilgrimage of the Life of Man*, ed. F. J. Furnivall, part 2, EETS ES lxxxiii (Oxford, 1901), pp. 555–61. In this account Lydgate is following closely his source, the second version of the French text: Guillaume de Deguileville, *Le Romant de trois pelerinaiges* (Paris, 1510), fols 73ᵛ–74ᵛ. For discussion of the genre of this work, and bibliography, see S. Wenzel, 'The Pilgrimage of Life as a Late Medieval Genre', *MS*, xxxv (1973), 370–88.

43 A full discussion of DeGuilleville's imagery of sight and vision is provided by Susan K. Hagen, *The Pilgrimage of the Life of Man: A Medieval Theory of Vision and Remembrance* (Ph.d. thesis, University of Virginia, 1976).

44 See Joy Russell–Smith, 'Walter Hilton and a Tract in Defence of the Veneration of Images', *Dominican Studies*, vii (1954), 180–214 (pp. 200–4).

45 For this story see Fulgentius, *Mythologiae*, ii.1 (ed. R. Helm, *Fabii Plancidis Fulgentii Opera* (Leipzig, 1898), pp. 15–17; trans. L. G. Whitbread, *Fulgentius the*

Mythographer (Ohio State University Press, 1971), p. 48). Restated by Ridevall, *Fulgentius Metaforalis*, i (ed. Liebeschütz, p. 66); Gower, *Confessio Amantis*, V, 1525–40 (ed. Macaulay, i, 443–4). For discussion of Gower's possible sources see H. C. Mainzer, *A Study of the Sources of the Confessio Amantis by John Gower* (D. Phil. thesis, Oxford, 1967), pp. 275–6, who refers to Alberic of London's *Poetarius*, Ridevall, Holcot, and Higden's *Polychronicon*. No classical source for the Syrophanes tale has been found: it may be an imaginative reworking of Wisdom 13.9–14.22.

46 Petronius, Fragment 27.1; cf. Statius, *Thebaid*, iii.661; Fulgentius, *Mythologiae*, ii.1; Servius on the *Aeneid*, ii.715; Orosius, *Historiae*, vi.1. Petronius and Statius are cited as sources of this statement in *Fulgentius Metaforalis*, i (ed. Liebeschütz, p. 67). For other references see Robinson's note to *Troilus and Criseyde*, IV, 1408 (*Chaucer: Works*, p. 831).

47 *Speculum Doctrinale*, xix.11 (*Speculum Maius*, ii, fol. 292ʳ); cf. Isidore, *Etymologiae*, VIII.xi, 90–1 (trans. Macfarlane, pp. 160–1).

48 *De Civitate Dei*, v.9. Cf. *Speculum Naturale*, iii.34 (*Speculum Maius*, i, fol. 32ʳ); *Summa Britonis*, ed. Daly, i, 257–8, s.v. *fatum*.

49 Here I use the (unfinished) edition of Trevet's commentary on Boethius by the late E. T. Silk.

50 Here Trevet is expanding on Isidore, *Etymologiae*, VIII.xi.92 (trans. Macfarlane, p. 161), which was cited by Vincent, *Speculum Doctrinale*, xix.11 (*Speculum Maius*, fol. 292ʳ), and the *Summa Britonis*, ed. Daly, i, 257–8.

51 For discussion see Hissette, *Enquête sur les 219 articles*; Van Steenberghen, *Aristotle in the West*, pp. 230–8; Leff, *Paris and Oxford Universities*, pp. 222–40; H. A. Oberman, *Archbishop Thomas Bradwardine: A Fourteenth-Century Augustinian* (Utrecht, 1957), pp. 6–7; David Knowles, *The Evolution of Medieval Thought* (London, 1962), pp. 272–7.

52 H. Denifle and A. Chatelain, *Chartularium Universitatis Parisiensis* (Paris, 1889 –97), i, 487.

53 Unfortunately, the *potentia Dei absoluta* has been described by several modern scholars as a subversive doctrine which undermined the traditional scheme of salvation and generated insecurity and skepticism. I can find no evidence in late-medieval theology of such sensational fears. For careful explanations of the two powers of God (*potentia absoluta* and *potentia ordinata*) see Oberman, *The Harvest of Medieval Theology*, pp. 30–40, and his article 'Fourteenth-Century Religious Thought: A Premature Profile', *Speculum*, liii (1978), 80–93 (esp. p. 85); also M. A. Pernoud, 'Innovation in William of Ockham's references to the *Potentia Dei*', *Antonianum*, xlv (1970), 65–97, and 'The Theory of the *Potentia Dei* according to Aquinas, Scotus and Ockham', ibid., xlvii (1972), 69–95. For Ockham's attack on fatalism and necessitation see *Ockham: Predestination, God's Foreknowledge, and Future Contingents*, trans. Adams and Kretzmann, esp. pp. 3–16; Leff, *William of Ockham*, p. 471.

54 Cf. Coleman, *Piers Plowman and the 'Moderni'*, pp. 23–4.

55 For discussion see Oberman, *Thomas Bradwardine*, pp. 49–64, 70–94; Leff, *Bradwardine and the Pelagians*, pp. 27–47.

56 Bradwardine, *De Causa Dei*, i.28: *De Fato* (ed. Savile, pp. 264–7).

57 This distinction relates to the two types of prediction, general and particular, which are discussed on pp. 46–7, 80–1.

58 *De Causa Dei*, i.29 (ed. Savile, pp. 267–71). See further the praise of the Stoics in John of Wales's *Compendiloquium*, pars vi, cap. 3 (ed. Wadding, p. 351), which draws on Augustine, *De Civitate Dei*, xi.4. For illustrations of Stoic enlightenment see Walter Burley, *Liber de Vita et Moribus Philosophorum*, ed. Knust, pp. 94–6, 106–8, 304, 310–12, 328–31, 354, 358–62, 386–8. In his book *Chaucer's Language and the Philosophers' Tradition*, J. D. Burnley discusses the 'architecture' of Chaucer's philosophical language, with special reference to Ciceronian stoicism.

Unfortunately, this study pays little attention to the dissemination and medievalization of Cicero's philosophy, or indeed to the complexity of the language of scholastic discourse in the fourteenth century.

59 H. A. Oberman and J. A. Weisheipl, 'The *Sermo Epinicius* ascribed to Thomas Bradwardine (1346)', *AHDLMA*, xxv (1958), 295–329 (pp. 308–10).

60 *De Causa Dei*, ii.3 (ed. Savile, pp. 449–51, 466–7).

61 Cf. especially the emphatic statement that stellar influences 'do not necessitate but dispose' human beings, made by John Ashenden, *Summa Iudicialis*, ii, dist. xii, cap. 3 (Bodleian Library, MS Bodley 369, fol. 378ᵛ).

62 Cf. the Middle English versions of the *exemplum* in *Three Prose Versions of the Secreta Secretorum*, ed. R. Steele, EETS ES lxxiv (Oxford, 1898), 38, 113, 217–8; *Secretum Secretorum: Nine English Versions*, ed. M. A. Manzalaoui, EETS, OS cclxxvi (Oxford, 1977), 10–11, 90, 197–8, 376–9.

63 *Speculum Naturale*, iii.34 (*Speculum Maius*, i, fol. 32ʳ). On Albert's astrological teaching see now B. B. Price, 'The Physical Astronomy and Astrology of Albertus Magnus', in *Albertus Magnus and the Sciences: Commemorative Essays 1980*, ed. J. A. Weisheipl, Pontifical Institute of Medieval Studies, Studies and Texts, xlix (Toronto, 1980), 155–85 (esp. pp. 174–85).

64 *S. Thomae Aquinatis Opuscula theologica*, ed. R. A. Verardo (Marietti, 1954), i, 155. Cf. the summary of its doctrine in J. A. Weisheipl, *Friar Thomas D'Aquino* (Oxford, 1975), pp. 399–400.

65 For discussion see Wedel, *Medieval Attitude toward Astrology*, pp. 8–11, 68, 72–3. See also Isidore's attack on the superstitious astrology practised by the *mathematici* who predict the nativities and disposition of men by the courses of the stars: *Etymologiae*, III.xxvii; III.lxxi.37–41; cf. the similar statement by Vincent of Beauvais, *Speculum Naturale*, xv:50: *Reprobatio fatalis constellationis* (*Speculum Maius*, i, fol. 190ᵛ).

66 J. D. North, *Richard of Wallingford: An Edition of his Writings with Introductions, English Translation and Commentary* (Oxford, 1976), ii, 88–9.

67 *Summa Iudicialis*, ii, prologus (Bodleian Library, MS Bodley 369, fol. 128ᵛ). Cf. Pseudo-Ptolemy, *Tetrabiblos*, ii.1 (trans. J. M. Ashmand (London, 1917), p. 58).

68 Cf. Oberman, *Thomas Bradwardine*, p. 24.

69 *De Causa Dei*, i.1, coroll. 32 (ed. Savile, pp. 29–37).

70 For Chaucer's possible knowledge of Sacrobosco see S. W. Harvey, 'Chaucer's Debt to Sacrobosco', *JEGP*, xxxiv (1935), 34–8; Walter B. Veazie, 'Chaucer's Text-Book of Astronomy, Johannes de Sacrobosco', *University of Colorado Studies*, ser.B, *Studies in the Humanities*, i (1939/40), 169–82.

71 Lynn Thorndike, *The Sphere of Sacrobosco and its Commentators* (Chicago, 1949), pp. 116–17, 142.

72 *Historia Destructionis Troiae*, bk.ii (ed. Griffin, pp. 16–17).

73 John of Wales's affection for antiquity is representative, and has been described well by T. G. Hahn: 'The disposition and accomplishments of the non-Christians impress John so favourably, that he always places the most advantageous construction upon their ideas or actions, even if he must stretch a point to make it fit. . . . though he sometimes admits, almost reluctantly, the unfortunate deficiency of this world that lacks access to Christianity, his immediate rejoinder is, how little we excel these pagans, even with our superior knowledge'. *God's Friends*, pp. 161, 163. In Wadding's edition of the *Compendiloquium* John's account of the philosophers' perfections occupies 54 pages (pp. 292–340), while his account of their abuses occupies a mere 10 (pp. 399–409).

74 See for example Vincent of Beauvais, *Speculum Historiale*, vi.62 (*Speculum Maius*, iv, fol. 66ʳ), citing Augustine, *De Civitate Dei*, x.27. For general discussion see Comparetti, *Vergil in the Middle Ages*, pp. 99–103.

75 *De Causa Dei*, i.1, coroll. 32 (ed. Savile, p. 35).

76 *Aurea Legenda Sanctorum*, cap. vi (ed. T. Graesse (Leipzig, 1850), p. 44. On

Chaucer's knowledge of the *Legenda* see now Sherry Reames, 'The Sources of Chaucer's *Second Nun's Tale*', *MP*, lxxvi (1978/9), 111–35.

77 *The Golden Legend or Lives of the Saints as Englished by William Caxton*, ed. F. S. Ellis (London, 1900–35), i, 27. Cf. *A Stanzaic Life of Christ*, ed. F. A. Forster, EETS OS, clxvi (Oxford, 1926), 20–1.

78 *Aurea Legenda*, cap. vi (ed. Graesse, p. 42; trans. Caxton, *The Golden Legend*, ed. Ellis, i, 26; cf. John of Wales, *Compendiloquium*, pars vii, cap. 2 (ed. Wadding, pp. 381–2); *Polychronicon Ranulphi*, i, 214–5, 218–9; *Stanzaic Life of Christ*, ed. Forster, pp. 16–18.

79 *Speculum Doctrinale*, xix.18: *Quod omnia potius vni Ioui esse attribuenda* (*Speculum Maius*, ii, fol. 292^v); cf. Augustine, *De Civitate Dei*, iv.11.

80 *Speculum Doctrinale*, xix.25–6 (*Speculum Maius*, ii, 293^v–4^r); cf. Augustine, *De Civitate Dei*, viii.6. See further John of Wales, *compendiloquium*, pars iii, dist. 4 (ed. Wadding, pp. 152–87); Walter Burley, *Liber de Vita et Moribus Philosophorum*, cap. lii (ed. Knust, pp. 214–34. See esp. p. 226, where he follows *De Civitate Dei*, viii.11); *Polychronicon Ranulphi*, iii, 340–59.

81 Vincent, *Speculum Historiale*, iv.66–71 (*Speculum Maius*, iv, fols 47^r–48^r), cf. *Speculum Morale*, lib. i, dist. civ, pars 3 (iii, fol. 102^r); *Polychronicon Ranulphi*, iii, 454–79. A useful summary of Higden's account is provided by David C. Fowler, *The Bible in Early English Literature* (London, 1977), pp. 224–7. On the sources of the story of Alexander and the Brahmans see George Cary, *The Medieval Alexander* (Cambridge, 1956), pp. 13–14, 91–5.

82 Troyes, Bibl. Mun., MS 1381, fol. 46^v; London, British Library, MS Royal 15.B.III, fol. 16^r; cf. Minnis, 'Medieval French and English Traditions of the *De Consolatione Philosophiae*', p. 324.

83 Cambridge, University Library, MS Ii.3.21, part ii, fol. 17^r.

84 *Comm. in De Cons. Phil.*, I pr.3 (ed. Silk).

85 *Roman de la Rose*, 5863–8 (ed. Langlois, ii, 274).

86 For other eulogistic accounts of the life and death of Socrates see Vincent of Beauvais, *Speculum Historiale*, iii.66 (*Speculum Maius*, iv, fol. 38^r); John of Wales, *Compendiloquium*, pars iii, dist. 3 (ed. Wadding, pp. 114–51); Burley, *Liber de Vita et Moribus Philosophorum*, cap. xxx (ed. Knust, pp. 108–142); *Polychronicon Ranulphi*, iii, 274, 290–5. One of John of Wales's sources is an 'expositor' of *De Consolatione Philosophiae*, who may be identified as William of Conches.

87 *Roman de la Rose*, 6211–45. The following account is based on Minnis, 'Medieval French and English Traditions of the *De Consolatione Philosophiae*', pp. 324–8.

88 Trans. Dahlberg, pp. 122–123.

89 MS Royal 15.B.III, fol. 72^v; CUL, MS Ii.3.21, pt. ii, fol. 17^v.

90 Trevet, *Comm. in De Cons. Phil.*, III pr. v (ed. Silk). Cf. Minnis, 'Medieval French and English Traditions', pp. 339–41.

91 For other eulogistic accounts of Seneca's life and death see Vincent, *Speculum Historiale*, ix.8 (*Speculum Maius*, iv, fol. 109^v); John of Wales, *Compendiloquium*, pars iv, cap. 17 (ed. Wadding, pp. 288–9); Burley, *Liber de Vita et Moribus Philosophorum*, cap. cxvii (ed. Knust, pp. 358–62). Some scholars went so far as to turn Seneca into a Christian martyr. See for example the Bruges gloss on John of Garland's *Morale Scolarium*, probably by the author himself: 'In this satire the author urges us to perseverance in the Catholic faith even until death, since nothing will be crowned unless it is properly fought out, and he admonishes by means of a certain very worthy poet, namely Seneca, who in the age of Nero fought boldly for Christ and suffered death, for he was Nero's teacher, and, as it is said, was converted by St Paul to the Catholic faith and was instructed solidly in the same'. *The Morale Scolarium of John of Garland*, ed. L. J. Paetow, Memoirs of the University of California, iv.2 (Berkeley, 1927), p. 241.

92 *Policraticus*, v.8 (ed. Webb, i, 317–8).

93 For discussion and bibliography see Coleman, *Piers Plowman and the 'Moderni'*,

pp. 108–126, 220–2; *St Erkenwald*, ed. Ruth Morse (Cambridge, 1975), pp. 16–25. But it should be emphasized that Morse's statement that Bradwardine's position concerning the salvation of infidels 'is provocative of despair' (p. 25), is insupportable.

94 *Communiloquium*, pars i, dist. 3, cap. 6 (fol. 21ᵛ); cf. *Speculum Historiale*, x.46 (*Speculum Maius*, iv, fol. 130ʳ).

95 *Polychronicon Ranulphi*, v, 2. The *Speculum Historiale* was the source of the story of Trajan in the anonymous *Fiore di filosofi*, to which Dante was indebted in his *Divine Comedy*, Purgatorio, canto x, 73–96. See Arturo Graf, *Roma nella memoria e nelle immaginazioni del Medio Aevo* (Turin, 1923), pp. 374–406.

96 *Aurea Legenda*, cap. xlvi (ed. Graesse, pp. 196–7); cf. the abbreviated version in Caxton, *The Golden Legend*, ed. Ellis, iii, 67–8.

97 Cf. *S. Gregorii Papae Vitae*, lib. ii (pr. Migne, *PL*, lxxv, cols 104–6).

98 This account of Langland's Trajan is based on my article 'Langland's Ymaginatif and Late-Medieval Theories of Imagination', *Comparative Criticism*, iii (1981), 71–103. See further R. W. Chambers, 'Long Will, Dante, and the Righteous Heathen', *Essays and Studies*, ix (1923), 50–69; T. P. Dunning, 'Langland and the Salvation of the Heathen', *Medium Ævum*, xii (1943), 45–54; G. H. Russell, 'The Salvation of the Heathen: The Exploration of a Theme in Piers Plowman', *JWCI*, xxix (1966), 101–116; Coleman, *Piers Plowman and the 'Moderni'*, pp. 108–46.

99 *Piers Plowman*, B-version, Passus XII, 285–92 (ed. Kane and Donaldson, pp. 482–3).

100 *Polychronicon Ranulphi*, v, 7. Trevisa's opinion concerning the achievement and destiny of good pagans in general, however, is far from clear. He criticises a story by Gregory Nazianzus which reveals Aristotle in a bad light, and recounts how the dying philosopher held an apple in his hand and had comfort of the smell, while teaching his scholars how they should live and come to God, and be with God without end: ibid., iii, 371. Yet he does not comment on the possibility of Aristotle's salvation. The source of Trevisa's anecdote about Aristotle and the apple, the *Liber de Pomo*, has recently been translated by M. F. Rousseau, *The Apple, or Aristotle's Death* (Milwaukee, Wisconsin, 1968).

101 *Aurea Legenda*, ed. Graesse, p. 197.

102 *St Erkenwald*, ed. Morse, pp. 8, 16–31.

103 For discussion of the term *ex puris naturalibus* see Oberman, *The Harvest of Medieval Theology*, pp. 47–50, 468; Johann Auer, *Die Entwicklung der Gnadenlehre in der Hochscholastik, vol. ii: Das Wirken der Gnade* (Freiburg, 1951), pp. 26–58.

104 For these identifications see Leff, *Bradwardine and the Pelagians*, pp. 127–254; Oberman, *Thomas Bradwardine*, pp. 28–48.

105 Cf. Smalley, *English Friars and Antiquity*, pp. 148–9, 186.

106 For Hoccleve's reference to Holcot see *Hoccleve's Works: The Minor Poems*, ed. F. J. Furnivall and I. Gollancz, EETS ES 61 and 73 (rev. reprint, Oxford, 1970), 33. Gower's possible knowledge of Holcot's commentary on Wisdom is discussed in Mainzer's unpublished thesis, *A Study of the Sources of the Confessio Amantis of John Gower*.

107 Paulo Molteni, *Roberto Holcot: Dottrina della grazia e della giustificazione, con due questioni quodlibetali inedite* (Pinerolo, 1967), pp. 174–204.

108 I *Sent.*, q. iv, art. 3, P-Q (*Super quattuor libros sententiarum quaestiones* (Lyon, 1497), unfol.).

109 On the nominalistic conception of natural law see especially Oberman, *The Harvest of Medieval Theology*, pp. 103–8; Leff, *William of Ockham*, pp. 622–3; A. McGrade, *The Political Thought of William of Ockham* (Cambridge, 1974), 177–85; Francis Oakley, 'Medieval Theories of Natural Law: William of Ockham and the Significance of the Voluntarist Tradition', *Natural Law Forum*, vi (1961), 65–83.

110 *Sap. Sal. praelectiones*, lectio 150 (on Wisdom 12.15–17), pp. 501–3.

111 Ed. Molteni, pp. 180–204.

112 Ibid., pp. 198–9.

113 For Ockham's similar, yet in some important respects different, doctrine of grace see Leff, *William of Ockham*, pp. 470–5, 476, 500.

114 Alois Meissner, *Gotteserkenntnis und Gotteslehre nach dem englischen Dominikanertheologen Robert Holkot* (Limburg, 1953), pp. 102–4.

115 Oberman, *The Harvest of Medieval Theology*, pp. 245–6.

116 Ibid., p. 246. By *meritum de congruo* is meant 'half merit', 'an act performed in a state of sin, in accordance with nature or divine law . . . and therefore accepted by God as satisfying the requirement for the infusion of first grace': *ibid.*, pp. 471–2. Cf. Leff, *William of Ockham*, pp. 494–5.

117 For discussion see especially Oberman, *The Harvest of Medieval Theology*, pp. 132–4, 240–8, 468; also his article ' "Facientibus quod in se est Deus non denegat gratiam": Robert Holcot O.P. and the Beginnings of Luther's Theology', *Harvard Theological Review*, lv (1962), 317–42.

118 *Sap. Sal. praelectiones*, lectio 29 (on Wisdom 2.21–2), p. 103.

119 Cf. Ockham's views, in *Ockham: Philosophical Writings*, ed. P. Boehner (London, 1957), pp. xliii–xlvi, 115–26; summarized by Leff, *William of Ockham*, pp. 335–6, 346, 359–98.

120 *Sap. Sal. praelectiones*, lectio 29, p. 103.

121 Cf. Oberman, *The Harvest of Medieval Theology*, pp. 241–3.

122 *Sap. Sal. praelectiones*, lectio 155 (on Wisdom 13.1–2), pp. 515–6; Cf. I Sent., q. iv, art. 3, M.

123 See Smalley's translation of this crucial passage in *English Friars and Antiquity*, p. 185. Cf. Holcot, I Sent., q. iv, art. 3, M.

124 *Sap. Sal. praelectiones*, lectio 103 (on Wisdom 7.27–8), p. 348.

125 Ibid., lectio 157 (on Wisdom 13.6–9), pp. 521–3.

126 *De Civitate Dei*, xviii.38.

127 I Sent., q. iv, art. 3, Q.

128 *Sap. Sal. praelectiones*, lectio 157, p. 522.

129 *Aurea Legenda*, ed. Graesse, p. 197.

130 But it should be noted that Holcot's views on the salvation of the heathen were by no means the most extreme of their kind. That dubious honour must surely go to Uthred of Boldon's opinion that all human beings, including pagans and infidels, enjoy a 'clear vision' of God at the moment just before death, when they must choose or reject Him. See M. E. Marcett, *Uthred de Boldon, Friar William Jordan, and Piers Plowman* (New York, 1938), pp. 37–42; M. D. Knowles, 'The Censured Opinions of Uthred of Boldon', *Proceedings of the British Academy*, xxxvii (1951), 305–42 (esp. pp. 313–7, 334).

CHAPTER 3

1 See especially J. S. P. Tatlock, 'The Epilog of Chaucer's *Troilus*', MP, xviii (1920/1), 625–59 (pp. 640–50), and Lewis, 'What Chaucer Really Did to *Il Filostrato*', in *Chaucer Criticism*, ii, 19–21; also T. P. Dunning, 'God and Man in *Troilus and Criseyde*', *English and Medieval Studies presented to J. R. R. Tolkien*, ed. N. Davis and C. L. Wrenn (London, 1962), 164–82; S. B. Greenfield, 'The Role of Calkas in *Troilus and Criseyde*', *Medium Ævum*, xxxvi (1967), 141–51.

2 Tatlock, 'The Epilog of Chaucer's *Troilus*', p. 643; cf. H. M. Cummings, *The Indebtedness of Chaucer's Works to the Italian Works of Boccaccio* (New York, 1965), pp. 126–7.

3 *Compendiloquium*, prologus (ed. Wadding, pp. 19–28).

4 Ibid., p. 425. On *gratia gratis data* see Oberman, *The Harvest of Medieval Theology*, p. 470, who points out that in a man this can co-exist with sin and does not

presuppose a state of grace; also Leff, *Bradwardine and the Pelagians*, pp. 142, 267–8.

5 *The Miller's Tale*, I, 3457–61; *Confessio Amantis*, VI, 1789–2366 (ed. Macaulay, ii, 215–230).

6 *Speculum Historiale*, iv.2–5 (*Speculum Maius*, iv, fol. 41ʳ–41ᵛ); *Polychronicon Ranulphi*, iii, 392–403.

7 *Speculum Historiale*, iv.65 (*Speculum Maius*, iv, fol. 47ʳ); *Polychronicon Ranulphi*, iv, 8–13.

8 *Speculum Historiale*, iv.11 (*Speculum Maius*, iv, fol. 42ʳ); *Polychronicon Ranulphi*, iii, 400–3.

9 *Polychronicon Ranulphi*, iii, 401–3.

10 Ibid., i, 16–20.

11 Ibid., i, 21.

12 Ibid., iii, 317–9.

13 For other examples see *Polychronicon Ranulphi*, i, 363; ii, 61, 77, 83, 91, 121, 161, 189, 195, etc. For discussion see A. J. Minnis, 'Late-Medieval Discussions of *Compilatio* and the Role of the *Compilator*', *PBB*, ci (1979), 385–421 (pp. 387–91).

14 *Apologia actoris*, cap. iv (ed. v. den Brincken, p. 470).

15 Ibid., cap. viii (p. 477); cf. Minnis, 'Late-Medieval Discussions of *Compilatio*', p. 389.

16 *Communiloquium*, prologus (fol. 3ʳ).

17 Cf. Wedel's definition of 'judicial astrology' in his *Medieval Attitude toward Astrology*, p. 11, note 2; cf. Wood, *Country of the Stars*, pp. 6, 15.

18 See Vincent's explanation of his use of the term *actor* in *Apologia actoris*, cap. iii (ed. v. den Brincken, p. 468); for general discussion of the relevant ideas see M.-D. Chenu, 'Auctor, actor, autor', *Bulletin du Cange*, iv (1927), 81–6.

19 *Speculum Naturale*, xv.50: *Reprobatio fatalis constellationis* (*Speculum Maius*, i, 190ᵛ–1ʳ).

20 J. A. Robson, *Wyclif and the Oxford Schools* (Cambridge, 1966), pp. 101–3.

21 Ibid., p. 102. Cf. the more elaborate defence at the end of his *Summa Iudicialis*, bk. iii, dist. xii, cap. 3 (MS Bodley 369, fols 377ᵛ–9ᵛ).

22 MS Bodley 369, fol. 1ʳ.

23 MS Bodley 369, fol. 1ᵛ.

24 For a description of this MS see G. Mathew, *The Court of Richard II* (London, 1968), pp. 40–1.

25 See the extract printed in *Four English Political Tracts of the Later Middle Ages*, ed. J. P. Genet, Camden Fourth Series (London, 1968), pp. 22–3.

26 Ed. Robinson, p. 546.

27 Ibid., p. 551. See further the discussions of this passage in Wood, *Country of the Stars*, pp. 15–17, and M. Manzalaoui, 'Chaucer and Science', in *Geoffrey Chaucer*, ed. D. Brewer, Writers and their Background (London, 1974), pp. 224–61 (pp. 235–6).

28 Cf. S. B. Greenfield, 'The Role of Calkas', who relates both these passages to Chaucer's depiction of Calkas the pagan astrologer.

29 *Sap. Sal. praelectiones*, pp. 3–4. Similarly, in the prologue to his *Breviloquium de sapientia sanctorum*, apparently a sequel to the *Compendiloquium*, John of Wales states that, because the gentile philosophers did not have knowledge of the true God, nor did they bear away the gifts of the God who revealed to them those things which they discovered, 'they became futile in their thinking, and, claiming to be wise, they became fools' (Romans 1.21–2); ed. Wadding, p. 429. The *Breviloquium* is very brief in comparison with the *Compendiloquium* and the *Communiloquium*, which would suggest that John enjoyed the company of the pagans, even though they were not the 'true philosophers'.

30 Cf. McAlpine, who argues that 'In *Troilus* . . . Chaucer gives a precise representation of the situation of the pagan who shares all the richness of his humanity with

the Christian but is without the aid of Christian revelation to interpret it. In the perspective of that revelation, pagan wisdom is not wrong, but it is seriously incomplete': *The Genre of Troilus*, pp. 179–80.

31 Cf. A. J. Minnis, 'John Gower, *sapiens* in Ethics and Politics', *Medium Ævum*, xlix (1980), 207–229 (pp. 210–11).

32 See esp. *The Testament of Cresseid*, 407–69, 540–74 (ed. Wood, pp. 119–21, 124–5).

33 *Benoît de Ste Maure: Roman de Troie*, 654–70, 25410–19, 25617–31, etc. (ed. L. Constans, (Paris, 1904–12), i, 35; iv, 124–5, 136–7); Guido, *Historia Destructionis Troiae*, bk. xxix (ed. Griffin, pp. 226–7). Cf. the brief reference in Joseph of Exeter, *Yliados libri sex*, ii, 542–4 (ed. Gompf, p. 97).

34 Perhaps it should be emphasized that this analysis does not in any way conflict with a Boethian point which the poem certainly makes, that Fortune, in a sense, rules over all things mortal and sub-lunary, and that all human happiness and aspiration is consequently insecure and mutable; therefore, one should love a godhead which is eternal, immutable and beyond change. While Chaucer was not a believer in absolute necessity of the kind espoused by certain pagans, he certainly accepted the notion of common Fortune, which governs all people in all ages (see esp. IV, 1–7). Moreover, as Boethius explained so well, fate is in fact divine providence seen from below, from the human point of view. All things are directed from above by divine providence: hence, Chaucer can speak (paganizing the Boethian idiom) of 'the fatal destyne/That Joves hath in disposicioun' (V, 1–2). But of course, all these ideas are perfectly compatible with belief in the freedom of the will (as is made clear in the fifth book of *De Consolatione Philosophiae*), and it is when Chaucer's pagans incline to the denial of this freedom that he parts company with them. I am grateful to Myra Stokes for valuable discussion of this point.

35 The free-will of Chaucer's characters is emphasized by H. R. Patch, 'Troilus on Determinism', in *Chaucer Criticism*, ed. Schoeck and Taylor, ii, 71–85, but he does not attempt to describe the full significance of Chaucer's literary paganism. Peter Elbow, in his *Oppositions in Chaucer* (Middletown, Conn., 1975), pp. 49–72, argues that at times Chaucer suggests determinism by emphasizing fortune and destiny, but at other times his characters make us think their actions are free. Criseyde, for example, seems to have free will, yet, when we look more closely, she is not free—she does what she does because she is what she is, because of her character. I would emphasize that Criseyde is free to the extent that she is responsible for her own actions, i.e. she has free will in the strict philosophical sense of the term. As medieval clerics say so often, character-traits may incline us to perform certain actions, but freedom of contradiction remains to us.

36 See W. C. Curry, *Chaucer and the Medieval Sciences*, 2nd ed. (London, 1960), pp. 258–65.

37 Many examples are offered throughout Wood's *Country of the Stars*.

38 J. D. North, '"Kalendres Enlumyned ben They": Some Astronomical Themes in Chaucer', *RES*, new series, xx (1969), 129–54, 257–83, 418–44.

39 Cf. Wood, *Country of the Stars*, pp. 47–9.

40 For these concepts see, for example, Bartholomaeus Anglicus, *On the properties of things*, iii.6 (Trevisa's translation, ed. M. C. Seymour et al. (Oxford, 1975), p. 96), which cites Pseudo–Augustine, *Liber de Anima et Spiritu*; also Étienne Gilson, *The Mystical Theology of St Bernard*, trans. A. H. C. Downes (London, 1940), p. 101, note 131. The disposition or 'affection' (*affectus*) was believed to be fourfold, comprising the affections of delight, misery, love and fear; these four are, as it were, the source and the common material of the virtues and vices.

41 See Pratt, 'Some Latin Sources of the Nonnes Preest'.

42 *Sap. Sal. praelectiones*, lectio 103 (on Wisdom 7.27–8), pp. 348–51.

43 Ibid., lectio 202 (on Wisdom 18.17–19), pp. 665–7.

44 *Il Filostrato*, vii, sts 84–102 (ed. Branca, pp. 213–4; trans. Havely, pp. 95–7).

45 Ed. Macaulay, ii, 156.

46 I cannot accept Henry H. Peyton's suggestion that 'Cassandra's divination is delivered with the diabolic intensity of a harpy': 'The Roles of Calkas, Helen and Cassandra in Chaucer's *Troilus*', *Interpretations*, vii (1975), 10–12. His unfavourable interpretation of her character is, in my opinion, mistaken.

47 It should be remembered that, according to a tradition which goes back to the *Agamemnon* of Aeschylus, Cassandra obtained the gift of prophecy from Apollo, who turned the blessing into a curse by causing her always to be disbelieved. However, this tradition did not find its way into Benoît, Joseph or Guido.

48 *Historia Destructionis Troiae*, bks vi, vii, xvi (ed. Griffin, pp. 66–7, 79, 148; trans. Meek, pp. 64–5, 77–8, 142–3).

49 Trans. Meek, p. 78.

50 *Historia Destructionis Troiae*, bk. viii (ed. Griffin, p. 87). The contrast between Guido's Cassandra and Medea is striking. The latter is learned in magic of a kind which involves necromancy, and 'the pagans of antiquity were willing to believe that she could very often force . . . the sun and moon to go into eclipse against the order of nature'—an event which, as Christians know full well, can occur only through divine intervention, as was the case at the crucifixion of Christ. See *Historia Destructionis Troiae*, bk. ii (ed. Griffin, pp. 15–17; trans. Meek, pp. 13–15).

51 To some extent the following account of Calkas supports the view of Greenfield, who argues that 'Chaucer is ridiculing the astrology-prophetism of Calkas . . . while at the same time using it to create an atmosphere of destinal determinism': 'The Role of Calkas', p. 145.

52 *Dictys and Dares*, trans. Frazer, pp. 31, 35, 146; Joseph of Exeter, *Yliados libri sex*, iv, 251–73 (ed. Gompf, p. 149; trans. Roberts, pp. 45–6).

53 For Benoît see Havely, *Chaucer's Boccaccio*, pp. 168–9; cf. *Historia Destructionis Troiae*, bks x and xix (ed. Griffin, pp. 97–9, 165; trans. Meek, pp. 95–6, 158–9).

54 *Historia Destructionis Troiae*, bk. xxv; cf. bk. xix, for the Trojans' (understandably) low opinion of him (ed. Griffin, pp. 196; 160–1).

55 *Historia Destructionis Troiae*, bk. x (ed. Griffin, pp. 97–9; trans. Meek, pp. 95–6).

56 *Il Filostrato*, i, sts 10–11 (ed. Branca, p. 28; trans. Havely, p. 25).

57 *Il Filostrato*, iv, st. 136 (ed. Branca, p. 147; trans. Havely, p. 71). Of course, it is possible to argue that this speech tells us as much about Criseyde's character as it does about her father's: see my discussion on pp. 83–5. But it cannot be dismissed as a wholly subjective, biased and self-revelatory view of Calkas, because of the extent to which it squares with the narrator's own point of view—a point of view which may be clarified by examination of Chaucer's divergences from Guido and Boccaccio in this instance.

58 *Summa Iudicialis*, ii, prologus (MS Bodley 369, fols 128ᵛ–9ʳ).

59 Trans. in an Appendix by Ashmand, *Ptolemy's Tetrabiblos*, p. 224.

60 *Tetrabiblos*, i.3 (trans. Ashmand, pp. 13–14).

61 See Wedel, *Medieval Attitude toward Astrology*, pp. 8–10, note 1.

62 *Summa Iudicialis*, ii, distinctiones ii–xi (MS Bodley 369, fols 130ᵛ–366ᵛ). Ashenden's account of prediction in the case of wars and 'combustions' is particularly interesting (distinctio xi, on fols 329ᵛ–366ᵛ).

63 For Aquinas and Bacon see Wedel, *Medieval Attitude toward Astrology*, pp. 72–3, 68; for Holcot see *Sap. Sal. praelectiones*, lectio 190 (pp. 626–7).

64 *Sap. Sal. praelectiones*, lectio 160 (on Wisdom 13.17–19), pp. 529–30.

65 Cf. note 57 above.

66 C. S. Lewis, *The Allegory of Love* (Oxford, 1936), p. 190. An excellent discussion of Criseyde's fears is included in Mark Lambert's essay 'Troilus, Books I–III: A Criseydan Reading', in *Essays on Troilus and Criseyde*, ed. Mary Salu, Chaucer Studies, iii (Woodbridge, 1981), 105–125.

67 *Sap. Sal. praelectiones*, pp. 540–1.

68 *Fulgentius Metaforalis*, ed. Liebeschütz, pp. 66–8.

69 Robertson, *Preface to Chaucer*, pp. 99–104, 112–3, 401, 447, 450–2, 478–82, 498–9; John Frankis, 'Paganism and Pagan Love in *Troilus and Criseyde*', in *Essays on Troilus*, ed. Salu, pp. 57–72.

70 *Sap. Sal. praelectiones*, lectio 163 (on Wisdom 14.11–14), pp. 537–40.

71 This is in essence the view of Robertson, *Preface to Chaucer*, pp. 477–9, 481.

72 Taking this scenario even further, one could cite Aquinas's remark that the majority of men are governed by their emotions, wherein the influence of the stars is clearly felt. 'The wise man rules the stars' in as much as he rules his own passions. See *Summa Theologiae*, I. 1a 115.4, cited by Wedel, *Medieval Attitude toward Astrology*, p. 68. Indulging his passions, Troilus is subjecting himself to the stars—a reprehensible reversal of the natural order and hierarchy. Certain Middle English verses quoted by North make the point succinctly:

> A resonable soule is more worthi than sterres,
> and is not harmed of hem but by ignoraunce.

Richard of Wallingford, i, 179.

73 This may be regarded as a variant of the arguments put forward by Robertson, *Preface to Chaucer*, pp. 499–500, and J. F. Adams, 'Irony in Troilus's Apostrophe to the Vacant House of Criseyde', *MLQ*, xxiv (1963), 61–5.

74 For discussion of the powers and limitations of the imagination as described by medieval thinkers see Minnis, 'Langland's Ymaginatif and Late-Medieval Theories of Imagination'.

75 K. C. Dean, '*Maritalis Affectio': Attitudes towards Marriage in English and French Medieval Literature* (Ph.d. thesis, University of California, Davis, 1979), pp. 156–7.

76 All these writers are characterised by Wigginton in his doctoral thesis, *Nature and Significance of the Late Medieval Troy Story*.

77 See Wigginton, pp. 59–60.

78 Joseph of Exeter, *Yliados libri sex* (ed. Gompf, pp. 128–30, 181; trans. Roberts, pp. 34–5, 66–7); *Historia Destructionis Troiae*, bks vii, xxiii (ed. Griffin, pp. 71–5, 183–6); cf. Wigginton, pp. 104–6.

79 Trans. Roberts, pp. 34–5.

80 *Historia Destructionis Troiae*, bk. xix (ed. Griffin, p. 164; trans. Meek, pp. 157–8).

81 See Baskerville, *Two Studies in the Redaction of the Medieval Troy Story*, p. 143.

82 *Historia Destructionis Troiae*, bk. xix (ed. Griffin, p. 166).

83 *Il Filostrato*, iv, st. 152 (ed. Branca, p. 151; trans. Havely, p. 73).

84 *Il Filostrato*, ii, st. 74 (ed. Branca, p. 62; trans. Havely, p. 38).

85 *Il Filostrato*, viii, st. 30 (ed. Branca, p. 224; trans. Havely, p. 101).

86 Wigginton, *Nature and Significance of the Late Medieval Troy Story*, p. 61.

87 Cf. Baskerville, *Two Studies in the Redaction of the Medieval Troy Story*, p. 138.

88 Cf. ibid., p. 117.

89 *Roman de Troie*, 20677–82 (ed. Constans, iii, 312; trans. Havely, p. 181).

90 Abundant documentation has been provided by Douglas Kelly, *Medieval Imagination: Rhetoric and the Poetry of Courtly Love* (Madison and London, 1978); cf. Minnis, 'Langland's Ymaginatif and Late-Medieval Theories of Imagination', p. 98, note 35.

91 *Historia Destructionis Troiae*, bk. xviii (ed. Griffin, pp. 165–6; trans. Meek, pp. 158–9).

92 The implication, of course, is that Briseida's emotions are leading her into impiety. Cf. with this Guido's tart comment on the lamentations of Hecuba, Polyxena, Cassandra and Andromache, on the death of Hector: 'It is inborn in women by nature to reveal their griefs in loud exclamations and to make them known with impious and grievous speeches' (trans. Meek, pp. 169–70).

93 In this episode Guido is following Benoît, but he has transformed his source.

Benoît's Calchas emphasizes that he obeyed the will of the gods with great reluctance, and his treason still pains his heart both night and day. Here is no condescension or moral superiority. Moreover, Calchas's love and concern for his daughter are manifest. See Havely's translation of the crucial passage, pp. 174–5.

94 *Historia Destructionis Troiae*, xix (ed. Griffin, p. 166; trans. Meek, p. 160).

95 *Polychronicon Ranulphi*, i, 19.

96 *Roman de Troie*, 20277–8 (ed. Constans, iii, 292; trans. Havely, p. 180).

97 *Polychronicon Ranulphi*, i, 18–21.

98 *Browning: Poetical Works 1833–64*, ed. Ian Jack (Oxford, 1970), p. 580.

99 For this point of view see especially E. T. Donaldson, 'Criseyde and her Narrator', *Speaking of Chaucer* (London, 1970), 65–83.

100 This conception of Troilus's character may have grown gradually in Chaucer's mind, for Troilus's hymn to love (III, 1744–71) and soliloquy on fate (IV, 958–1078), both derived from Boethius, were not present in what R. K. Root regarded as the earliest version of the poem: see Root's edition of *The Book of Troilus and Criseyde by Geoffrey Chaucer* (Princeton, 1945), pp. lxxi–lxxiii. However, B. Windeatt has argued convincingly that 'To say that the *Troilus* existed for a while without the philosophical passages is comparable to saying that St Paul's Cathedral existed for a while without its dome, that is, until the plan implied by the rest of the structure was completed': 'The Text of the *Troilus*', *Essays on Troilus*, ed. Salu, pp. 1–22 (p. 21).

101 Cf. Patch, who remarks that in IV, 953–1085 Troilus gives 'way to his feelings rather than his intellect': 'Troilus on Determinism', *Chaucer Criticism*, ed. Schoeck and Taylor, ii, 77.

102 *Comment. in De Cons. Phil.*, II pr. 1 (ed. Silk).

103 One might compare Criseyde's outburst concerning earthly mutability, on being told about Troilus's jealousy, in III, 813–36.

104 Condemned proposition 21, printed by Denifle and Chatelain, *Chartularium Universitatis Parisiensis*, i, 545.

105 Therefore, Ida Gordon misses the point in claiming that this speech is a parody of Boethius: *The Double Sorrow of Troilus* (Oxford, 1970), pp. 45–6.

106 *In Topica Ciceronis*, lib. i (Migne, *PL*, lxiv, col. 1048D).

107 Chenu, *Toward understanding St Thomas*, p. 94.

108 *Boethius: Tractates, De Consolatione Philosophiae*, ed. and trans. H. F. Stewart, E. K. Rand and S. J. Tester (Cambridge, Mass., 1973), p. 405. This edition and translation of *De Consolatione Philosophiae* has been used throughout this book.

109 At the end of his soliloquy Chaucer describes Troilus as having been 'Disputyng with hymself' (IV, 1084). On the technical scholastic meaning of the term *disputatio* see Chenu, *Toward understanding St Thomas*, pp. 88–93.

110 *Three Prose Versions of the Secreta*, ed. Steele, p. 65. Cf. the similar statements in other versions ed. Steele, pp. 21, 196.

111 Perhaps it should be emphasized at this point that no neat and strict distinction can be made between pagan monotheism and pagan polytheism in *Troilus*, since the main characters often refer to an almighty god yet just as often swear by the planet-gods. This is a common feature of late-medieval classicism and literary paganism, deriving from, for example, the statement made by Augustine in *De Civitate Dei*, iv.11 that the pagan doctors believed the multitude of gods to be but one and the same Jupiter; quoted by Vincent of Beauvais, *Speculum Doctrinale*, xix.18: *Quod omnia potius vni Ioui viderentur esse attribuenda* (*Speculum Maius*, ii, 292ᵛ–3ʳ). Other pagans were content simply to believe that Jupiter was the king of the gods: see *De Civitate Dei*, iv.9. Many late-medieval clerics seem to have assumed that, in pagan antiquity, fatalism of the worst kind could co-exist with either polytheism or monotheism as defined above, although of course there was no essential connection, since the best of the virtuous heathen believed in one god and in the freedom of the will.

112 This feature of the poem has been discussed extensively, but there has been a regrettable tendency to disparage Pandarus's acts of friendship on the grounds that they are lacking in real virtue: see especially Alan T. Gaylord, 'Friendship in Chaucer's *Troilus*', *The Chaucer Review*, iii (1969), 239–46; Robert G. Cook, 'Chaucer's Pandarus and the Medieval Ideal of Friendship', *JEGP*, lxix (1970), 407–24. Those who regard Pandarus as a true friend include S. B. Neff, 'Chaucer's Pandarus', *Western Humanities Review*, iv (1950), 343–8, and E. E. Slaughter, 'Chaucer's Pandarus: Virtuous Uncle and Friend', *JEGP*, xlviii (1949), 186–95.

113 In my opinion, the view of J. B. Maguire and H. A. Kelly that Troilus and Criseyde were secretly married is a striking instance of misplaced ingenuity: Maguire, 'The Clandestine Marriage of Troilus and Criseyde', *The Chaucer Review*, viii (1974), 275–6; Kelly, *Love and Marriage in the Age of Chaucer* (Ithaca, 1975), pp. 225–42. Neither can I accept Gordon's view that 'Chaucer's silence about marriage is of a kind that implicitly raises the question of the illicitness of the love': *The Double Sorrow of Troilus*, p. 52.

114 It may be added that, in secular and non-homiletic medieval literary contexts, marriage is very rarely a criterion for the worthiness of the love being presented—one immediately thinks of the troubadours, Guillaume de Machaut, Chaucer's own *Book of the Duchess*, and Thomas Malory. In such contexts, the contrast is between chaste or virtuous or faithful love and foolish love or promiscuity, not between marriage and fornication. It is highly unlikely, therefore, that Chaucer was anxious about this aspect of his story. I am indebted to Myra Stokes for valuable discussion of this point.

115 Gordon, *The Double Sorrow of Troilus*, p. 37.

116 By this I mean simply that, in this instance, Chaucer's syncretism seems just and reasonable; I am not adumbrating a 'harmony of contraries' argument of the type formulated so elaborately by Donald W. Rowe, *O Love, O Charite! Contraries Harmonized in Chaucer's Troilus* (Carbondale and Edwardsville, S. Illinois, 1976). I endorse the comments on Rowe's approach made by Ian Bishop, *Chaucer's Troilus and Criseyde* (Bristol, 1981), p. 111, note 43.

117 On these prologues see Minnis, 'Medieval French and English Traditions of the *De Consolatione Philosophiae*', p. 314.

118 *Comment. in De Cons. Phil.*, III pr. 7 (ed. Silk).

119 See E. Langlois, 'Archipiada', *Mélanges de philologie romane dediés à Carl Wahlund* (Macon, 1896), 173–9; Pierre Courcelle, *La Consolation de philosophie dans la tradition littéraire*, Études Augustiniennes (Paris, 1967), pp. 258–9, 280; R. A. Dwyer, 'Villon's Boethius', *Annuale Medievale*, xi (1970), 74–80.

120 *Sap. Sal. praelectiones*, lectiones 155–6, pp. 517–20.

121 Cf. E. T. Donaldson, 'The Ending of *Troilus*', *Speaking of Chaucer*, pp. 84–101 (p. 92).

122 As is implied by Frankis, 'Paganism and Pagan Love', pp. 66–9.

123 *Polychronicon Ranulphi*, i, 18–21.

124 *Chaucer: Works*, ed. Robinson, p. 265.

125 For references and illuminating discussion see John M. Steadman, *Disembodied Laughter: Troilus and the Apotheosis Tradition* (Berkeley and Los Angeles, 1972), pp. 1–41; also J. A. W. Bennett, 'Some Second Thoughts on the *Parlement of Foules*', in *Chaucerian Problems and Perspectives: Essays presented to Paul E. Beichner*, ed. E. Vasta and Z. P. Thundy (Notre Dame, Indiana, and London, 1979), pp. 132–46 (pp. 132–7).

126 Cf. Minnis, 'A Note on Chaucer and the *Ovide Moralisé*', p. 254.

127 *Le Roman de Thebes*, 4711–950 (ed. L. Constans (Paris, 1890), i, pp. 230–42; cf. the expanded version printed in vol. ii, Appendice I, pp. 16–17).

128 *Lydgate's Siege of Thebes*, ed. A. Erdmann, EETS ES cviii (Oxford, 1911), 166.

129 *Teseida*, xi, st. 1 (ed. Roncaglia, p. 316; trans. Havely, *Chaucer's Boccaccio*, p. 144); cf. Steadman, *Disembodied Laughter*, pp. 16–20.
130 *Teseida*, x, sts 95, 99 (ed. Roncaglia, pp. 310, 311; trans. B. M. McCoy, *The Book of Theseus by Giovanni Boccaccio* (New York, 1974), p. 279).
131 Chiose al libro x (ed. Roncaglia, p. 449; trans. McCoy, p. 286). On Chaucer's possible knowledge of Boccaccio's commentary on his own work see especially Boitani, *Chaucer and Boccaccio*, pp. 113–6, 190–7.
132 *Teseida*, xi, st. 3 (ed. Roncaglia, p. 316; trans. McCoy, p. 289; cf. Havely, p. 144).
133 Cf. Steadman, *Disembodied Laughter*, pp. 40–1.
134 See especially Arcita's catalogue of the virtues which, in his view, make him worthy of Elysium: *Teseida*, x, sts 96–9 (ed. Roncaglia, pp. 310–11; trans. McCoy, p. 279).
135 Cf. Tatlock, 'The Epilog of Chaucer's *Troilus*', pp. 640–7.

CHAPTER 4

1 On the other hand, the Knight has been seen as a crude mercenary and a cold-blooded killer, a product of the growing commercialization of warfare: see Terry Jones, *Chaucer's Knight: The Portrait of a Medieval Mercenary* (London, 1980). An utterly convincing refutation of these views has been provided by Maurice Keen, 'Chaucer's Knight, the English Aristocracy, and the Crusade', in *English Court Culture in the Later Middle Ages: Proceedings of the Colston Symposium, University of Bristol, 5–8 April* (forthcoming).
2 The significance of the age of each of the characters is brought out well by D. Brooks and A. Fowler, 'The Meaning of Chaucer's *Knight's Tale*', *Medium Ævum*, xxxix (1970), 123–46, and J. A. Burrow, 'Chaucer's *Knight's Tale* and the Ages of Man' (unpublished).
3 On style and characterization in *Il Teseida* see especially Boitani, *Chaucer and Boccaccio*, pp. 1–60.
4 On Chaucer's knowledge of the *Anticlaudianus* see especially E. P. Hammond, *Chaucer: A Bibliographical Manual* (repr. New York, 1933), p. 84; T. R. Lonsbury, *Studies in Chaucer* (New York, 1892), ii, 344–52; M. J. Donivan, 'The *Anticlaudianus* and Three Passages in the *Franklin's Tale*', *JEGP*, lvi (1957), 52–9.
5 This notion has been expressed in various ways by a few critics, but never (to the best of my knowledge) in the form offered here. I have found particularly stimulating Brooks/Fowler and Burrow (cit. note 2 above), and also P. M. Kean, *Chaucer and the Making of English Poetry* (London and Boston, 1972), ii, 3–52; Alan Gaylord, 'The Role of Saturn in the *Knight's Tale*', *The Chaucer Review*, viii (1974), 171–90 (esp. pp. 175, 182–3).
6 Cf. Boitani, *Chaucer and Boccaccio*, p. 47.
7 I cannot accept R. M. Jordan's view that 'There is no clear reason why Palamon should be the Knight of Venus and Arcite the Knight of Mars rather than vice versa': *Chaucer and the Shape of Creation* (Cambridge, Mass., 1967), pp. 172–3.
8 Some of the arguments offered here concerning the differences in the cousins' characters were to some extent anticipated by H. N. Fairchild, 'Active Arcite, Contemplative Palamon', *JEGP*, xxvi (1927), 285–93. Unfortunately, he imposes a Christian ideology on pagan characters, failing to take account of their historical position. Most critics agree that Arcite and Palamon are similar in many respects; there is, however, considerable disagreement concerning the quality of differentiation between them. See the helpful summary of the various positions provided at the beginning of L. Y. Roney's thesis, *Scholastic Philosophies in Chaucer's Knight's Tale* (Ph.d. thesis, University of Wisconsin, Madison, 1970).

9 *Ovidius Moralizatus*, ed. Engels, p. 15; cf. the anonymous *De Deorum Imaginibus Libellus*, iii (ed. as an appendix by Liebeschütz, Ridevall's *Fulgentius Metaforalis*, pp. 117–8). See further the account of medieval descriptions of Mars in Twycross, *The Representation of the Major Classical Divinities*, pp. 208–59.

10 *Reductorium Morale*, v.25 (in the Venice edition of 1583, p. 122).

11 *On the Properties of Things*, viii.13 (ed. Seymour et al., i, 481).

12 Alain de Lille, *Anticlaudianus*, IV, 420–6 (ed. R. Bossuat, Textes philosophiques du moyen âge, i (Paris, 1955), p. 119; trans. J. J. Sheridan, *Anticlaudianus, or The Good and Perfect Man*, Pontifical Institute of Mediaeval Studies (Toronto, 1973), p. 133).

13 North, *Richard of Wallingford*, i, 200–1, 214–5, 232–3.

14 *Summa Iudicialis*, i, dist. iv, cap. 3 (MS Bodley 369, fols 44ᵛ–6ᵛ). Cf. the brief account in Vincent of Beauvais, *Speculum Naturale*, xv.27 (*Speculum Maius*, i, fol. 188ᵛ); also Curry, *Chaucer and the Medieval Sciences*, pp. 123–4.

15 See Twycross, *The Medieval Anadyomene*.

16 *Ovidius Moralizatus*, ed. Engels, p. 22. Cf. the *Libellus*, v (ed. Liebeschütz, p. 118). No Venus 'picture' appears in the partial text of Ridevall's *Fulgentius Metaforalis* edited by Liebeschütz, but one is included in the 'longer version', on which see Allen, 'The "Fulgentius Metaphored" of John Ridewall', pp. 25–8. An edition of Ridevall's picture of Venus is being prepared by Dr Nigel Palmer of Oriel College, Oxford.

17 On Chaucer's descriptions of the temples of Venus and Mars see especially Boitani, *Chaucer and Boccaccio*; also his article 'Chaucer's Temples of Venus', *Studi Inglesi*, ii (1975), 9–31.

18 *Mythologiae*, ii.i (ed. Helm, pp. 66–7).

19 Mythographus Tertius, ii.1 (in *Scriptores rerum mythicarum*, ed. Bode, pp. 228–9. For the identification of this writer as Alberic of London see E. Rathbone, 'Master Alberic of London, "Mythographus Tertius Vaticanus"', *Mediaeval and Renaissance Studies*, i (1941–3), 35–8. Cf. the essentially similar view of Venus held by Mythographus Secundus, iii.30–3 (ed. Bode, pp. 84–5).

20 *On the Properties of Things*, viii.14 (ed. Seymour, i, 481–2); cf. *Reductorium Morale*, v.26 (pp. 122–3); Vincent of Beauvais, *Speculum Naturale*, xv.29 (*Speculum Maius*, i, fol. 188ᵛ).

21 From the anonymous Middle English translation of the *Exafrenon prognosticacionum temporis* (ed. North, *Richard of Wallingford*, i, 233).

22 *Summa Iudicialis*, i, dist. iv, cap. 5 (MS Bodley 369, fols 47ʳ–8ᵛ).

23 On late-medieval 'affective piety' see especially D. Gray, *Themes and Images in the Medieval English Religious Lyric* (London and Boston, 1972), pp. 18–30.

24 *Reductorium Morale*, v.26 (pp. 122–3).

25 Cf. Curry, *Chaucer and the Mediaeval Sciences*, pp. 131–4.

26 Ibid., pp. 134–7. However, Curry is quite wrong in thinking that Saturn champions the cause of Venus by granting her knight ultimate success, since Chaucer makes it perfectly clear that both Venus and Mars are satisfied with Saturn's solution (see I, 2446; 2471–76). Cf. Gaylord, 'The Role of Saturn', p. 190, note 47.

27 *On the Properties of Things*, viii.17 (ed. Seymour et al., i, 493). For medieval attitudes to Diana see Twycross, *The Representation of the Major Classical Divinities*, pp. 499–564.

28 *Ovidius Moralizatus*, ed. Engels, pp. 28–9.

29 *On the Properties of Things*, viii.12 (ed. Seymour et al., i, 480). For medieval attitudes to Jupiter see Twycross, *The Representation of the Major Classical Divinities*, pp. 167–207.

30 *Reductorium Morale*, v.24 (pp. 121–2). Cf. Richard of Wallingford's *Exafrenon*, ed. North, i, 200–1, 231–3, 214–5.

31 *Summa Iudicialis*, i, dist. iv, cap. 2 (MS Bodley 369, fols 42ᵛ–44ᵛ); cf. Vincent of

Beauvais, *Speculum Naturale*, xv.27; *Speculum Doctrinale*, xv.47 (*Speculum Maius*, i, fol. 188ᵛ; ii, fol. 263ᵛ).

32 *Ovidius Moralizatus*, ed. Engels, pp. 10–11. Cf. the *Libellus*, ii (ed. Liebeschütz, p. 117). See further Bernard Silvester's interesting etymology of the name 'Theseus': 'Theseus is called *deus bonus*: 'the good god'—*theos* is *deus*, 'god', and *eu* is *bonum*, 'good'. He is called a god because of the theoretical knowledge of the divine, and is called good because of the practical knowledge which teaches the human good, that is, the honest life'. *Commentary on the First Six Books of Virgil's Aeneid by Bernardus Silvestris*, trans. E. G. Schreiber and T. E. Maresca (Lincoln and London, 1979), p. 83. Cf. Robertson, *Preface to Chaucer*, pp. 260–2, who unfortunately finds in this interpretation support for his allegorical approach to *The Knight's Tale*. In my opinion, Silvester's details constitute an interesting abstract and ideological parallel to the way in which Chaucer conceived of the character of Theseus in terms which were historical, literal and concrete.

33 *Ovidius Moralizatus*, ed, Engels, pp. 6, 11; cf. Mythographus Tertius, iii.4 (ed. Bode, p. 162); Mythographus Secundus, proemium (p. 74); also (more generally) Vincent of Beauvais, *Speculum Doctrinale*, xv.47 (*Speculum Maius*, iii, fol. 263ᵛ).

34 See for example Ridevall, *Fulgentius Metaforalis*, iii (ed. Liebeschütz, pp. 81–2); Mythographus Tertius, iii.2 (ed. Bode, p. 160).

35 However, this action cannot be taken as an instance of special cruelty, *pace* Jones, *Chaucer's Knight*, pp. 175–6, and H. J. Webb, 'A Reinterpretation of Chaucer's Theseus', *RES*, xxiii (1947), 289–96. According to the medieval laws of war relating to a town taken by assault, Theseus was perfectly justified: see Maurice Keen's chapter 'Sieges' in his *The Laws of War in the Later Middle Ages* (London, 1965), pp. 119–33.

36 *Fulgentius Metaforalis*, iii (ed. Liebeschütz, pp. 82–3). Cf. Mythographus Tertius, iii.3 (ed. Bode, p. 161).

37 *Anticlaudianus*, IV, 445–51 (ed. Bossuat, p. 120; trans. Sheridan, p. 134).

38 'þis Iubiter by his goodnes abatiþ þe malice of Saturnus'; 'by his presence he abatiþ þe kynde malice of Saturnus': *On the Properties of Things*, viii.12 (ed. Seymour, i, 480); cf. Vincent of Beauvais, *Speculum Naturale*, xv.27 (*Speculum Maius*, i, fol. 188ᵛ); Ashenden, *Summa Iudicialis*, i, dist. iv, cap. 2 (MS Bodley 369, fols 42ᵛ–4ᵛ); Bersuire, *Reductorium Morale*, v.24 (pp. 121–2).

39 Cf. Jones, *Chaucer's Knight*, p. 195; R. Neuse, 'The Knight: The First Mover in Chaucer's Human Comedy', *University of Toronto Quarterly*, xxxi (1961/2), 299 –315 (p. 306).

40 Critical opinion on Theseus has been sharply divided. For the view, which I share, that he is an admirable and noble ruler, see for example R. K. Root, *The Poetry of Chaucer* (rpt. New York, 1950), p. 171; C. Muscatine, *Chaucer and the French Tradition* (Berkeley and Los Angeles, 1957), p. 183; E. T. Donaldson, *Chaucer's Poetry: An Anthology for the Modern Reader* (New York, 1958), p. 104; Robertson, *Preface to Chaucer*, pp. 260–66; R. L. Hoffman, *Ovid and the Canterbury Tales* (Pennsylvania, 1966), p. 46; Elbow, *Oppositions in Chaucer*, p. 79; Boitani, *Chaucer and Boccaccio*, pp. 144–7; Burlin, *Chaucerian Fiction*, pp. 101–2, 104–5, 110–11; Burnley, *Chaucer and the Philosophers' Tradition*, pp. 25–7, 30–1, 44, 80, 116. Unfavourable interpretations include: Webb, 'A Reinterpretation of Chaucer's Theseus'; Dale Underwood, 'The First of the *Canterbury Tales*', *ELH*, xxvi (1959), 455–69; Neuse, 'The Knight: The First Mover'; T. K. Meier, 'Chaucer's Knight as "Persona": Narration as Control', *English Miscellany*, xx (1969), 11–21; Kathleen A. Blake, 'Order and the Noble Life in Chaucer's *Knight's Tale*', *MLQ*, xxxiv (1973), 3–19; Jones, *Chaucer's Knight*, pp. 192–211.

41 On late-medieval conceptions of the link between ethics and politics, and of the importance of such doctrine for a ruler, see Minnis, 'John Gower, *sapiens* in Ethics and Politics'.

42 *Chaucer: Works*, ed. Robinson, pp. 510–5. This ignoble incident is mentioned also

in the *House of Fame*, 405–26 (pp. 285–6), where the narrator says of 'fals' Theseus, 'The devel be hys soules bane!' But no trace of this attitude can be found in *The Knight's Tale*. Cf. W. Frost, 'An Interpretation of Chaucer's *Knight's Tale*', *RES*, xxv (1949), 289–304.

43 *Communiloquium*, pars i, dist. 2, cap. 1 (fols 11ᵛ–12ʳ); cf. John of Salisbury, *Policraticus*, iv.1 (ed. Webb, i, 235–6; trans. Dickinson, p. 4). For praise of Plurarch as Trajan's teacher see for example Walter Burley, *De Vita et Moribus Philosophorum*, cap. cxix (ed. Knust, pp. 364–8).

44 John of Wales illustrates this with the *exemplum* of Trajan and the wronged widow, which is quoted on p. 53 above. The impartiality of Theseus is unquestionable. Chaucer omitted the episode in *Il Teseida* where Mars, disguised as Teseo, appears before Arcita to exhort him to fight harder in the tournament: he did not wish his character Theseus to seem to take sides in the feud, even in this indirect way, or indeed to condone the cousins' strife.

45 See *Communiloquium*, pars i, dist. 3, cap. 5 (fols 19ᵛ–21ʳ); cf. John of Salisbury, *Policraticus*, iv.8 (ed. Webb, i, 263–4; trans. Dickinson, pp. 38–9).

46 *St Erkenwald*, ed. Morse, pp. 60–2.

47 *Polychronicon Ranulphi*, v, 4–7.

48 On these standards see Keen, *The Laws of War*, passim.

49 *Teseida*, vii, sts 8–14 (ed. Roncaglia, pp. 182–3; trans. McCoy, pp. 168–9).

50 *Teseida*, viii, st. 100 (ed. Roncaglia, p. 246; trans. McCoy, p. 230).

51 *Teseida*, x, st. 6 (ed. Roncaglia, p. 285; trans. McCoy, p. 262).

52 Such irony was detected by Webb, 'A Reinterpretation of Chaucer's Theseus'. Frost rejected Webb's arguments as 'partial, misleading and incomplete': 'An Interpretation of Chaucer's *Knight's Tale*', pp. 289–304. For Keen's rejection of the more elaborate argument in Jones's book *Chaucer's Knight*, see note 1 above.

53 *Teseida*, xii, sts 5–19 (ed. Roncaglia, pp. 343–6; trans. McCoy, pp. 314–6).

54 *Teseida*, xii, sts 34–7 (ed. Roncaglia, pp. 350–1; trans. McCoy, pp. 319–20).

55 On the importance of causality as a fourteenth-century topic see W. J. Courtenay, 'The Critique on Natural Causality in the Mutakallimun and Nominalism', *Harvard Theological Review*, lxvi (1973), 77–94; also his 'Covenant and Causality in Pierre d'Ailly', *Speculum*, xlvi (1971), 94–119. On some thirteenth-century precedents see Chapter 3 of my book *Medieval Theory of Authorship*.

56 *Secreta Secretorum*, ed. Steele, pp. 64–5.

57 Ibid., p. 65.

58 Bradwardine stresses this aspect of God's power in *De Causa Dei*, i.1, cor. 32; ii.3 (ed. Savile, pp. 42–4, 449–72). Perhaps Chaucer regarded this as too Christian a belief, and hence too historically improbable, to ascribe to his noble pagan. But note that, in the *Secreta Secretorum*, 'Aristotle' expresses such a belief: if the stars tell of evil, we can pray to the 'heghe destynour' to put aside the evils that are to come (ed. Steele, p. 65).

59 For discussion of Chaucer's point of view see B. C. Koonce, *Chaucer and the Tradition of Fame: Symbolism in The House of Fame* (Princeton, 1966), and J. A. W. Bennett, *Chaucer's Book of Fame: An Exposition of The House of Fame* (Oxford, 1968).

60 *Sap. Sal. praelectiones*, lectio 18 (on Wisdom 2.4), pp. 68–9.

61 Ibid., p. 66; cf. his discussion of two additional points from *De Consolatione Philosophiae* III pr. 6, on pp. 66–7.

62 Cf. the discussion in Steadman, *Disembodied Laughter*, pp. 130–1.

63 *Teseida*, xii, sts 14–15 (ed. Roncaglia, p. 345; trans. McCoy, p. 315).

64 *Sap. Sal. praelectiones*, lectio 18 (p. 65).

65 *De Civitate Dei*, v.18 (ed. B. Dombart and A. Kalb, Corpus Christianorum, Series Latina, xlvii–iii (Turnholt, 1955), i, 151; trans. John Healey (London and New York, 1945), i, 166).

66 *Teseida*, xii, st. 15 (ed. Roncaglia, p. 345; trans. McCoy, p. 315).

67 *De Civitate Dei*, v.18; cf. cap. 17 (ed. Dombart and Kalb, i, 149–54; trans. Healey, i, 164–8).

68 The exemplum of Brutus is narrated at considerable length in Trevet's commentary on *De Consolatione Philosophiae* II pr. 7, wherein the general influence of Augustine's approach to the material is obvious.

69 *De Civitate Dei*, v.19 (ed. Dombart and Kalb, i, 156; trans. Healey, i, 170).

70 *Speculum Morale*, lib. iii, pars iii, dist. 8: *De peccato inanis gloriae* (*Speculum Maius*, iii, fol. 185ᵛ); *Communiloquium*, pars i, dist. 1, cap. 11: *Quanta sustinuerunt et fecerunt antiqui pro salute reipublice* (fol. 9ᵛ; cf. fols 10ʳ–10ᵛ); *Compendiloquium*, prohemium; also ii.2 (ed. Wadding, pp. 21, 78–9). In his *Manipulus Florum*, s.v. *gloria eterna*, Thomas of Ireland cites *De Civitate Dei*, v.22 (pp. 438–9, 442–3); see further his authorities on *gloria bona* and *gloria mala sive vana* (pp. 430–2, 432–8).

71 Bersuire, *Dictionarius seu Repertorium Morale*, s.v. *fama* (Venice, 1583), p. 100; cf. Koonce, *Chaucer and the Tradition of Fame*, pp. 20–2, note 17. See further Bersuire's entry under *gloria* (pp. 170–3), wherein a distinction is made between eternal glory, which is the same as beatitude, and worldly glory, which is greatly deceptive, short in duration, never satisfied (as is illustrated by the insatiable ambition of Alexander and Nabuchodonosor), utterly distracting, and ends sadly. Cf. Vincent of Beauvais, *Speculum Doctrinale*, iv.128: *De inani gloria*, and v.67–8, on glory and fame according to the philosophers and poets (*Speculum Maius*, ii, fols 68ʳ, 80ʳ); also *Speculum Morale*, lib. iii, pars iii, dist. 8: *De peccato inanis gloriae* (iii, fols 185ʳ–6ᵛ), and dist. 9: *De speciebus inani gloria, et de filiabus eiusdem* (iii, fols 186ᵛ–8ʳ —incorrectly foliated).

72 In this context, these terms may be regarded as synonymous: see Bersuire, *Dictionarius*, p. 100: 'Fama idem est, quod bonum nomen, bonus rumor, vel bona opinio de aliquo'.

73 Milton, *Lycidas*, 70–1. For discussion of the origins of Milton's concepts see J. S. Coolidge, 'Boethius and "That Last Infirmity of Noble Mind"', *PQ*, xlii (1963), 176–82.

74 See Boitani, *Chaucer and Boccaccio*, pp. 49–51, who claims that Emilia is 'undoubtedly the most fascinating of all the characters in the *Teseida*'.

75 *Teseida*, viii, st. 98 (ed. Roncaglia, p. 246; trans. McCoy, p. 229).

76 *Teseida*, viii, st. 100 (ed. Roncaglia, p. 246; trans. McCoy, p. 230).

77 *Teseida*, viii, st. 127 (ed. Roncaglia, pp. 253–4; trans. McCoy, p. 235).

78 *Teseida*, ix, sts 10–12; x, sts 69–71 (ed. Roncaglia, pp. 260–1; 302–3; trans. McCoy, pp. 243, 274).

79 This suggestion could be countered with the argument that the problem in question is not susceptible of easy solution. One of the cousins has to lose, whatever happens; consequently, what could even a benevolent god (e.g. Jupiter or the Christian God Himself) have done? Two kinds of reply may be offered, the first being that Chaucer was concerned to emphasize that the malevolent Saturn was ruling the roast, thereby alerting the reader to the issues described on pp. 139–141 above. Therefore, the question of what Jupiter could or could not have done simply does not arise. Secondly, one could reply that, in the case of the Christian God, the problem caused by different gods promising different things would not have occurred in the first place, since He is single, complete and consistent, in contradistinction with the pagan gods, who act on personal whim in a manner which is unco-ordinated and divisive. In sum, Chaucer did not intend us to consider the problem divorced from its historical pagan context. I am grateful to John Burrow for valuable discussion of this point.

80 *Teseida*, vii, 23–41 (ed. Roncaglia, pp. 185–90; trans. McCoy, pp. 171–5).

81 Cf. Boitani, *Chaucer and Boccaccio*, pp. 81–2, who notes that the 'dramatic' and 'delphic ambiguity' of Arcite's prayer and the god's response 'differs from Boccaccio's vagueness'.

82 See above pp. 34–5.

83 This is, of course, to read the relevant part of *The Knight's Tale* from the human point of view. On considering the situation from the gods' point of view, a rather different reading offers itself, although the basic point concerning the ambiguity of the oracle remains unchanged. Both Mars and Venus grant favours to their respective devotees, then discover that they have promised contradictory things— had Mars planned at the outset to give Arcite victory in battle alone, Venus would not have been upset. It is, therefore, Saturn who turns the response of Mars into an ambiguous answer: i.e., this is a case of retrospective ambiguity! Moreover, it should be noted that there may be another ambiguous oracle in the tale (again, of this retrospective kind). Mercury urges Arcite to return to Athens in the following manner:

> 'To Atthenes shaltou wende,
> Ther is the shapen of thy wo an ende'
> (I, 1391–2)

This is ambiguous, since it can mean either:
1. In Athens your woe shall end and you shall be joyful, or
2. There you shall meet your end or death, which will put paid to your woe—and any other emotion whatever! This episode is particularly significant because it is unprecedented in *Il Teseida*, where Arcita makes the decision to return to Athens without divine prompting. Could Chaucer have been inspired by a reminiscence of the passage in the *Roman de Thebes* where Apollo, speaking in a manner which the anonymous poet describes as obscure and deceptive, tells Oedipus that if he journeys to Thebes he will learn all about his parentage?

> 'Pour tant, se tu vers Thebes vas,
> De ton pere nueves orras'.

Le Roman de Thebes, 167–8 (ed. Constans, i, 10). In Lydgate's version the ambiguous response is put in the third person, but the grim irony is maintained. The fiend orders Oedipus

> in hast / taken his viage
> Toward Thebes / wher of his lynage
> He heren shal / and be certefied.

Lydgate's *Siege of Thebes*, 555–7 (ed. A. Erdmann, EETS ES cviii (Oxford, 1910), p. 25). For discussion of the crucial episode in the *Roman* see McGalliard, *Classical Mythology in certain Mediaeval Treatments of the Legends of Troy, Thebes and Aeneas*, pp. 180–2.
84 *Lydgate's Troy Book*, part 3, ed. H. Bergen, EETS ES cvi (Oxford, 1910), p. 767.
85 *Lydgate's Siege of Thebes*, ed. Erdmann, p. 25.
86 *Teseida*, ed. Roncaglia, p. 197; trans. McCoy, p. 179.
87 *On the Properties of Things*, viii.12 (ed. Seymour et. al., i, 479). Cf. Richard of Wallingford's *Exafrenon* (ed. North, *Richard of Wallingford*, i, 200–1, 212–5, 233; John Ashenden's *Summa Iudicialis*, i, dist. iv, cap. 1 (MS Bodley 369, fol. 41ʳ–42ᵛ), which may be compared with Ptolemy's *Tetrabiblos*, ii.9 (trans. Ashmand, pp. 85–6); Vincent of Beauvais, following William of Conches, in *Speculum Naturale*, xv.27 (*Speculum Maius*, i, fol. 188ᵛ). For general discussion of Saturn in medieval literature see Klibansky, Panofsky and Saxl, *Saturn and Melancholy*, pp. 159–95.
88 *Reductorium Morale*, v.23 (p. 121); *Ovidius Moralizatus*, ed. Engels, p. 6.
89 *Anticlaudianus*, IV, 482–3 (ed. Bossuat, p. 121). In his commentary on the *Anticlaudianus* (c.1212), Radulphus de Longo Campo expands on this consider-

ably: *Radulphus de Longo Campo in Anticlaudianum Alani Commentum*, ed. Jan Salowski (Wrocław and Warsaw, 1972), pp. 84–6.

90 Critical opinion on the role of Saturn is sharply divided. Helpful summaries of the differing views are included in Gaylord, 'The Role of Saturn'. Those who emphasize the planet-god's malevolent aspects include Curry, *Chaucer and the Medieval Sciences*, pp. 127–30; Muscatine, *Chaucer and the French Tradition*, p. 190; D. B. Loomis, 'Saturn in Chaucer's *Knight's Tale*', in *Chaucer und seine Zeit. Symposion für Walter F. Schirmer*, ed. Arno Esch (Tübingen, 1968), pp. 149–61; Wood, *Country of the Stars*, pp. 74–5; Gaylord, 'The Role of Saturn'; Burnley, *Chaucer's Language and the Philosophers' Tradition*, p. 38. Those who emphasize his sage wisdom include Twycross, *The Representation of the Major Classical Divinities*, pp. 148–50; Brooks and Fowler, 'The Meaning of Chaucer's *Knight's Tale*', p. 126; Kean, *Chaucer and the Making of English Poetry*, ii, 38–41; McCall, *Chaucer among the Gods*, pp. 79–80; Burrow, 'Chaucer's *Knight's Tale* and the Ages of Man'.

91 Quoted by Klibansky, Panofsky and Saxl, *Saturn and Melancholy*, p. 166.

92 *Fulgentius Metaforalis*, ed. Liebeschütz, p. 71.

93 *Ovidius Moralizatus*, ed. Engels, pp. 9–10.

94 Kean, *Chaucer and the Making of English Poetry*, ii, 32–4.

95 As argued, for example, by McCall, *Chaucer among the Gods*, pp. 80, 173.

96 It may be added that Saturn seems to have been responsible for the complications which render Arcite's injury fatal: Curry, *Chaucer and the Medieval Sciences*, pp. 139–48. Note also the role of Saturn in *The Legend of Hypermnestra*: it was the 'badde aspectes' which she had 'of Saturne, / That made hire for to deyen in prisoun . . .' (*Legend of Good Women*, 2597–8).

97 *Ovidius Moralizatus*, ed. Engels, p. 11.

98 See Bennett, 'Some Second Thoughts on *The Parlement of Foules*', p. 133.

99 *The Book of Theseus*, trans. McCoy, p. 14.

100 *Sap. Sal. praelectiones*, lectio 2 (pp. 8–9).

101 With regard to the musical metaphor (used in describing harmony and concord), cf. John of Wales, *Communiloquium*, pars i, dist. i, cap. 2 (fols 4ʳ–5ʳ).

102 Plato's commendation of the philosopher-ruler is cited by John of Wales also, in a chapter on the usefulness of philosophy in the *regimen vitae*. A state cannot be governed without just laws, he emphasizes, and philosophy is the inventor of laws. Moreover, certain ancient rulers had philosophers as counsellors: Alexander the Great had Aristotle, Nero had Seneca, and Trajan had Plutarch. *Compendiloquium*, pars i, cap. 6 (p. 53); cf. the *Communiloquium*, pars i, dist. iii, cap. 7 (fols 22ʳ–3ᵛ), on the importance to a prince of knowledge (*scientia*).

Adams, J. F.,   'Irony in Troilus's Apostrophe to the Vacant House of Criseyde', *MLQ*, xxiv (1963), 61–5.

Aiken, P.,   'Vincent of Beauvais and Dame Pertelote's Knowledge of Medicine', *Speculum*, x (1935), 281–7.

'The Summoner's Malady', *SP*, xxxiii (1936), 10–14.

'Chaucer's Legend of Cleopatra and the *Speculum Historiale*', *Speculum*, xiii (1938), 232–8.

'Vincent of Beauvais and the Green Yeoman's Lecture on Demonology', *SP*, xxxv (1938), 1–9.

'Vincent of Beauvais and Chaucer's *Monk's Tale*', *Speculum*, xvii (1942), 56–68.

'Vincent of Beauvais and Chaucer's Knowledge of Alchemy', *SP*, xli (1944), 371–89

Alain de Lille,   *Anticlaudianus*, ed. R. Bossuat, Textes philosophiques du moyen âge, i (Paris, 1955).

Anticlaudianus, or The Good and Perfect Man, trans. J. J. Sheridan, Pontifical Institute of Mediaeval Studies (Toronto, 1973).

Allen, J. B.,   'Hermann the German's Averroistic Aristotle and Medieval Poetic Theory', *Mosaic*, ix/3 (1976), 67–81.

'Commentary as Criticism: The Text, Influence and Literary Theory of the "Fulgentius Metaphored" of John Ridewall', in *Acta Conventus Neo-Latini Amstelodamensis: Proceedings of the Second International Congress of Neo-Latin Studies, Amsterdam 19–24 August 1973*, ed. P. Tuynman et al. (Munich, 1979), pp. 25–47.

Aquinas, Thomas,   *De Iudiciis Astrorum*, in *Opuscula Theologica*, i, ed. R. A. Verardo (Marietti, 1954).

Division and Methods of the Sciences, trans. A. Maurer, 3rd ed. (Toronto, 1963).

Summa Theologiae, Blackfriars ed. (London and New York, 1963–).

Ashenden, John,   *Summa Iudicialis*, in Bodleian Library, MS Bodley 369.

Atwood, E. B.,   *English Versions of the Historia Trojana* (Ph.d. thesis, University of Virginia, 1932).

Auer, Johann,   *Die Entwicklung der Gnadenlehre in der Hochscholas-*

Augustine, St.,	*tik, vol. ii: Das Wirken der Gnade* (Freiburg, 1951). *De Civitate Dei*, ed. B. Dombart and A. Kalb, Corpus Christianorum, Series Latina, xlvii–iii (Turnholt, 1955). *The City of God*, trans. J. Healey, ed. R. V. G. Tasker (London and New York, 1945).
Bartholomaeus Anglicus,	trans. John Trevisa, *On the Properties of Things*, ed. M. C. Seymour et al. (Oxford, 1975).
Baskerville, M.,	*Two Studies in the Redaction of the Medieval Troy Story: Guido delle Colonne's Historia Destructionis Troiae and the Alliterative Destruction of Troy* (Ph.d. thesis, Columbia University, 1978).
Baudry, L.,	*Lexique philosophique de Guillaume d'Occam* (Paris, 1957).
Bennett, J. A. W.,	*Chaucer's Book of Fame: An Exposition of The House of Fame* (Oxford, 1968). 'Some Second Thoughts on the *Parlement of Foules*', in *Chaucerian Problems and Perspectives: Essays presented to Paul E. Beichner*, ed. E. Vasta and Z. P. Thundy (Notre Dame, Indiana, and London, 1979), pp. 132–46.
Benoît de Ste Maure,	*Roman de Troie*, ed. L. Constans (Paris, 1904–12).
Benson, C. David.,	*The History of Troy in Middle English Literature* (Woodbridge, 1980).
Bernard Silvester,	*Commentary on the First Six Books of Virgil's Aeneid*, trans. E. G. Screiber and T. E. Maresca (Lincoln and London, 1979).
Bersuire, Pierre,	*Dictionarius seu Repertorium Morale* (Venice, 1583). *Reductorium Morale* (Venice, 1583). *Reductorium Morale, lib. xv: Ovidius Moralizatus, cap. i: De Formis Figurisque Deorum*, ed. J. Engels, Werkmaterial iii (Utrecht, 1966).

Biblia Sacra cum Glossa Ordinaria et Postilla Nicolai Lyrani (Lyon, 1589).

Blake, Kathleen A.,	'Order and the Noble Life in Chaucer's *Knight's Tale*', *MLQ*, xxxiv (1973), 3–19.
Bloomfield, M. W.,	'Chaucer's Sense of History', *JEGP*, li (1952), 301–13. 'Distance and Predestination in *Troilus and Criseyde*', rpt. in *Chaucer Criticism*, ed. Schoeck and Taylor, ii, 196–210.
Bishop, Ian,	*Pearl in its Setting* (Oxford, 1968). *Chaucer's Troilus and Criseyde* (Bristol, 1981).
Boccaccio, Giovanni,	*Genealogia Deorum Gentilium*, bks xiv and xv, trans. C. O. Osgood, *Boccaccio on Poetry*, The Library of Liberal Arts (Indianapolis and New York, 1956). *Il Filostrato*, ed. V. Branca, in *Tutte le opere di Giovanni Boccaccio, vol. ii*, I Classici Mondadori (Verona, 1964), pp. 17–228. *Teseida delle nozze d'Emilia*, ed. A. Roncaglia, Scrittori d'Italia, clxxxv (Bari, 1941).

	The Book of Theseus, trans. B. M. McCoy (New York, 1974).
	see also Havely, N. R.
Bode, G. H.,	*Scriptores Rerum Mythicarum Latini Tres Romae nuper reperti* (Celle, 1834).
Boehner, P.,	*Collected Articles on Ockham*, ed. E. M. Buytaert, Franciscan Institute Publications, Philosophy Series, xii (New York, 1958).
Boethius,	*In Topica Ciceronis*, Migne, *PL*, lxiv, cols 1039 –1174.
	Tractates; De Consolatione Philosophiae, ed. and trans. H. F. Stewart, E. K. Rand and S. J. Tester (Cambridge, Mass., 1973).
Boitani, P.,	'Chaucer's Temples of Venus', *Studi Inglesi*, ii (1975), 9–31.
	Chaucer and Boccaccio, Medium Ævum Monographs, New Series, viii (Oxford, 1977).
Bradwardine, Thomas,	*De Causa Dei contra Pelagium et de virtute causarum ad suos Mertonenses*, ed. H. Savile (London, 1618).
	Sermo Epinicius, ed. H. A. Oberman and J. A. Weisheipl, 'The *Sermo Epinicius* ascribed to Thomas Bradwardine (1346)', *AHDLMA*, xxv (1958), 295 –329.
Brewer, D.,	'What is the *Nun's Priest's Tale* really about?', *Trames*, Coll. anglais, ii (1979), 9–23.
Brito, William,	*Summa Britonis sive Guillelmi Britonis Expositiones Vocabulorum Biblie*, cd. L. W. Daly and B. A. Daly (Padova, 1975).
Browning, Robert,	*Poetical Works 1833–64*, ed. Ian Jack (Oxford, 1970).
Burley, Walter,	*Liber de Vita et Moribus Philosophorum*, ed. H. Knust (Tübingen, 1886).
Brooks, D., and Fowler, A.,	'The Meaning of Chaucer's *Knight's Tale*', *Medium Ævum*, xxxix (1970), 123–46.
Burlin, R. B.,	*Chaucerian Fiction* (Princeton, 1977).
Burnley, J. D.,	*Chaucer's Language and the Philosophers' Tradition*, Chaucer Studies, ii (Cambridge, 1979).
Burrow, John,	'Chaucer's *Knight's Tale* and the Ages of Man' (unpublished).
	'The Alterity of Medieval Literature', in *New Literary History*, x (1979), 385–90.
Callus, D. A.,	'The Function of the Philosopher in Thirteenth-Century Oxford', *Miscellanea Mediaevalia*, iii (Berlin, 1964), 153–62.
Cary, George,	*The Medieval Alexander* (Cambridge, 1956).
Caxton, William,	*The Golden Legend or Lives of the Saints*, ed. F. S. Ellis (London, 1900–35).
Chambers, R. W.,	'Long Will, Dante, and the Righteous Heathen', *Essays and Studies*, ix (1924), 50–69.

Chanson de Roland, La, ed. C. Segre, Documenti di filologia, xvi (Milan and Naples, 1971).

Chaucer, Geoffrey,   *The Works of Geoffrey Chaucer*, ed. F. N. Robinson, 2nd ed. (London, 1957).

Troilus and Criseyde, ed. R. K. Root (Princeton, 1945).

Chenu, M.-D.,   'Auctor, actor, autor', *Bulletin du Cange*, iv (1927), 81–6.

'Antiqui, Moderni', *RSPT*, xvii (1928), 82–94.

'Les "philosophes" dans la philosophie chrétienne médiévale', *RSPT*, xxvi (1937), 27–40.

Toward Understanding St Thomas, trans. A.-M. Landry and D. Hughes (Chicago, 1964).

La Théologie comme science au XIIIᵉ siècle, 3rd ed., Bibliothèque Thomiste, xxxiii (Paris, 1969).

Cleanness, ed. J. J. Anderson (Manchester, 1977).

Coleman, Janet,   *Piers Plowman and the 'Moderni'*, Edizioni di storia e Letteratura (Rome, 1981).

Comestor, Peter,   *Historia Scholastica*, Migne, *PL*, cxcviii, cols 1049–1722.

Comparetti, D.,   *Vergil in the Middle Ages*, trans. E. F. M. Benecke (London, 1895).

Cook, Robert G.,   'Chaucer's Pandarus and the Medieval Ideal of Friendship', *JEGP*, lxix (1970), 407–24.

Cooke, John D.,   'Euhemerism: A Medieval Interpretation of Classical Paganism', *Speculum*, ii (1927), 396–410.

Courcelle, P.,   *La Consolation de philosophie dans la tradition littéraire*, Études Augustiniennes (Paris, 1967).

Courtenay, W. J.,   'Covenant and Causality in Pierre d'Ailly', *Speculum*, xlvi (1971), 94–119.

'The Critique on Natural Causality in the Mutakallimun and Nominalism', *Harvard Theological Review*, lxvi (1973), 77–94.

Crompton, James,   *Lollard Doctrine with special reference to the Controversy over Image Worship and Pilgrimages* (B. Litt. thesis, University of Oxford, 1948).

Cross, F. L.,   *The Oxford Dictionary of the Christian Church*, 2nd ed. (Oxford, 1974).

Crow, M. N., and
Olson, C. C.   *Chaucer Life-Records* (Oxford, 1964).

Cummings, H. M.,   *The Indebtedness of Chaucer's Works to the Italian Works of Boccaccio* (New York, 1965).

Curry, W. C.,   *Chaucer and the Medieval Sciences*, 2nd ed. (London, 1960).

Dante Alagherii,   *Epistolae*, ed. P. Toynbee, 2nd ed. by C. G. Hardie (Oxford, 1966).

Il Convivio, ed. B. Cordati (Turin, 1968).

Dares,   see Frazer, R. M.

De Deorum Imaginibus Libellus, ed. as an appendix by Liebeschütz in his edition of John Ridevall's *Fulgentius Metaforalis*, pp. 117–28.

Dean, K. C.,   '*Maritalis Affectio*': *Attitudes towards Marriage in English and French Medieval Literature* (Ph.d. thesis, University of California, Davis, 1979).

Dedeck-Héry, V. L.,   'Jean de Meun et Chaucer: traducteurs de la *Consolation* de Boèce', *PMLA*, xlii (1937), 967–91.

De Deguileville,
Guillaume,   *Le Romant de trois pelerinaiges* (Paris, 1510).

Delany, Sheila,   *Chaucer's House of Fame: The Poetics of Skeptical Fideism* (Chicago and London, 1972).

Demats, P.,   *Fabula: Trois études de mythographie antique et médiévale*, Publications romanes et françaises, cxxii (Geneva, 1973).

Denifle, H., and
Chatelain, A.,   *Chartularium Universitatis Parisiensis* (Paris, 1889 –97).

De Wit, Pamela,   *The Visual Experience of Fifteenth-Century English Readers* (D. Phil. thesis, University of Oxford, 1977).

Dicts and Sayings of the Philosophers, The, ed. C. F. Bühler, EETS OS (Oxford, 1941).

Dictys,   see Frazer, R. M.

Donaldson, E. T.,   *Chaucer's Poetry: An Anthology for the Modern Reader* (New York, 1958).

    Speaking of Chaucer (London, 1970).

Donivan, M. J.,   'The *Anticlaudianus* and Three Passages in the *Franklin's Tale*', *JEGP*, lvi (1957), 52–9.

Douie, D. L.,   *Archbishop Pecham* (Oxford, 1952).

Dronke, Peter,   *Fabula: Explorations into the Uses of Myth in Medieval Platonism* (Leiden and Köln, 1974).

Dunning, T. P.,   'Langland and the Salvation of the Heathen', *Medium Ævum*, xii (1943), 45–54.

    'God and Man in *Troilus and Criseyde*', in *English and Medieval Studies presented to J. R. R. Tolkien*, ed. N. Davis and C. L. Wrenn (London, 1962), pp 164 –82.

Dwyer, R. A.,   'Villon's Boethius', *Annuale Mediaevale*, xi (1970), 74–80.

    Boethian Fictions (Cambridge, Mass., 1976).

Elbow, Peter,   *Oppositions in Chaucer* (Middletown, Conn., 1975).

Fairchild, H. N.,   'Active Arcite, Contemplative Palamon', *JEGP*, xxvi (1927), 285–93.

Fontenrose, Joseph,   *The Delphic Oracle: Its Responses and Operations, with a Catalogue of Responses* (Berkeley and Los Angeles, 1978).

Fowler, A.,   see Brooks, D.

Fowler, David C.,   *The Bible in Early English Literature* (London, 1977).

Frankis, John,   'Paganism and Pagan Love in *Troilus and Criseyde*', in *Essays on Troilus and Criseyde*, ed. M. Salu, pp. 57–72.

Frazer, R. M., *The Trojan War: The Chronicles of Dictys and Dares the Phrygian* (Bloomington and London, 1966).

Frost, W., 'An Interpretation of Chaucer's *Knight's Tale*', *RES*, xxv (1949), 289–304.

Fulgentius, *Fabii Plancidis Fulgentii Opera*, ed. R. Helm (Leipzig, 1898).

Gardner, John, *The Poetry of Chaucer* (Carbondale, Illinois, 1977).

Gaylord, Alan T., 'Friendship in Chaucer's *Troilus*', *The Chaucer Review*, iii (1969), 239–46.

'The Role of Saturn in the *Knight's Tale*', *The Chaucer Review*, viii (1974), 171–90.

Genet, J. P., *Four English Political Tracts of the Later Middle Ages*, Camden Fourth Series (London, 1968).

Giles of Rome, *De Erroribus Philosophorum*, ed. J. Koch and trans. J. O. Riedl (Milwaukee, 1944).

Gilson, Étienne, *The Mystical Theology of St Bernard*, trans. A. H. C. Downes (London, 1940).

Gordon, Ida, *The Double Sorrow of Troilus* (Oxford, 1970).

Gordon, R. K., *The Story of Troilus* (New York, 1964) [Includes a complete translation of Boccaccio's *Il Filostrato*]

Gower, John, *The English Works*, ed. G. C. Macaulay, EETS ES lxxxi and lxxxii (Oxford, 1900–1).

Graf, Arturo, *Roma nella memoria e nelle immaginazioni del medio evo* (Turin, 1923).

Gray, Douglas, *Themes and Images in the Medieval English Religious Lyric* (London and Boston, 1972).

Green, R. H., 'Dante's "Allegory of the Poets" and the Mediaeval Theory of Poetic Fiction', *Comparative Literature*, ix (1957), 118–28.

Greenfield, S. B., 'The Role of Calkas in *Troilus and Criseyde*', *Medium Ævum*, xxxvi (1967), 141–51.

Guelley, R., *Philosophie et théologie chez Guillaume d'Ockham* (Louvain and Paris, 1947).

Guido delle Colonne, *Historia Destructionis Troiae*, ed. N. E. Griffin, The Medieval Academy of America, Publication no. xxvi (Cambridge, Mass., 1936).

Historia Destructionis Troiae, trans. Mary E. Meek (Bloomington and London, 1974).

Guillaume de Lorris, see Jean de Meun

Hagen, Susan K., *The Pilgrimage of the Life of Man: A Medieval Theory of Vision and Remembrance* (Ph.d. thesis, University of Virginia, 1976).

Hahn, T. G., *God's Friends: Virtuous Heathen in Later Medieval Thought and English Literature* (Ph.d. thesis, University of California, Los Angeles, 1974).

Hammond, E., *Chaucer: A Bibliographical Manual* (repr. New York, 1933).

Harvey, S. W., 'Chaucer's Debt to Sacrobosco', *JEGP*, xxxiv (1935), 34–8.

Havely, N. R., *Chaucer's Boccaccio*, Chaucer Studies, iii (Wood-

	bridge, 1980) [Includes a translation of *Il Filostrato* and extracts from *Il Teseida*.]
Hazelton, R.,	'*The Manciple's Tale*: Parody and Critique', *JEGP*, lxii (1963), 1–31.
Henryson, Robert,	*The Poems and Fables*, ed. H. H. Wood (Edinburgh, 1958).
Higden, Ralph,	*Polychronicon Ranulphi Higden; together with the English translations of John Trevisa and of an unknown writer of the fifteenth century*, ed. C. Babington and J. R. Lumby (London, 1865–86).
Hilton, Walter,	*An Edition, from the Manuscripts, of Book ii of Walter Hilton's Scale of Perfection* (Ph.d. thesis, University of London, 1962).
	De Tolerandis Imaginibus, in London, British Library, MS Royal 11.B.X, fols 178^r–83^v.
Hirsch, E. D.,	*The Aims of Interpretation* (Chicago and London, 1976).
Hissette, R.,	*Enquête sur les 219 articles condamnés à Paris le 7 Mars 1277*, Philosophes médiévaux, xxii (Louvain and Paris, 1977).
Hoccleve, Thomas,	*The Minor Poems*, ed. F. J. Furnivall and I. Gollancz, EETS ES lxi and lxxiii (rev. repr. Oxford, 1970).
Hoffman, R. L.,	*Ovid and the Canterbury Tales* (Pennsylvania, 1966).
Holcot, Robert,	*Sapientiae Regis Salomonis praelectiones* (Basel, 1586).
	Super quattuor libros sententiarum quaestiones (Lyon, 1497).
?Holcot, Robert,	*Le 'Tractatus de principiis theologiae' attribué a Guillaume d'Ockham*, ed. L. Baudry (Paris, 1936).
Hugutio,	*Magnae Derivationes*, in Oxford, MS Bodley 376.
Isidore of Seville,	*Etymologiae*, ed. W. M. Lindsay (Oxford, 1911).
Jacob of Voragine,	*Aurea Legenda Sanctorum*, ed. T. Graesse (Leipzig, 1850).
Jauss, H. R.,	*Alterität und Modernität der mittelalterlichen Literatur* (Munich, 1977).
	'La Transformation de la forme allégorique entre 1180 et 1240: d'Alain de Lille à Guillaume de Lorris', in *L'Humanisme médiéval dans les littératures romanes*, Centre de Philologie et de Littératures Romanes de l'Université de Strasbourg, Actes et Colloques, iii (Paris, 1964) 107–46.
	'The Alterity and Modernity of Medieval Literature', *New Literary History*, x (1979), 385–90.
Jean de Meun,	*Le Roman de la Rose*, ed. E. Langlois (Paris, 1914–24).
	The Romance of the Rose by Guillaume de Lorris and Jean de Meun, trans. Charles Dahlberg (Princeton, 1971).

Jefferson, B. L.,	*Chaucer and the 'Consolation of Philosophy' of Boethius* (Princeton, 1917).
Jenaro-MacLennan, L.,	*The Trecento Commentaries on the Divina Commedia and the Epistle to Cangrande* (Oxford, 1974).
John of Garland,	*Morale Scolarium*, ed. L. J. Paetow, Memoirs of the University of California, vol. iv, no. 2 (Berkeley, California, 1927).
	Parisiana Poetria, ed. and trans. T. Lawler (New Haven and London, 1974).
John of Salisbury,	*Policraticus*, ed. C. C. J. Webb (Oxford, 1909).
	The Statesman's Book of John of Salisbury, trans. John Dickinson (New York, 1927).
John of Wales,	*Communiloquium*, in *Summa de regimine vite humane s. margarita doctorum* (Lyon, 1511), fols 1ʳ–139ᵛ.
	Compendiloquium, in *Florilegium de Vita et Dictis Philosophorum et Breviloquium de Sapientia Sanctorum*, ed. Luke Wadding (Rome, 1655) pp. 19–426.
John the Deacon,	*S. Gregorii Papae Vitae*, in Migne, *PL*, lxxv, cols 59–242.
Jones, Terry,	*Chaucer's Knight: The Portrait of a Medieval Mercenary* (London, 1980).
Jordan, R. M.,	*Chaucer and the Shape of Creation* (Cambridge, Mass., 1967).
Joseph of Exeter,	*Yliados Libri Sex*, ed. L. Gompf in *Joseph Iscanus: Werke und Briefe*, Mittellateinische Studien und Texte, iv (Leiden and Köln, 1970).
	The Iliad of Dares Phrygius, trans. Gildas Roberts (Cape Town, 1970).
Kaminsky, A. M.,	*Chaucer's Troilus and Criseyde and the Critics* (Ohio University Press, 1980).
Kean, P. M.,	*Chaucer and the Making of English Poetry* (London and Boston, 1972).
Keen, Maurice,	*The Laws of War in the Later Middle Ages* (London, 1965).
	'Chaucer's Knight, the English Aristocracy, and the Crusade', in *English Court Culture in the Later Middle Ages: Proceedings of the Colston Symposium, University of Bristol, 5–8 April 1981* (forthcoming).
Kelly, Douglas,	*Medieval Imagination: Rhetoric and the Poetry of Courtly Love* (Madison and London, 1978).
Kelly, H. A.,	*Love and Marriage in the Age of Chaucer* (Ithaca, 1975).
	'Aristotle-Averroes-Alemannus on Tragedy: The Influence of the "Poetics" on the Latin Middle Ages', *Viator*, x (1979), 161–209.
Kittredge, G. L.,	'Chaucer's Lollius', *Harvard Studies in Classical Philology*, xxviii (1917), 47–133.
Klibansky, R., Panofsky, E., & Saxl, F.,	*Saturn and Melancholy* (London, 1964).

Knowles, M. D.,	'The Censured Opinions of Uhtred of Boldon', *Proceedings of the British Academy*, xxxvii (1951), 305–42.
	The Evolution of Medieval Thought (London, 1962).
Koonce, B. C.,	*Chaucer and the Tradition of Fame: Symbolism in the House of Fame* (Princeton, 1966).
Köpf, U.,	*Die Anfänge der theologischen Wissenschaftstheorie im 13. Jahrhundert*, Beiträge zur historischen theologie, xlix (Tübingen, 1974).
Lambert, Mark,	'*Troilus*, Books I–III: A Criseydan Reading', in *Essays on Troilus and Criseyde*, ed. Mary Salu, pp. 105–25.
Langland, William,	*Piers Plowman: The B-Version*, ed. G. Kane and E. T. Donaldson (London, 1975).
Langlois, E.,	'Archipiada', *Mélanges de philologie romane dediés à Carl Wahlund* (Mâcon, 1896), pp. 173–9.
Leff, Gordon,	*Bradwardine and the Pelagians*, Cambridge Studies in Medieval Life and Thought, New Series, v (Cambridge, 1957).
	Paris and Oxford Universities in the Thirteenth and Fourteenth Centuries (New York and London, 1968).
	William of Ockham (Manchester, 1975).
Lewis, C. S.,	*The Allegory of Love* (Oxford, 1936).
	'What Chaucer really did to *Il Filostrato*', rpt. in *Chaucer Criticism*, ed. Schoeck and Taylor, ii, 16–33.
Liber de Pomo, trans. M. F. Rousseau, *The Apple, or Aristotle's Death* (Milwaukee, 1968).	
Lofmark, Carl,	*Rennewart in Wolfram's 'Willehalm'* (Cambridge, 1972).
Lonsbury, T. R.,	*Studies in Chaucer* (New York, 1892).
Loomis, D. B.,	'Saturn in Chaucer's *Knight's Tale*', in *Chaucer und seine Zeit. Symposion für Walter F. Schirmer*, ed. Arno Esch (Tübingen, 1968), pp. 149–61.
Lumiansky, R. M.,	'The Story of Troilus and Briseida according to Benoît and Guido', *Speculum*, xxix (1954), 727–33.
Lydgate, John,	*Lydgate's DeGuilleville's Pilgrimage of the Life of Man*, ed. J. Furnivall, EETS ES lxxvii, lxxxiii and xcii (Oxford, 1899–1904).
	Siege of Thebes, ed. A. Erdmann, EETS ES cviii (Oxford, 1911).
	The Troy Book, ed. H. Bergen, EETS ES xcvii, ciii, cvi and cxxvi (Oxford, 1906–35).
Macfarlane, Katherine,	*Isidore of Seville's Treatise on the Pagan Gods: Origenes viii.11* (Ph.d. thesis, University of Washington, 1978).
Macrobius,	*Commentary on the Dream of Scipio*, trans. W. H. Stahl (New York and London, 1952).
Maguire, J. B.,	'The Clandestine Marriage of Troilus and Criseyde', *The Chaucer Review*, viii (1974), 275–6.

Mainzer, H. C.,	*A Study of the Sources of the Confessio Amantis by John Gower* (D.Phil. thesis, University of Oxford, 1967).
Manning, S.,	'The Nun's Priest's Morality and the Medieval Attitude toward Fables', *JEGP*, lix (1960), 403–16.
Marcett, M. E.,	*Uhtred de Boldon, Friar William Jordan, and Piers Plowman* (New York, 1938).
Marchalonis, S.,	'Medieval Symbols and the *Gesta Romanorum*', *The Chaucer Review*, viii (1973), 311–19.
McAlpine, M. E.,	*The Genre of Troilus and Criseyde* (Ithaca and London, 1978).
McCall, John P.,	*Chaucer among the Gods: The Poetics of Classical Myth* (University Park, Penn., and London, 1979).
McGalliard, J. C.,	*Classical Mythology in certain Mediaeval Treatments of the Legends of Troy, Thebes, and Aeneas: A Study in the Literary Paganism of the Middle Ages* (Ph.d. thesis, Harvard University, 1930).
McGrade, A.,	*The Political Thought of William of Ockham* (Cambridge, 1974).
Meier, T. K.,	'Chaucer's Knight as "Persona": Narration as Control', *English Miscellany*, xx (1969), 11–21.
Meissner, Alois,	*Gotteserkenntnis und Gotteslehre nach dem englischen Dominikanertheologen Robert Holkot* (Limburg, 1953).
Minnis, Alastair,	'"Authorial Role" and "Literary Form" in Late-Medieval Scriptural Exegesis', *PBB*, xcix (1977), 37–65.
	'Late-Medieval Discussions of *Compilatio* and the Role of the *Compilator*', *PBB*, ci (1979), 385–421.
	'Literary Theory in Discussions of *Formae Tractandi* by Medieval Theologians', *New Literary History*, xi (1979/80), 133–45.
	'John Gower, *sapiens* in Ethics and Politics', *Medium Ævum*, xlix (1980), 207–29.
	'The Influence of Academic Prologues on the Prologues and Literary Attitudes of Late-Medieval English Writers', *MS*, xliii (1981), 342–83.
	'Langland's *Ymaginatif* and Late-Medieval Theories of Imagination', *Comparative Criticism*, iii (1981), 71–103.
	'Aspects of the Medieval French and English Traditions of the *De Consolatione Philosophiae*', in *Boethius: His Life, Thought and Influence*, ed. M. T. Gibson (Oxford, 1981), pp. 312–61.
	'Chaucer and Comparative Literary Theory', in *New Perspectives in Chaucer Criticism: Proceedings of the Second International Conference of the New Chaucer Society*, ed. D. M. Rose (Norman, Oklahoma, 1981), pp. 53–69.
	Medieval Theory of Authorship: Scholastic Literary

	Attitudes in the Later Middle Ages (London, 1982).
Muscatine, C.,	*Chaucer and the French Tradition* (Berkeley and Los Angeles, 1957).
Mythographus Secundus,	see Bode, G. H.
Mythographus Tertius,	see Bode, G. H.
Neff, S. B.,	'Chaucer's Pandarus', *Western Humanities Review*, iv (1950), 343–8.
Neuse, R.,	'The Knight: The First Mover in Chaucer's Human Comedy', *University of Toronto Quarterly*, xxxi (1961/2), 299–315.
Nicholas of Lyre,	see *Biblia Sacra*.
North, J.D.,	'"Kalendres Enlumyned ben They": Some Astrological Themes in Chaucer', *RES*, new series, xx (1969) 129–54, 258–83, 418–44.
	Richard of Wallingford: An Edition of his Writings with Introductions, English Translations and Commentary (Oxford, 1976).
Norton-Smith, John,	*Geoffrey Chaucer* (London and Boston, 1974).
Oakley, Francis,	'Medieval Theories of Natural Law: William of Ockham and the Voluntarist Tradition', *Natural Law Forum*, vi (1961), 65–83.
Oberman, H. A.,	*Archbishop Thomas Bradwardine: A Fourteenth-Century Augustinian* (Utrecht, 1957).
	'"Facientibus quod in se est Deus non denegat gratiam": Robert Holcot O. P. and the Beginnings of Luther's Theology', *Harvard Theological Review*, lv (1962), 317–42.
	The Harvest of Medieval Theology: Gabriel Biel and Late-Medieval Nominalism (Grand Rapids, Michigan, 1967).
	'Fourteenth-Century Religious Thought: A Premature Profile', *Speculum*, liii (1978), 80–93.
Oberman, H. A., & Weisheipl, J. A.,	'The *Sermo Epinicius* ascribed to Thomas Bradwardine (1346)', *AHDLMA*, xxv (1958), 295–329.
Olson, C. C.,	see Crow, M. N.
Ovide Moralisé, vols i and iv, ed. C. de Boer, Verhandelingen der Koninkijke Akademie van Wetenschappen te Amsterdam, Afdeeling Letterkunde, xv & xxxvii (Amsterdam, 1915 and 1936).
Owst, G. R.,	*Literature and Pulpit in Medieval England* (Oxford, 1966).
Panofsky, E.,	see Klibansky, R.
Pantin, W. A.,	'John of Wales and Medieval Humanism', in *Medieval Studies presented to Aubrey Gwynn* (Dublin, 1961), pp. 297–319.
Patch, H. R.,	'Troilus on Determinism', rpt. in *Chaucer Criticism*, ed. Schoeck and Taylor, ii, 71–85.
Patience, ed. J. J. Anderson (Manchester, 1969).

Peck, R. A.,   'Chaucer and the Nominalist Questions', *Speculum*, liii (1978), 745–60.

Peyton, Henry H.,   'The Roles of Calkas, Helen and Cassandra in Chaucer's *Troilus*', *Interpretations*, vii (1975), 10–12.

Pernoud, M. A.,   'Innovation in William of Ockham's references to the *Potentia Dei*', *Antonianum*, xlv (1970), 65–97.

'The Theory of the *Potentia Dei* according to Aquinas, Scotus and Ockham', *Antonianum*, xlvii (1972), 69–95.

Petersen, K. O.,   *Sources of the Nonnes Preestes Tale*, Radcliffe College Monographs, x (Boston, 1896).

'Chaucer and Trivet', *PMLA*, xviii (1903), 173–93.

Poag, J. F.,   *Wolfram von Eschenbach* (New York, 1972).

Polo, Marco,   *Travels*, trans. R. E. Latham (Harmondsworth, 1958).

Pratt, R. A.,   'Chaucer and *Le Roman de Troyle et de Criseida*', *SP*, liii (1956), 509–39.

'Chaucer and the Hand that Fed Him', *Speculum*, xli (1966), 619–42.

'Chaucer and *Les Cronicles* of Nicholas Trevet', in *Studies in Language, Literature, and Culture of the Middle Ages and Later*, ed. E. B. Atwood and A. A. Hill (Austin, 1969), pp. 303–11.

'Some Latin Sources of the Nonnes Preest on Dreams', *Speculum*, lii (1977), 538–70.

Price, B. B.,   'The Physical Astronomy and Astrology of Albertus Magnus', in *Albertus Magnus and the Sciences: Commemorative Essays 1980*, ed. J. A. Weisheipl, Pontifical Institute of Medieval Studies, Studies and Texts, xlix (Toronto, 1980), 155–85.

(Pseudo-) Ptolemy,   *Tetrabiblos*, trans. J. M. Ashmand (London, 1917).

Raby, F. J. E.,   *The Oxford Book of Medieval Latin Verse* (Oxford, 1959).

Radulphus
de Longo Campo,   *In Anticlaudianum Alani Commentum*, ed. Jan Salowski (Wrocław and Warsaw, 1972).

Rathbone, E.,   'Master Alberic of London, "Mythographus Tertius Vaticanus', *Mediaeval and Renaissance Studies*, i (1941–3), 35–8.

Reames, Sherry,   'The Sources of Chaucer's *Second Nun's Tale*', *MP*, lxxvi (1978/9), 111–35.

Ridevall, John,   *Fulgentius Metaforalis*, ed. H. Liebeschütz, Studien der Bibliothek Warburg, iv (Leipzig, 1926).

Robertson, D. W.,   *A Preface to Chaucer* (Princeton, 1962).

'Chaucerian Tragedy', rpt. in *Chaucer Criticism*, ed. Schoeck and Taylor, ii, 86–121.

Robson, J. A.,   *Wyclif and the Oxford Schools* (Cambridge, 1966).

Roman de Thebes, ed. L. Constans (Paris, 1890).

Roman de Troie en Prose, vol. i, ed. L. Constans and E. Faral (Paris, 1922).

Roney, L. Y.,   *Scholastic Philosophies in Chaucer's Knight's Tale*

	(Ph.d. thesis, University of Wisconsin, Madison, 1970).
Root, R. K.,	'Chaucer's Dares', *MP*, xv (1917), 1–22.
	The Poetry of Chaucer (rpt. New York, 1950).
Rowe, Donald W.,	*O Love, O Charite! Contraries Harmonized in Chaucer's Troilus* (Carbondale and Edwardsville, S. Illinois, 1976).
Ruggiers, Paul G.,	'Notes towards a Theory of Tragedy in Chaucer', *The Chaucer Review*, viii (1973), 88–99.
Russell, G. H.,	'The Salvation of the Heathen: The Exploration of a Theme in *Piers Plowman*', *JWCI*, xxix (1966), 101–16.
Russell-Smith, Joy,	'Walter Hilton and a Tract in Defence of the Veneration of Images', *Dominican Studies*, vii (1954), 180–214.

Saint Erkenwald, ed. R. Morse (Cambridge, 1975).

Salu, Mary,	*Essays on Troilus and Criseyde*, Chaucer Studies, iii (Woodbridge, 1981).
Sandkühler, B.,	*Die frühen Dantekommentare und ihr Verhaltnis zur mittelalterlichen Kommentartradition*, Münchner Romanistische Arbeiten, xix (Munich, 1967).
Saxl, F.,	see Klibansky, R.
Schoeck, R., & Taylor, J.,	*Chaucer Criticism* (Notre Dame, Indiana, 1960–1).

Secreta Secretorum, ed. R. Steele, *Three Prose Versions of the Secreta Secretorum*, EETS ES lxxiv (Oxford, 1898).

	ed. M. A. Manzalaoui, *Secretum Secretorum: Nine English Versions*, EETS OS ccliivi (Oxford, 1977).
Sidney, Sir Philip,	*An Apology for Poetry*, ed. G. Shepherd (London, 1965).
Silk, E. T.,	*Cambridge MS Ii.3.21 and the Relation of Chaucer's Boethius to Trivet and Jean de Meun* (Ph.d. thesis, Yale University, 1930).
Slaughter, E. E.,	'Chaucer's Pandarus: Virtuous Uncle and Friend', *JEGP*, xlviii (1949), 186–95.
Smalley, Beryl,	*The Study of the Bible in the Middle Ages* (Oxford, 1952).
	English Friars and Antiquity in the Early Fourteenth Century (Oxford, 1960).
Southern, R. W.,	*Western Views of Islam in the Middle Ages* (Cambridge, Mass., 1962).
Spicq, P. C.,	*Esquisse d'une histoire de l'exégèse latine au moyen âge*, Bibliothèque Thomiste, xxvi (Paris, 1944).

Stanzaic Life of Christ, A, ed. F. A. Foster, EETS OS clxvi (Oxford, 1926).

Steadman, J. M.,	'Flattery and the Moralitas of the *Nonnes Preestes Tale*', *Medium Ævum*, xxviii (1959), 172–9.
	Disembodied Laughter: Troilus and the Apotheosis Tradition (Berkeley and Los Angeles, 1972).
Tatlock, J. S. P.,	'The Epilog of Chaucer's *Troilus*', *MP*, xviii (1920/1), 625–59.

Thomas of Ireland,   *Manipulus Florum*, printed as *Flores omnium pene doctorum . . . alphabetico ordine digesti* (Paris, 1556).

Trevet, Nicholas,   *Commentary on Boethius, De Consolatione Philosophiae*, ed. by E. T. Silk (unfinished at the time of Professor Silk's death).

Trevisa, John,   see Bartholomaeus Anglicus and Higden, Ralph.

Tupper, F.,   'The Envy Theme in Prologues and Epilogues', *JEGP*, xvi (1917), 551–72.

Twycross, M. A.,   *The Representation of the Major Classical Divinities in the Works of Chaucer, Gower, Lydgate and Henryson* (B. Litt. thesis, University of Oxford, 1961).
The Medieval Anadyomene: A Study in Chaucer's Mythography, Medium Ævum Monographs, new series, i (1972).

Ulrich of Strassburg,   *La Summo de Bono*, livre i, ed. J. Daguillon, Bibliothèque Thomiste, xii (Paris, 1930).

Underwood, Dale,   'The First of the Canterbury Tales', *ELH*, xxvi (1959), 455–69.

Usk, Thomas,   *The Testament of Love*, in *Supplement to the Works of Geoffrey Chaucer, vol. vii: Chaucerian and Other Pieces*, ed. W. W. Skeat (Oxford, 1897), pp. 1–145.

Van Steenberghen, F.,   *Aristotle in the West: The Origins of Latin Aristotelianism*, trans. L. Johnston (Louvain, 1955).

Veazie, Walter B.,   'Chaucer's Text-Book of Astronomy, Johannes de Sacrobosco', *University of Colorado Studies*, ser. B, *Studies in the Humanities*, i (1939/40), 169–82.

Vignaux, Paul,   *Justification et prédestination au XIVe siècle* (Paris, 1934).
Nominalisme au XIVe siècle (Montreal and Paris, 1948).

Vincent of Beauvais,   *Apologia totius operis* [the prologue to the *Speculum Maius*], ed. A.-D. v. den Brincken, 'Geschichtsbetrachtung bei Vincenz von Beauvais', *Deutsches Archiv für Erforschung des Mittelalters*, xxxiv.2 (1978), 465–99.
Speculum Maius (Venice, 1591).

Webb, H. J.,   'A Reinterpretation of Chaucer's Theseus', *RES*, xxiii (1947), 289–96.

Wedel, T. O.,   *The Mediaeval Attitude toward Astrology, particularly in England*, Yale Studies in English, lx (New Haven, 1920).

Weisheipl, J. A.,   'Classification of the Sciences in Medieval Thought', *MS*, xxvii (1965), 54–90.
Friar Thomas d'Aquino (Oxford, 1975).
see also Oberman, H. A.

Wenzel, S.,   'The Pilgrimage of Life as a Late Medieval Genre', *MS*, xxxv (1973), 370–88.

Wetherbee, W.,   *Platonism and Poetry in the Twelfth Century* (Princeton, 1972).

Whitbread, L. G.,   *Fulgentius the Mythographer* (Ohio State University Press, 1971).

Wigginton, W. B.,   *The Nature and Significance of the Late-Medieval Troy Story: A Study of Guido delle Colonne's Historia Destructionis Troiae* (Ph.d. thesis, Rutgers University, 1965).

William of Aragon,   *Commentary on Boethius, De Consolatione Philosophiae*, in Cambridge, University Library, MS Ii.3.21, pt. ii.

William of Conches,   *Commentary on Boethius, De Consolatione Philosophiae* (second redaction), in London, British Library, MS Royal 15.B.III.

William of Ockham,   *Philosophical Writings*, ed. P. Boehner (London, 1957).
Predestination, God's Foreknowledge, and Future Contingents, trans. M. M. Adams and N. Kretzmann (New York, 1969).

Winsatt, W. K.,   'Vincent of Beauvais and Chaucer's Cleopatra and Croesus', *Speculum*, xii (1937), 375–81.

Windeatt, B.,   'The Text of the *Troilus*', in *Essays on Troilus and Criseyde*, ed. Salu, pp. 1–22.

Wood, Chauncey,   *Chaucer and the Country of the Stars* (Princeton, 1970).

Wright, L. B.,   *Middle Class Culture in Elizabethan England* (London, 1964).

Wycliffite Bible,   *The Holy Bible: Made from the Latin Vulgate by John Wycliffe and his Followers*, ed. J. Forshall and F. Madden (Oxford, 1950).

Young, K.,   *The Origin and Development of the Story of Troilus and Criseyde* (London, 1908).

Index

Printed in the United Kingdom
by Lightning Source UK Ltd.
128073UK00002B/76-78/A